BEHIND THE SCENES OF
MOTOR RACING

KEN GREGORY

Behind the Scenes of Motor Racing

*

Foreword by
STIRLING MOSS

MOTORACES BOOK CLUB
MACGIBBON & KEE
London 1963

TO STIRLING
AND TO THE MEMORY OF
PETER, STUART
AND IVOR

CONTENTS

ILLUSTRATIONS

FOREWORD

I first met Ken Gregory years ago, when he was in the Competition department of the R.A.C., working long hours to help motor sport along a difficult path. Now, ten years later, he is working even longer hours, helping me along with my racing.

Being a professional racing driver is a nerve-racking job, not because of the races, but because of the life it entails. This life would be impossible without his help. In this book, Ken has brought back many happy memories, also some of the difficult times. I think the reader will get a look at a side of racing which few people realize exist, and if they follow our sport I feel they will learn a lot of interesting things.

STIRLING MOSS

CHAPTER ONE

MY PLUNGE INTO RACING

LOOKING back on it all now, the most surprising thing to me about my career in the world of motor racing is the fact that I entered it quite by chance. When I finished a seven-year career in the Services, beginning at the age of fifteen as a cadet in the Royal Army Ordnance Corps, and ending as a Sergeant Pilot in the Glider Pilot Regiment, I did not specifically seek a civilian occupation in so unlikely a field for employment as motor racing.

I might just as easily have ended up in something like football or boxing promotion, travelling or insurance; it simply happened that, at the time I called at the Ecclestone Square depot of the British Legion, there was a vacancy at the Pall Mall offices of the Royal Automobile Club.

The fact that it was in the Competitions Department didn't mean a thing to me at the time, yet here was an 'Open Sesame' to the sport of sports for which many a motor-racing enthusiast might have gone green with envy. When I called at No. 83 Pall Mall for interview the job sounded routine enough. The duties involved sifting various inquiries, the issue of competition licences, keeping the R.A.C. Records book up to date, and others. I gladly accepted the post, little knowing where it was to lead me, content only in having secured a job which promised to be interesting.

Dean Delamont had joined the department just previously, and we both worked under Colonel Stanley Barnes, Competitions Manager of the R.A.C. and a former racing and trials driver. There was plenty to do. The demand for new or re-issued competition licences was constant, and people were rushing in and out all day long with a wide variety of inquiries.

Soon, with familiarity, the flow of faces constantly before me began to take on identities. Most of them were racing drivers, or trials or rally men. One sturdy, fresh-complexioned fellow with a grin and a gruff voice was Eric Brandon, whose habit was to carry a '100' box of Player's in his pocket. Another cheerful character with a ready and sardonic humour was, I learned, W. J. White-house, commonly known in the racing fraternity as 'Big Bill'; a fair-headed, handsome Belgian speaking impeccable English was John Claes, once well known as a bandleader (remember 'Johnny Claes and his Clay Pigeons'?); while the nineteen-year-old with a mop of dark hair and the alert look was Stirling Moss . . .

The passer-by walking in Pall Mall and eyeing the calm, digni-fied buildings of the R.A.C. can never visualize what a hive of industry they are within. As the spring of 1949 advanced, the general ferment in the Competitions Department mounted almost to a frenzy, and the sole topic on every caller's lips seemed to be the same—just 'Silverstone, Silverstone, Silverstone'!

The name struck an instant chord with me. Not for its connection with motor racing, but as the wartime aerodrome it used to be, before ever racing cars careered around its perimeter tracks and runways. When flying Horsa troop transport gliders late in the war I had been stationed at a Northants aerodrome called Finmere; Silverstone, six miles to the south-west, was our closest neighbour, and one which I frequently passed whilst carrying out my duties as Regimental Transport Sergeant.

On 14 May, 1949, I found myself there in very different circum-stances. No thunder of V12 Rolls-Royce motors as Lancaster bombers warmed up this time, but instead the snarl of fierce Italian Maseratis, French Talbots and British E.R.A.s filled the air. The second British Grand Prix for Formula 1 cars was about to take place, and as the R.A.C., Britain's national motor club, were the organizers, we minions of Pall Mall were naturally at the circuit in full force.

As one small cog in the great organizational machine, my duties were in the Race Control office, where the main occupation seemed to be answering incessant telephone calls from all quarters of the circuit. At that time I knew little of the actual sport of motor racing, and in truth I knew little more when that busy Saturday was over! I only knew that it had been abominably hot in the con-crete blockhouse, formerly the aerodrome control office, which housed Race Control, that bells had rung incessantly all day, from the paddock, from the corner marshals, from the first-aid posts, from the fire points, checking and rechecking—and that I was over-whelmingly tired.

That cheery Swiss driver, Baron Emanuel de Graffenried, won the British Grand Prix in his Maserati, but I saw little of his performance, or of Bob Gerard's valiant fight with a pre-war E.R.A. The phone bells were still ringing in my ears hours afterwards, yet deep down I was conscious that I had enjoyed myself. There was considerable satisfaction in being a link, no matter how small, in the organization, and playing a part in making the complex operation of running a major international motor race a success, and I found myself looking forward to the next 'frenzy'.

Later that season, Dean Delamont, by then the Assistant Manager of the R.A.C. Competitions Department, took me down to the British Automobile Racing Club's September meeting at Goodwood, this being the first important fixture at which I was able to be a spectator. I found it highly exciting, particularly the tremendous struggle between Peter Walker in the E.R.A. E type, and Reg Parnell with the 4CLT Maserati in two races.

It was at this meeting that I first saw Stirling Moss in action. He was driving a Cooper with 995 c.c. J.A.P. twin-cylinder engine installed, and won the Madgwick Cup event after a wonderful drive from Eric Brandon and Bill Whitehouse in similar cars. As that day marked his twentieth birthday, this success brought extra zest to his celebrations.

Not long after that, Dean Delamont took me along to a committee meeting of the 500 Club. This body, often dubbed the 'Poor man's motor club' in fun, by reason of its primary aims to promote cheaper racing, had interested me ever since I came across their file at the R.A.C. They were immensely enthusiastic and since their formation in 1946 had set the 500 c.c. racing movement on so firm a footing that four years later it was granted international status as Formula 3.

Like many another, I really wanted to build a '500' myself, and in this ambition Dean Delamont was with me, nursing sundry bold ideas on design which he was later to see fulfilled in the famous 'swing axle' Kieft and the Erskine Staride. At that time, Dean was assisting the 500 Club in an advisory capacity, and at that first meeting which I attended, held at Gerald Spink's house in Surbiton, considerable discussion ended in my being appointed as assistant to the secretary, taking on the administration of the Club, under the direction of the committee, for the sum of £1 per week.

My first task on their behalf was the organization of the annual dinner and dance. This was held at the Rubens Hotel in Victoria, and was quite a small, informal affair when compared with today's B.R.S.C.C. function. Yet it was immensely important to me in marking the first occasion on which I met those two highly promising young drivers, Stirling Moss and Peter Collins, on a social level.

At that time membership of the Club seemed to be split up into the very young and the comparatively old, who were living on their pre-war memories and tended to stick together. It was thus that three of the younger people, Stirling, Peter and myself, banded together at one table, and thoroughly enjoyed ourselves. I hadn't brought a girl friend, but Peter and Stirling had made up for this by bringing at least two each. During the dinner, Mrs Kay Petre, herself a pre-war racing driver, presented Peter Collins with the trophy for winning the 100-mile race at Silverstone in 1949 with his Cooper 500, using a Norton engine—he having started the vogue for Nortons when the J.A.P. engine was the usual wear.

Peter was an extremely pleasant person, very gay, completely carefree and, even in those days, very much the cavalier-type as he was right up to the end. Stirling was more serious, and even then was giving indications of that single-mindedness of purpose which was to take him right to the top of the racing tree. That night, however, he had another little problem on his mind. He was very much looked after by his father in those days, and 'Dad' wanted Stirling to go home to the farm in Maidenhead with him and Mrs. Moss immediately after the dinner/dance.

His twenty-year-old son, on the other hand, wanted to see his girl friend home first, and make his own way back to Maidenhead later on. He put the problem to me, then himself suggested the solution. 'Why not go and tell Father that you've asked me to come and have coffee with you at your flat? Then everything will be O.K. and I can take the girl friend home.' So I entered into the deception, not without flinching as I looked into Alfred Moss's eyes. But I fancied I caught a twinkle in them as he said, 'All right then—don't keep him too long.'

The 500 Club's next meeting was held in Victoria, on the

premises of Halsey Electrics, committee member Eric Brandon being a director of this concern. It was probably the most momentous meeting in the history of the Club, having a vital effect on its future.

Stan Coldham of Forest Hill, one of the keenest members and an excellent driver, announced that he had been down to Brands Hatch, on the A20 London–Maidstone road near Fawkham, Kent, where they had just laid down a new tarmacadam road circuit for motor-cycle racing, over the site of the old grass track. There he had met Joe Francis, Managing Director of Brands Hatch, and discussed with him the possibility of the 500 Club running car race meetings on the new one-mile circuit.

We quickly followed this up, entered into negotiations with Francis, and finally it was agreed with Brands Hatch that the 500 Club would promote a number of meetings there in 1950, the first to take place on 16 April. Thus what was termed 'the cradle of 500 c.c. racing' came into existence. As this was five years after 500 c.c. racing had been born, the simile was not all that apt, but Brands Hatch certainly became the hub of the movement, greatly assisting its expansion and helping to produce numerous new British racing drivers destined for international fame. That agreement with the Brands Hatch people was the best day's work the Club had ever done, and great credit must go to Stan Coldham for pioneering the close link between the now famous Kentish circuit and the 500 c.c. racing movement.

The job of organizing the meetings there fell principally upon me. Organizing a race meeting is no small undertaking, as I found out by trial and error. The tasks were many and varied. Regulations had to be drafted and sent out to all Club members, entries secured, selected and divided, if necessary, into heats; marshals and other officials appointed, the R.A.C.'s safety rules applied, insurance coverage arranged, the race programme made up and sent out for printing, and numerous other things.

Dean Delamont helped a lot in drawing up the regulations, being an expert at such matters, while John Gale, the Club Secretary and a man of great organizing ability, did much advisory work too, and proved a most able Clerk of the Course at that first meeting.

Yes, there was plenty to do, particularly as I was fully occupied

B

all day at the R.A.C. and did 500 Club work in the evenings and week-ends at my Hampstead flat. Even then, I had to stick my neck out and take on something else! One evening I was working at the flat when the phone rang. The man at the other end said his name was Cyril Kieft, from Bridgend, South Wales. He'd built a 500 c.c. racing car, wanted to race it in the very near future, and 'could I recommend a driver?'

Well, I'd always wanted the chance to drive a racing car, so impulsively the first thing I said was 'Yes—me!' To my astonishment Cyril Kieft didn't even seem surprised. 'All right,' he said, 'we'll arrange an early meeting; in the meantime, put in an entry for Brands Hatch on April 16th with yourself as driver and Kieft as entrant.' I could hardly believe my ears! He went on to discuss engines, and whether the car should have a Vincent or a J.A.P. I knew little of the practical side of things then, and said, 'Let's have a Vincent'—more because the name appealed than anything else. That was as far as we got on that first phone call, but subsequently we met for further discussions, and became very great friends.

A week before the inaugural Brands Hatch meeting, I went down to Goodwood with Stirling Moss for the Easter Monday fixture there. After a successful try-out with an H.W.M. at Odiham airfield in Hants, Stirling had signed-up with John Heath and George Abecassis of H.W. Motors to drive for them in Formula 2 events during the 1950 season. Goodwood was his first race for H.W.M. It was a terrible day, with rain pelting down and a howling gale blowing, but Stirling drove extremely well, gaining a second place to Duncan Hamilton's Maserati in one race.

We stayed that week-end at John Brierley's hotel, the White Swan at Stoughton, Moss and I sharing a room. With several other of the '500 crowd' also staying there, the usual pranks were inevitable, and we suffered our share. We had been out on the Friday evening, getting back about 10 p.m. Ken Carter, Billy Carter, Gordon Bedson, Bill Whitehouse, Stan Coldham and Co. were still in the bar, and when we went upstairs we sensed that something 'fishy' was going on.

Looking round suspiciously, we couldn't find anything particularly wrong, beyond the fact that they'd filled our beds with holly, and stuck those ceramic things that you usually find in hotels beneath the sheets. We sorted this lot out, undressed and got into bed. We hadn't been there half an hour when I yelled across, 'Blimey, Stirling—something's hot!' And he agreed vehemently, feeling just the same. They had filled our pyjamas with cayenne pepper!

So to the first Brands Hatch meeting of the 500 Club on 16 April, 1950—and my first drive in a racing car, the Vincent-engined Kieft. There was a substantial entry to contest the four races, two of which we had to divide into three heats and a final each. Encouraged by bright sunshine, the boys had a magnificent day's racing over the one-mile 'kidney bean'-shaped circuit, run anti-clockwise in those days.

Don Parker, Ken Carter and Bill Whitehouse all won races, but as for newcomer K. A. Gregory (Kieft), he didn't figure in the results at all, I'm afraid. But I found the experience of racing at Brands most exciting, and one of the comforting features of that particular meeting was, I suppose, that probably seventy-five per cent of the entry were also newcomers to racing, while the track, of course, was new to all.

The Kieft, which had a light alloy channel frame and wheels and rubber bush suspension, ran well enough, but the Vincent engine was better, I think, in its own element, between two wheels, and could not match the output of the dirt-track J.A.P. units, running on alcohol at 14 or so to 1 compression ratio. Had I said 'J.A.P.' instead of 'Vincent' in that first phone conversation with Cyril Kieft, the early days of his 500 might have been more successful.

After all our efforts at Brands Hatch on 16 April, it was extremely pleasing to read Rodney Walkerley's views on the meeting in *The Motor* of 26 April, 1950. Amongst the many kind things he said were: '. . . I must say a very well-organized meeting it was. The spectators to the number of 10,000 (at a guess), had what is unique in motor racing, a view of the entire circuit, from wherever they were stationed, from start to finish, and I cannot off-hand think of anywhere else that such a thing is possible (not even Pau or Monte Carlo). . . . The racing was of a high order. Several times we had battles fought out from start to finish not only among the leaders but back in the field. . . . This circuit is going to be a really fine

thing for 500 c.c. devotees, and I cannot think of a better afternoon's money's worth for the paying customer or a better training
ground for the Grand Prix aspirant.'

At the end of April, H.W.M.s went to the Continent for the
first time, for the Paris Grand Prix at Montlhéry. Moss and Abecassis were to drive, and I was desperately anxious to go and see
the race, but couldn't afford to. Alfred Moss was kind enough to
buy my ticket and take me over with him and Mrs Moss for the
day, an action typical of him. Stirling got up to third place in the
race after 33 laps, behind Grignard's Talbot and a Delage, but
then had to retire with engine trouble.

Soon came Britain's biggest meeting of the year—the 'Royal
Silverstone', with the European G.P. as the principal race, and
King George VI, the Queen and Princess Margaret gracing the
meeting with their presence.

I was much too busy doing my job with the R.A.C. there to
attempt any racing, and two Kiefts were driven by Colin Strang
and Lord Strathcarron. They had no luck in the 500 c.c. race,
which was won by Wing Cdr. Frank Aikens in his Triumph-
engined Iota after Stirling's Cooper-J.A.P. died on the last lap,
coasting silently over the line in second place, scraping home by a
length from Peter Collins's Cooper!

I didn't see much of that race, nor of the glorious red Alfa Romeos which dominated the Grand Prix, watched by the Royal
Family from a special stand at Stowe corner. The day was chiefly
memorable to me for the crowds, and my own private 'flap' as a
result of them. While I could not race at Silverstone, I was keen to
do so elsewhere, and as a meeting was being held at Mons, in Belgium, the following day, I had undertaken to drive the Kieft there,
in the 500 c.c. race. What a lot of trouble I let myself in for!

Immediately the 500 c.c. event at Silverstone—luckily the first
of the day—was over, the Vincent-engined Kieft was wheeled
across the track to the outside, and loaded on to a 30-cwt. Bedford
van, lent by Don Bilton. A friend of mine then drove it down to
Dover in order to catch the night boat across to Dunkirk.

Meanwhile I went back to my duties at Silverstone, the plan being that, as soon as the racing was over, I would drive down to

Dover with all speed, and cross with the lorry to Dunkirk that night. The plan completely misfired. Attendance at Silverstone was immense, and as in those days the local constabulary weren't used to handling the traffic, fantastic road jams developed as the public tried to leave the car parks.

We who were stuck in the centre couldn't get out for hours, and after a few desperate but hopeless attempts, I phoned my friend at Dover and told him not to wait but take the boat, as I would have to make other arrangements for getting over. Then Stirling Moss told me he intended to catch a very early plane on Sunday from Northolt to Brussels, so I made plans to travel on the same plane. Alas, I overslept, woke up with a start when that plane had already gone, and rang up the airport in a panic. I found I had just fifty minutes to wash and shave, get dressed, and drive from Hampstead to Northolt!

By scrambling madly around, then flogging my poor old Ford Eight to the utmost, I just made it in time, got on the plane, and thankfully reached Brussels. Of course, there was nobody going to Mons by then, so I had to hire a taxi for the journey of about thirty-five miles. I hadn't enough money for such a luxury, but there was no option, and I just hoped that when I got to the circuit I could borrow from somebody to pay the driver.

My taxi-man must have guessed my predicament, for when we got to Mons he drove me straight to the circuit and, regardless of having no passes, armlets or anything, miraculously got his taxi right into the pits! When he could go no farther, he firmly walked with me onwards, until we met Johnny Claes, who paid him out, to my great relief.

By then it was midday, the 500 c.c. race was due to start at 2.30 p.m., and I had not even seen the circuit. Claes had tried the Kieft on the course with a view to taking it over if I did not arrive, but was so disappointed with it that he declined to drive it anyway. Certainly it was in poor fettle after Silverstone the previous day, and there had been no time to improve it, but I was determined to drive, learning the circuit as the race progressed.

For some unknown reason, I was allotted a second-row starting position, but when the starting flag went down and the cars rushed *en masse* down the long straight to the first corner, I had dropped back somewhat, being a bit too scared to press on 'into the un-known' with the others. Suddenly, however, I felt myself in the middle of the corner, trying to get round it too fast. I spun, but managed to keep the engine going, and set off once again. Came the next corner and, shame on me, I spun again, and this time the engine stopped.

This was no way to learn a circuit, but worse was to come. I managed to restart the Kieft and rejoined the race—everybody else now miles ahead, of course—and came to a right-hand corner which I managed to negotiate safely. But it was rapidly followed by another corner to the left, which I just didn't make. The Kieft careered nose-first through some straw bales and headed straight for the front door of a house on the outside of the corner. The poor car literally wedged its front between the lintel of the door and the walls, and I hit my nose on the steering wheel and got a bit of a shock, but nothing serious at all.

Unfortunately for me, this house was serving as the emergency hospital for that side of the circuit, and the medical staff had been on duty more or less since dawn, with all sorts of equipment to hand, and nobody to use it on. The arrival of a 'customer' right at their front door was too good a chance to miss!

The first thing I knew was that one very excited person rushed up and jabbed me with a hypodermic needle; it was also the last I knew for some little time! I was taken into the house and deposited on a table, and when I woke up I beheld a huge man looming over me, his face brown as a berry and with a vast bushy beard and whiskers; he was dressed in a Franciscan monk's habit, with a roped sash around his middle, and his feet were in brown sandals. And I thought, 'Crikey, this is the lot, boy!'

But he soon revealed himself to be extremely human, he and the other people in the house being kindness itself. They gave me all sorts of things to eat and drink, and finally took me upstairs to a room overlooking the circuit so that I could see the rest of the race in comfort. Just as I settled down, Stan Coldham's Cooper broke down near the corner, so he joined me at the window, where we watched the gay, carefree Harry Schell win the race in his blue and white Cooper, followed by Bill Aston.

I had to be back at work at the R.A.C. by 9 a.m. Monday, so I asked John Claes to collect my starting money for me. This amounted to about £50, which may sound generous for an inexperienced amateur, but left little change by the time the two-way journey by lorry, and personal travel and expenses, had been paid for.

Early in June the Kieft was entered for the Midland A.C.'s Shelsley Walsh hillclimb. 'Shelsley' had been a revered name in British racing for years, and I was very keen to see this famous hill. It was very short and concentrated—a mere 1,000 yards from start to finish, demanding maximum concentration from the driver.

I didn't put up much of a time in the Kieft, but when I got to the top I felt absolutely worn out. The first thing I wanted, above all else, was a cigarette—and mine were in my jacket, down in the paddock.

There was nothing for it but to scrounge one; I looked around and approached a vaguely familiar figure in pale blue overalls. I said 'Excuse me' and when he turned round I saw it was Peter Collins.

'Cigarette?—sure,' he said, producing his packet. As I took one I was ashamed to see how much my hands were shaking. I hoped Peter wouldn't notice, until he gave me a light, when I saw that his hands, too, were trembling. Relieved, I remarked on it, and Peter laughed. 'Don't worry, everybody gets that—we call it the Shelsley shivers!'

My next trip abroad was to Rheims. That splendid circuit in France's champagne country is renowned, of course, as the regular scene of the classic French Grand Prix. In 1950, however, the one and only Formula 3 race to be staged there was promoted as a 'curtain raiser' to the Grand Prix. I took the same Kieft that I had 'raced' at Mons, and brought along a second Kieft, fitted with a Norton single-cam engine. This was to be driven by Les Leston, making, if not his very first Formula 3 appearance, then certainly one of his earliest.

A 'rolling' type start was used, and as little trouble had been taken by the organizers to issue practice times or grid positions, we more or less pushed our cars where we wanted them. While we were still getting positioned, the pilot car suddenly started off, and everybody went after it in a wild scramble.

Rheims is quite a long circuit, measuring 4·86 miles round in those days, when it still passed through the village of Gueux, and the field of 500s quickly strung out. Retirements soon whittled down their number and after a while I found myself running with not another car in sight, and remember thinking with wild optimism: 'This is a cinch—I'm the only car still running. Keep going, Gregory, and you're bound to win.'

Les Leston's Kieft seized its engine and he coasted to a halt near La Garenne, and shortly after, I breasted the hill beyond that corner when my chain broke. I pulled off-course, reached for the pair of pliers I carried under the seat and ran back to Leston's car. I whipped his chain off, fitted it to my car and got going again, feeling vaguely heroic and still kidding myself that I was the only runner left.

Then half-way down the Thillois straight a hole burned in the top of the piston, and that finished my pleasant little delusion. Alf Bottoms in his J.B.S. won the race from a Swedish Effyh and Ken Carter's Cooper.

Amidst this racing activity, I was becoming more and more embroiled in 500 Club matters, and had now been promoted to Assistant Secretary, my salary rising from £1 to £3 per week. My main employers were still, of course, the R.A.C., but what with darting hither and thither, arranging my tickets, shipping, currency, carnets and so on through the Touring Department, and overdoing the private telephoning, Colonel Barnes was not very pleased, and I received the first of a number of severe dressings-down from him.

It was at the R.A.C. late one summer afternoon that Leslie Johnson, then well known as a Jaguar works driver and proprietor of the E.R.A. concern at Dunstable, called on me. He told me he wanted to produce a very special 500 c.c. racing car embodying E.R.A.-designed engine and transmission, to be called the F-type E.R.A. His plans included the marketing of this car on a hire-purchase basis.

As a result, Bill Whitehouse and I had dinner with Johnson and discussed the project at length. Nothing ever came of the Formula 3 F-type E.R.A. owing to various reasons, but while we were with Leslie Johnson I took the opportunity of asking him if he could use his influence with the Jaguar Company, and persuade them to give Stirling Moss a drive in the forthcoming Tourist Trophy race at the new Dundrod circuit in Northern Ireland.

Johnson's reply shook me. He said he did not consider Stirling was by any means ready to drive such a car as the competition XK120 Jaguar. The upshot was that Stirling was eventually offered a drive in T. H. (Tommy) Wisdom's private XK120, Tommy himself being down to drive a Jowett Jupiter.

On the Saturday of the T.T., I was down at Brands Hatch, practising for the following day's 500 Club race meeting. In between lapping, several of us gathered around a car radio in the paddock, listening to the T.T. race broadcast, and it was no small satisfaction for me to hear that Stirling Moss was way out in front, leading Leslie Johnson's and Peter Whitehead's works Jaguars! The race was run in atrocious weather, rain pouring down from start to finish, but it was there, at Dundrod, that Stirling first demonstrated his mastery of a car in the wet.

As a '500 boy', his victory in the T.T. was very well received at Brands Hatch. That night he flew over from Belfast, and next day he drove his Cooper at Brands. He won a heat of his race, but the car went off-colour in the final. With a T.T. victory that week-end, however, and a birthday party that night, arranged at the Greenways Club near Maidstone by his father, nothing could dampen Stirling's high spirits.

As for me, I was supposed to drive a Kieft-Norton at Brands again, sharing it with George Wicken. Unfortunately George ran into mechanical troubles during his race, and I found myself without a car for the Junior Championship race. Luckily, my friend Jack Leary lent me his impeccably prepared Mk. IV Cooper-J.A.P. and although I didn't do too well in my heat, I finished fifth and qualified for the final.

Waiting for the final to start, I felt extremely nervous, and when the flag fell, I wasn't very quick off the mark. However, by the time we were rounding Clearways I lay third, with David Brake's black and white Cooper leading. I managed to get through into second place, then followed Brake for several rounds, wondering when, where, how and if I could pass him.

Eventually, as we came into Clearways, David's Cooper ran

rather wide to the right (Brands Hatch was run anti-clockwise in those days, remember) and I managed to slip through on the inside and get ahead. Once there, I had a stab of alarm; I'd never led a race before, and realized that I'd have to go faster than ever if I wanted to stay there, yet on the other hand mustn't overdo it, lest I spin off and throw everything away. Somehow I managed not to do anything silly, pressed on, and eventually saw the 'Last Lap' board, with the starter getting the chequered flag ready. I won the race, with David Brake second and Robin Montgomerie-Charrington third, all in Coopers. What a fine feeling it was to win something!

When I got back to the paddock, the boys grabbed hold of me, gave me a severe bumping and threw me up in the air several times —just their gentle way of celebrating my win! I felt extremely elated, and well primed to join in celebrating Stirling's birthday party that evening.

In the final 1950 meeting at Brands Hatch, I drove a newer Kieft with lighter suspension units and general structure, and much improved bodywork. I do most heartily subscribe to the theory that if a thing looks right, it is right, and consider aesthetics to be vitally important in a racing car. Painted in silver, that Kieft looked much more attractive than the old one, and though that didn't mean that it flashed round the circuit at record speeds, it made me feel better and probably caused me, unconsciously, to drive better. I am not alone in this feeling, and am happy to cite the case of the great Sir Henry Segrave, who couldn't bear the scruffy appearance of his Sunbeam in one of the early French Grands Prix, so had it repainted at his own expense. Not, as he said, that its performance was improved any thereby, but it just made him feel better.

After finishing second in my heat of the Open Championship race, a little contretemps with Ian Burgess's Cooper (he is today the 'headmaster' of the Cooper driving school at Brands) put me out of the final. I was behind Ian on the inside as we rushed up to the then uphill Paddock Bend, and darted between him and the grass verge as we emerged; then the Cooper, completing a wider arc, came across my front, its nearside rear wheel riding over my Kieft's offside front wishbone. The impact put the Kieft's steering well out of line, and I had to retire.

Six weeks later I was out at Montlhéry track, near Paris, on a record-hunting foray with the long-chassis Kieft. Stirling Moss, Cyril Kieft, Jack Neill, Steve Lancefield and I made up the party, and with both International Class I and J records in mind, we brought two Norton engines with us, one a double-knocker 350, the other a single o.h.c. 500, both prepared by Lancefield.

Conditions were pretty desperate on 21 November for record-breaking; it was cold, intermittently wet, and decidedly windy, but the attempt went through. Stirling worked out the best speed line on the banked *Piste de Vitesse*, which co-drivers Neill and I then followed. We were unnecessarily perturbed when the Dunlop men inflated the tyres to 28 lb. per sq. in., and there was morning frost, too, to worry us, but we succeeded in breaking thirteen records before the engines called it a day. Six were in Class J (350 c.c.) when Moss and I drove, from the 50 km. at 78·44 m.p.h. to the 200 km. at 77·11 m.p.h., after which a contact breaker spring broke, and it was decided to pop the bigger unit in.

We broke seven Class I figures, from the 50 k.m. at 90·06 m.p.h. to the 200 miles at 86·99 m.p.h., Jack Neill taking a spell at the wheel with Stirling and me. Our best speed of all was 91·4 m.p.h. for the 100 miles. When a big end went, our run finished, but we weren't terribly sorry about this, for apart from the cold and the unpleasant cross wind, the special scuttle fuel tank had sprung a leak, and was dripping methanol steadily on to our legs.

In between runs with the Kieft, we amused ourselves driving Cyril Kieft's vast V8 Cadillac around the track, but after about fifteen fairly fast laps a nasty knock developed in the engine, and the 'Caddy' showed general signs of overheating; Cyril Kieft didn't seem much worried, so we left it to cool off, then put some more water in, and got on with the record-breaking.

Afterwards, Stirling and I set off for Paris in the Cadillac, but alas, we had covered barely two miles, and were just tackling a steepish hill, when there came a sort of sullen bang under the bonnet, and we stopped very suddenly. There was nothing for it but to return to Montlhéry, so we hitched a ride back in an ancient Citroën, containing one farmer, two pigs, six hens and several bottles of wine. There was just room for us as well.

We then took over the Guy transporter, stopping to tie on the disabled Cadillac, which Cyril Kieft steered. By now it was dark and we were very late. Stirling drove hard, keeping the headlights full on as we tore towards Paris, and I felt very sorry for Cyril at the other end of the tow rope. Now the French object strongly to the use of white headlights, and there was many an indignant toot from other motorists.

At one crossing a gendarme waved his baton furiously at the lights, blowing blasts on his whistle and practically catching fire with rage, but Stirling kept going. Perhaps it was as well, but at the time I was doubtful! 'Suppose he gets his gun out and takes a shot at us?—I wouldn't put it past him,' I said. Stirling grinned and opened out still further. 'He'll hit the "Caddy" first, I expect!' he said.

CHAPTER TWO

LINING UP WITH STIRLING

KIEFT plans for 1951 were ambitious. Cyril Kieft had invited Stirling to drive for him in Formula 3 races, but Stirling wasn't keen—not if the 1950-type car was to be used. Meantime, however, he had met a Bohemian but talented character named Ray Martin, who ran a small mews garage in Victoria, and was busily occupied there, repairing cars. Many of his customers seemed to be jazz fiends, and this was not surprising since Ray himself used to conduct a jazz band with considerable zest.

It is here, too, that the late John A. Cooper, sports editor of *The Autocar* until his sad death in 1954 and a very keen 'jazz student', comes into the picture. John (Autocar) Cooper was a clever engineer, with bold ideas when it came to racing cars, and not unnaturally he, Ray Martin and Stirling Moss frequently got together to talk motor racing and music, often joined by Dean Delamont.

Planning a '500' to beat all '500s', they had roughed out a hypothetical specification, startling for its rear swing axle on which the wheels were canted inwards even at rest; the suspension was by rubber strands, and everything about the design was ultra-light. When Cyril Kieft's offer was made to Stirling, the idea came to them—if Kieft would finance it, Martin could build the car at Victoria under their surveillance. Cyril Kieft agreed to the proposition, Cooper and Delamont finalized the design, and Martin wrought it in the metal.

The new Kieft, as all agreed it would be called, had a tubular frame, wishbone front suspension, and swing axle rear, the springing medium being horizontal strands of aero-elastic, linked by thin wire cables to the hub carriers with guide pulleys at the crucial right-angle turn. Stirling's twenty-first birthday present from his father, the double-knocker Norton engine which Ray had formerly installed in the Cooper, supplied the power, while the driver (Stirling, of course) sat well forward in a very compact body, shaped rather like a bomb cut down the middle. Borrani wire wheels, which

Moss purchased in Italy for the equivalent of £7 each, were fitted, and overall weight was well under five cwt.

While it was being built, Stirling and I had become directors of the Kieft Car Construction Co. Ltd., the plan being to develop the first car until it was fully race-worthy, and then to produce replicas in limited quantity for sale. As the spring of 1951 advanced, so the work on the Kieft grew more frenzied. John and Dean were constantly in and out, between their everyday jobs, Stirling was dashing hither and thither getting parts, while Ray Martin was working prodigious hours to complete it, in between looking after his other customers. I remember countless nocturnal sessions on the car, when poor Mrs Martin's upstairs flat would be crowded out, and endless cups of tea consumed there while various design points were thrashed out.

It was hoped that the new Kieft 500 would be ready in time for the Formula 3 Luxembourg G.P. on 3 May, but this proved impossible, so Stirling agreed to drive the old 1950 type. It ran poorly, and he retired from his heat after five laps only. Typifying his rigid sense of honour and sporting outlook, Stirling returned his starting money to the organizers, feeling his showing was too poor to merit any.

By dint of further all-night work, the Kieft was at last ready in time for the international meeting at Goodwood on Whit Monday. Moss was in Italy driving for H.W.M.s in the Formula 2 Monza G.P. on the Sunday, so I qualified the car at Goodwood on Saturday, finding its acceleration and general handling an absolute revelation after the old Kieft. It was fabulously light, and even with careful cornering I could pick up whole seconds from the rival Coopers along the short straights.

Stirling flew back from Monza after driving a wonderful race there, finishing third behind the works Ferraris of Ascari and Villoresi. He arrived at Goodwood just half an hour before the first heat of the Formula 3 race was due to start, and we were all so overjoyed at seeing him that I regret to say nobody remembered to put a hard plug in after the warming-up lap. The result was a miserable eighth place, just scraping into the final, after Stirling had stretched the throttle cable in trying to get really moving.

The Kieft's apparent slow pace certainly lulled the opposition, and the crowd, into discounting it as a serious rival to the Coopers. Indeed, the initial public reception of this odd-looking vehicle was cool to say the least. But we renewed the throttle cable, and put the proper plug in this time—and what a change there was after the final!

The Ecurie Richmond boys, Eric Brandon and Alan Brown, in their Coopers took the lead initially, but Stirling passed Brown after two laps, then set about Eric. He caught him on lap 4, the pair passing the pits almost dead level, to everybody's wild excitement, then, as they came up to Madgwick, the Kieft nosed ahead, passing on the actual turn, and leaving the Cooper almost standing as it accelerated away. Coming past the pits on the next lap, Stirling grinned across at me, and patted the Kieft's stubby 'bonnet' approvingly, while poor Brandon, flogging along behind, made despairing gestures to his pit crew.

We won by no less than 27 sec.—and what a 'moment divine' that was for Ray Martin after all his work, standing there almost asleep on his feet after not seeing his bed for two nights. There wasn't much time for celebration, though, as the car was due to race at Genoa the following Sunday.

Lionel Leonard took the Kieft to Italy in Stirling's Bedford van, and shortly after arrival at Genoa this was broken into. Obviously the Italians were no respecters of British green then, for they didn't bother with the car at all, but made off with Lionel's prize camel-hair overcoat instead!

Stirling led the Formula 3 race at Genoa until one of the rear suspension wire cables broke near the end. We remedied this trouble when the Kieft was back in England by replacing the wires with light roller chains running over tiny sprockets. Stirling and I then had to buckle down to several lengthy sessions with Cyril Kieft, who naturally now wanted to get the '500' into production. As there were no complete working drawings, the car had to spend some of its time at the Bridgend works as a 'master' for the production cars, which meant missing a few races.

Stirling was having a terrifically busy season with the H.W.M. team, dashing between England and the Continent, enjoying it all immensely, getting some marvellous experience, and building up a fine reputation for himself. Just how far he had climbed up the motor-racing ladder was brought home to us with a bang late in June 1951.

He was over in Germany with John Heath and Lance Macklin for the Formula 2 Avus race, when I received a telephone call from Desmond Scannell, Secretary of the B.R.D.C., saying he'd received an important telegram for Stirling, and as I was his close friend, perhaps I could contact him quickly. The telegram was from Enzo Ferrari, and offered Stirling a drive with the Ferrari team in the French and British Grands Prix—a tremendous honour, and an indication of the esteem felt for him on the Continent.

How to contact Stirling? H.W.M. arrangements were always pretty 'last minute' and Stirling himself hadn't known where he would be staying in Berlin before leaving. I therefore contacted a friend of mine who was a Reuter's Agency correspondent, asking if he could trace Stirling through Reuter's Berlin office. He immediately got a Telex message through to Berlin, and in only twenty minutes they had located Moss, and sent back his hotel address and phone number to me!

Very soon we were in contact, and I told him of the Ferrari offer. Needless to say, I was pretty excited, but can you imagine Stirling's own emotions? I heard the word 'crikey' come over the wire, there was a pause, then he said he could do nothing about the French G.P. at Rheims, as he was committed to driving for John Heath at Avus on the same day, and wouldn't break his word. As to the British G.P., he'd love to drive a Ferrari.

Next thing, to get in touch with Ferrari—but Signor Enzo wouldn't accept such an arrangement. He wanted somebody to drive both at Rheims *and* Silverstone. In the end he signed on Froilan Gonzalez, the tubby Argentinian, who drove two brilliant races in the 4½-litre V12 Ferrari, lying second at Rheims until he handed over to Ascari, and winning the British G.P., becoming the first man to beat the fabulous Alfa Romeos in six years. Just think —it might have been Stirling!

Obviously he was terribly disappointed at having to refuse the offer, but his principles were such that he just wouldn't entertain the idea of 'letting John Heath down', which was the way he looked at it. Yet I feel sure that, had he put the problem to him, Heath would have released him from his Avus commitments without hesitation. As it was, a strict sense of duty lost Moss a golden opportunity to get into the highest class of motor racing—the Grand Prix class—with a wonderful car. And this was in mid-1951, remember, when as things turned out Stirling didn't drive his first pukka Grand Prix car until April 1954—and even then it was a privately owned and not a works car.

To make the pill more bitter to swallow, the Avus race was a flat-out affair round the banked track, not at all suited to the H.W.M.s which arrived with road-racing gear ratios. Their engines just flew to pieces trying to hold the special streamlined German Veritas and B.M.W. cars, Stirling's breaking a connecting rod before three laps were completed.

That 1951 British Grand Prix won by Gonzalez was an unforgettable race. The R.A.C. had moved Race Control that year from the aircraft control office to a caravan, situated at the end of the pits, right at the exit from Abbey Curve. Whilst there, I nipped out now and then to watch the racing, and was naturally particularly keen to see how Gonzalez drove, since he was occupying the cockpit which, I felt, could well have been Stirling's.

I had heard that the Argentinian was spectacular, but was not prepared for what I saw. Nearly every lap he came round, Gonzalez was practically broadside coming out of Abbey. I had never seen anything so spectacular or frightening before; he seemed simply to aim the big Ferrari at the apex, then he picked it up by the steering wheel and forced it round by the sheer strength of his great arms.

But I couldn't help thinking—if Gonzalez in a Ferrari can beat Fangio in an Alfa Romeo at Silverstone, then Stirling Moss might have done the same. . . . The only compensation that day was that Stirling had won the curtain-raiser 500 c.c. race with the Kieft, leaving the rival Coopers and J.B.S. far behind—another feather in the Martin-Cooper-Delamont cap.

After Silverstone came Zandvoort and the Dutch G.P. meeting. I went across with Stirling, and saw his two impressive drives with the Kieft and the H.W.M. He won the 500 c.c. race by 9 sec. and was third in the Grand Prix for Formula 1 cars with the Formula 2 H.W.M. He had been hanging on to Etancelin's 4½-litre Talbot when the latter burst a tyre, so up went the H.W.M. into second position. Suddenly he rushed to the pits with misfiring; Alf Francis whipped the bonnet off and changed a plug, and with the old man 'Phi-phi' Etancelin due round at any moment, Stirling tore off again, leaving his bonnet behind.

A real shouting match then ensued between Heath and Francis, with Alfred Moss and me joining in, for we were all 'het up' at the thought of Stirling lying second in a Grand Prix. But it was a waste of breath, for the H.W.M. was still misfiring, Etancelin's Talbot caught it, and Stirling was lucky to stammer his way round to the finish.

Stirling's next date was the Formula 3 race preceding the German G.P. on the Nurburgring the following week-end. Sally Weston, who had been with our party at Zandvoort, went on to Germany with him and his father, but I had to get back to England and my work. By this time I had acquired somewhat higher status in the Competitions Department of the R.A.C., being now concerned with the organizational side of things.

The 500 Club, meanwhile, had undergone a certain significant change too, having changed its name to the Half-Litre Club. This was the result of complaints from the longer-established '500 Club' in Albemarle Street, a social body run by Richard Attenborough and John Mills. It seems that several of our members, believing that the Albemarle Street establishment was just another of our Club amenities, had been going there and enjoying proper members' privileges—an embarrassing situation which we solved in the only possible way—by changing our own name.

By now I had become the Secretary of the Club, which was thriving exceedingly and absorbing all my spare time, bringing more and more complaints from Stanley Barnes about the number of people calling on me at Pall Mall to discuss Half-Litre Club affairs in what should have been R.A.C. time.

I got the full story of Stirling's troubles in Germany when he and the others returned to England. In practice for the Formula 3 race, the Kieft had gone remarkably quickly, the rear swing axle being very suited to Nurburg's twists and turns. Stirling has always said that it is not so much power that one needs there as roadholding, and that was something the Kieft really had.

Unfortunately on race day he was feeling extremely ill, possibly through food poisoning of some kind; he was suffering from nausea, headache, chills and periodic shivering, but he gritted his teeth and, looking greener than the Kieft, turned out for the race. Perhaps being anxious to get the whole thing over as soon as possible, he came round on lap 1 some 22 seconds in the lead. He increased this to 39 sec. on lap 2, but on the next round the Kieft's steering arm broke and Stirling skated to a standstill.

He was unhurt, but back at the pits his mother and father did not know this, and were naturally extremely worried, remembering how ill he was; while John Cooper, also in the pits, had gone white with anxiety. Then, in the midst of this tension, Sally Weston, who had been watching the race elsewhere with Fangio, tripped gaily into the pit and asked how Stirling was. She was told by his father and mother that he was missing, and then unfortunately remarked, 'Oh well, I must go and finish the steak I'm having with Fangio,' and went off, showing apparent unconcern. The family never forgave her for that remark, even though reassuring news of Stirling shortly came through.

Coming up on 18 August was the Half-Litre Club's 100-mile race at Silverstone, and Cyril Kieft had agreed that I would drive the swing-axle Kieft, a prospect which excited me.

As a director of the Kieft Co., I was naturally interested in sales of the production models now being built at Bridgend. There was a certain sales resistance due, I believed, to the fact that only Stirling Moss had raced and won with the Kieft. Potential purchasers were all too often likely to argue: 'Oh well, you could put Moss on a bedstead and he'd win anyway. Let's see how somebody else gets on in the thing.'

The entry was so colossal that we had to split the 100-mile race into two separate events, an interesting point, considering that 'the 500 boys' were supposed to be such a mercenary lot, since there was no starting money paid, and very little prize money, while an entry fee was also payable.

I ran in the second 100-miler, together with thirty-eight other cars, and we shared the disadvantages of a circuit with plenty of rubber and oil on it, but the advantage of knowing exactly how fast we had to go to beat the speeds of the winners and placemen in the first race.

There was the usual scuffle for the lead at first, but I lay well behind. I was just settling down, and thought to myself, as I came down the long straight to the Copse hairpin, 'It's a lovely day, the sun is shining, the Kieft is going well . . .' and was really beginning to enjoy myself when suddenly a green Cooper came up and passed on my nearside, then tucked in right in front of me to line up for the hairpin, braking hard.

I slammed my brakes on, but to my horror the front wheels locked solid, I saw blue smoke curling off the tyres as they graunched their way across the concrete, the Kieft seeming almost to accelerate; it hit the green Cooper a good solid 'wham' and knocked it right off the circuit. It was Bob Gerard's car, and I felt terribly sorry for Bob, because I had literally put him out of the race.

After that, I settled to a steady race, speeding up as I gained confidence with the car, until, as the race neared its end, Alfred Moss and Ray Martin in my pit began dancing and waving and giving obvious 'step on it' signals. So I drove as hard as I could, and eventually passed the chequered flag, to learn that I was placed second, 5·4 sec. behind Les Leston's J.B.S. and 28 sec. ahead of Eric Brandon's Cooper. Had I opened out earlier, I might have caught Les, but as it was, neither of us equalled Alan Brown's winning speed of 70·94 m.p.h. in the first 100-mile race so that he became the winner of the Yorke Trophy, Leston was second and I was third.

Had Stirling been driving the Kieft he would obviously have won at a canter, but he was, in fact, over in Italy on very important business indeed, visiting Enzo Ferrari to discuss the question of driving the new 2½-litre lightweight Ferrari in the Bari G.P. Agreement was reached, and Stirling and his father duly arrived at the port of Bari for the race on 2 September, only to receive a rude shock. Ferrari, it seemed, had decided that Piero Taruffi would drive the car instead of Stirling, who was left flat without a wheel.

This was to have great repercussions on Stirling's racing career, for thereafter he steadfastly refused to drive a works Ferrari. When I became his manager, it was my job to try as far as possible to place him in the car with the best chance of winning, which very often was a Ferrari, but he wouldn't budge. Today, of course, he further insists that the Formula 1 car he drives must be British, which narrows the choice even further.

But to return to 1951. September meant the second Dundrod T.T. race, and this time Stirling was driving in the works Jaguar team. I went over to Ulster with Derek Annable, and we managed to get into the same hotel as Stirling and his parents. Stirling had brought his faithful Morris Minor MMM771 over—it had now done about 45,000 really hardworking miles—and his father and mother borrowed it to run up to the circuit.

They were half-way there when the Minor's fan flew off and went straight through the radiator, letting all the water out and generally messing things up. Their tempers weren't improved at all when Stirling said: 'Huh!—that's what happens when I lend you a car—you break it. Now you can jolly well get it repaired!' So that trip from the hotel to the circuit cost Alfred about twenty pounds, one way and another.

The T.T. was run in dry weather this time, but it was very blustery, with a high wind. Stirling won by over 2½ minutes from Peter Walker, both driving XK120C Jaguars, but the day was overshadowed by the death of Eric Winterbottom, who crashed in a 2-litre Frazer-Nash. Eric was the popular host of the Albert Hotel on Kingston Hill, where the 500 Club used regularly to congregate, and we all missed him immensely.

After his second T.T., Stirling galloped off to Italy for a race at Modena with the H.W.M., then wound up his season with meetings at Goodwood, Winfield in Scotland, and Brands Hatch, scoring wins at all three. After that we both felt that a holiday would be just the thing, albeit the one we selected was something of a 'busman's holiday'—to drive down to Barcelona and see the Spanish Grand Prix.

This was an excellent opportunity to conduct a long road test with one of the new 1952 models then just announced, so we looked around for a suitable one. Through Tom Mulcaster, the editor of the Rootes Group magazine *Modern Motoring and Travel*, whose daughter Elsie was with the R.A.C. Competitions Department, we were introduced to Norman Garrad, Sales and Competitions Manager of Sunbeam-Talbot Ltd.

With the object of writing our report on the run for the Rootes magazine, I asked if we could have the use of a Sunbeam-Talbot '90' and Norman Garrad was extremely helpful, arranging for one of the Earls Court demonstration cars to be made available to us as soon as the Motor Show was over. Thus it was that early one morning, in a nice new Sunbeam-Talbot with 800 miles on the clock, we set off for Dover and the long run down to Barcelona.

It was a dull grey morning, and the sea at Dover looked very rough, but I had been explaining to Stirling how I'd never been seasick in my life, so what about some breakfast before going on the boat? Stirling said, yes, he thought that was a good idea, so we went to the local hotel and tucked into bacon and eggs. Then we boarded the boat which, as soon as it left the shelter of Dover harbour, was tossed around the sea like a pea in a tin can.

The result was that I felt extremely ill, lost all the benefits of my breakfast and had never longed so hard to see the coast of France before. It didn't affect Stirling at all; he was perfectly all right, and proved by far the better traveller on this occasion. Thus I began my holiday in a dismal mood, but some good-natured chaff from Stirling and the return to *terra firma* soon put me right. We had a wholly uneventful journey down through Montelimar, Perpignan, then across the frontier and into Barcelona itself.

Next day we went up to the organizers' office to collect passes, and armed with a letter of introduction from the R.A.C., I introduced Stirling to various officials and asked for passes. Much of their initial cordiality melted away, and they were far from helpful, but eventually, after tremendous persuasion and much volubility on all sides, they parted with some tickets—entitling us to sell ice cream! We thought this a little unconventional, but were assured that all would be well; never, indeed, have I seen such a strange collection of passes as those worn by the British visitors to get into the circuit. One of the oddest was that of Gregor Grant, editor of *Autosport*, who sported a press pass from Prescott!

The race itself was wonderful, being the vital 'decider' for the 1951 World Championship, for which Fangio, driving an Alfa Romeo, and Ascari in a Ferrari were close contenders. After defeating the Alfas at Silverstone, Ferraris did it again in the German and Italian G.P.s and everyone expected them to do it a fourth time at Barcelona. But as it happened, the Ferraris used too small a size of wheel, and along the very fast straights were throwing treads left, right and centre, so that Fangio won the Spanish G.P. and the World Championship, and Alfa Romeo won their very last race with the famous supercharged Type 159.

After the Grand Prix, we went to see a bullfight. In order not to interrupt their fights, the car race was run in the morning so that it finished in good time for the Spaniards to take a light lunch and a slight *siesta*, then make their way to the bull arena. Stirling and I were accompanied by a Spanish friend of ours named Aurelio Valls, who was working for the Spanish Embassy in London, and came over to Barcelona to watch the Grand Prix.

Bullfights in Spain are divided, it seems, into two categories, one for the great professionals—a sort of 'Formula 1'—and the other for second grade or learner *toreadors*. October, we learned, was in the latter part of the bullfighting season, and the full-grade boys apparently don't fight then, so we had to make do with a show by the lesser men.

I am afraid the bullfight rather disgusted Stirling, who did not like the sport at all; as for myself, although I felt it was a spectacle one shouldn't miss just once in a lifetime, I shall not worry if I never see another bullfight. During the course of the afternoon, there were six bulls to be killed, and it is the custom at the fights to dedicate the death of each animal to a person or group of persons. On this occasion one of the bulls was dedicated to Juan Manuel Fangio, and another to the Alfa Romeo mechanics who had prepared his winning car. I thought this was rather a nice touch, even though it was a gruesome sport.

After Barcelona, we set off for the Monza circuit near Milan in Italy. Stirling had arranged to carry out extended tests of that complicated load of trouble, the 16-cylinder B.R.M., and I stayed with him for a couple of days to watch. Then I made my way homeward as the Sunbeam had to be returned, stopping in Paris to meet a friend named Ronnie Samuels, to whom I had promised a lift home when we met in Spain. He and I decided to go shopping in Paris before leaving for Dunkirk, so we set off for the Galeries Lafayette area in the city centre, parked the Sunbeam and locked it, and walked off to the shops.

Our purchases made, we emerged to find it was pouring with rain, so dashed back to the car, laden with parcels, getting rapidly soaked in the lashing rain. I felt in my pocket for the car key—to find it had gone! I searched in every pocket frantically but not a hope. Horrified, we retraced our steps to the crossing, and I gazed hopelessly at the wide, glistening road with cars continually splashing by.

Then, to my utter joy and astonishment, I spotted the key, lying in the centre of the road! Two taxi-drivers must have thought me crazy, for I just dived between them and grabbed the key with a whoop of triumph. Once more we made the mad dash back to the Sunbeam, this time to climb thankfully inside, soaked to the skin but very relieved.

So we arrived safely in London, and with regret I handed the Sunbeam-Talbot back to the Rootes people, then sat down to prepare the road test article. Stirling vetted this when he came back from Monza, and it was later published by *Modern Motoring and Travel*. The car was afterwards used in competition by Stirling, then purchased from Rootes by Alfred Moss.

On my return to work at the R.A.C., practically the first thing I had to undertake was the organization of the 1951 Veteran Car Run to Brighton, a task delegated to me by Colonel Stanley Barnes. This necessitated several meetings with the Committee of the Veteran Car Club of Great Britain, who are very closely concerned with the Run, and are a tower of strength in its promotion, in the verification of the ages of competing cars, and other vital factors. I had also to go down to Brighton several times for sessions with the Chief of Police, the Chief of Public Relations and the Entertainments Officer, to finalize arrangements.

One of the greatest problems of the Veteran Run lies in trying to dissociate the tender vehicles from the actual veterans on the road. It is felt that the tender cars, following their charges in close attendance, are partially responsible for the large road blocks which ensue. Many ways have been tried to overcome this difficulty, but none have succeeded, because you just can't stop a man from following his precious veteran with a tender of some kind, in order to give assistance whenever needed.

In 1951, I didn't appreciate just how much veteran cars might need assistance, but later on, when I drove in the Run myself, I realized why most of the tender cars broke the instructions not to follow their charges on the day.

The Run itself took place in pouring rain, as was so often the case—'The Wettest Ever' said one report, and 'Weterans' another —but even so, spirits weren't dampened overmuch, and the event went off well, without any ill-effects or hitches.

As 1951 drew to a close, Stirling and I looked back and realized what a hectic season it had been. He had driven H.W.M.s, Jaguars and Kiefts in a whirl of races at home and abroad. Co-ordinating his activities month after month had meant a great deal of planning and complicated travel arrangements. He was, in fact, beginning to feel the burden of being a professional racing driver, and the need for someone who could take on his administrative worries, and could also be a travelling companion and a friend to him.

He was well aware of my love for organizing, of my work with the R.A.C. and the Half-Litre Club; we were close friends, and I had long been accepted virtually as one of the family by the Mosses at Tring. As a result, after several discussions, Stirling offered me a job as his manager in 1952.

I accepted.

CHAPTER THREE

1952—TOUGH GOING

IT WAS both with reluctance yet eager anticipation that I entered Colonel Barnes's office one day early in 1952, and gave notice that I wished to leave the employ of the R.A.C. in order to join Stirling Moss as personal manager. Reluctance because I had learned a very great deal in the Pall Mall offices, and enjoyed the friendly and helpful atmosphere there; anticipation because of my hopes for the future, closely concerned with one whom I considered an outstandingly brilliant driver and a coming World Champion.

Next I resigned the Secretaryship of the Half-Litre Club, my place being taken by Ken Carter; then Stirling and I got down to some preliminary planning for the coming season. There was an immense amount to think about—which cars to drive, which races to support, negotiations with fuel and oil concerns, the B.R.M., accommodation problems, the Kieft directorships, a new project by Leslie Johnson. . . .

I was bursting to get at grips with them all, but taking priority, very early in the New Year, was a variety of motoring contest new to Stirling Moss—the classic Monte Carlo Rally.

After our drive to Barcelona the previous October, Norman Garrad of Rootes had taken the opportunity of signing-up Moss to drive a Sunbeam-Talbot 90 in the Monte Carlo Rally. In his usual way, Stirling took this undertaking very seriously, and chose as his crew a sound pair in John A. Cooper of *The Autocar* and Desmond Scannell, Secretary of the British Racing Drivers Club. Then, in order to get himself into A1 physical trim for the event, Stirling, who has always had a mania for keeping fit, decided we would go winter sporting for the first time. Neither of us had ever been on skis, and Stirling felt that now was the time, to acclimatize himself for the ice and snow which was anticipated in the big Rally.

Thus it was that, early in January, we went off together in a new Jowett Javelin which Stirling had persuaded his mother she ought to have. We arranged to go to Kitzbühel in the Austrian Tyrol, and drove via France and Switzerland. Late on the second night we reached a little town called Buchs, close to the Swiss-Austrian border, and put up at the Station Hotel, where the proprietor spoke excellent English and remembered the name of Moss for his performances at Berne and Erlen with the H.W.M.s. He asked why we didn't stay on the Swiss side for our skiing, rather than journey the extra 150 or so miles across the frontier to Kitzbühel. We said we thought it would be too expensive, but he rang up a little village called Unterwasser, up in the mountains about ten miles away, and was able to get us excellent terms.

Arriving at Unterwasser, we lost no time in hiring skis and sticks —we had our own boots—and without a thought for the future rushed straight on to the funicular railway and up to the top. From there we managed somehow to slither, slide and scramble across a little valley to a building and a further ski tow, where they fixed a big leather strap round your bottom and you stood in your skis, the lift then pulling you right up into the mountain, almost up to heaven itself, it seemed.

Stirling pushed me on to this thing first, and said he would follow, and I hadn't gone more than 200 yards up when I came an awful 'purler'. I managed to scramble out of the way, because Stirling was only about thirty feet behind, and he went sailing past until eventually he decided it was getting too steep altogether, and pulled off.

Then the truth struck us. Neither of us knew how to ski, yet there we were, three parts of the way up a mountain, and the only apparent way down was by ski. It was easy enough to get started on them—only too easy—but as Stirling said, he couldn't find the brake pedal! So discretion won the day, we took our skis off, walked down, and caught the funicular to the bottom.

The next morning we joined the Swiss ski school, and from then on enjoyed every single minute of our holiday. Stirling proved particularly good, and quickly learnt the art of skiing. On the other hand, whilst I enjoyed it, I was slower to learn, though almost managing to keep up with Stirling. This sometimes had disastrous effects, particularly on the day when I was trying to keep up with him down the normal ski run, and then ran out of control and hit a low boundary wall, snapping one of my skis completely in half, close to my foot.

That holiday put Stirling in remarkably good health, fit to face the rigours of what proved to be a very severe Monte Carlo Rally. Tremendous blizzards raged in the Alpes Maritimes and the Col de Braus, and very few competitors got through with a clean sheet. Stirling did, however, and finished second in the entire Rally, only four marks behind the winner, Sidney Allard.

Back home again, we got down to preparations for the season. One problem which often worried Stirling was the high cost of hotel accommodation on the Continent, not to mention the inconvenience. Only those who have done it themselves can realize just how fed up you become of living in and out of a suit-case all the time. The average family or person recalls packing a suit-case as an annual event; picture what it is like when you do this, not once a year, but often as much as two or three times a week.

If travelling, for example, from a race at Zandvoort in Holland to, say, Monza, it means two days' travelling, and each time you stop you have to unpack, then pack again. If your itinerary is worked out in advance, you may already have booked the hotel; if not, you must seek one out, and all in all it becomes quite a nightmare after a few weeks. As an instance, between March and October 1951, Stirling raced consecutively at Goodwood, Marseilles, San Remo, the Mille Miglia, Luxembourg, Silverstone, Monza, Goodwood, Genoa, Berne, Aix-les-Bains, Rome, Douglas, Le Mans, Berlin, Rouen, Silverstone, Mettet (Belgium), Zandvoort, Nurburgring, Freiburg (Germany), Erlen (Switzerland), Bari (Italy), the Curragh (Eire), Dundrod, Modena, Goodwood, Winfield (Scotland), and Brands Hatch, the latter being the sole occasion on which he didn't need his suit-case and an hotel!

We decided that the way to solve the problem was to have a caravan specially fitted out, to stock it with tinned foods and other requisites, and to tow it behind Stirling's car—one of the first Jaguar XK120 hardtops—from meeting to meeting. By this means we would have a base, should save a lot of money, and travelling from country to country would be much pleasanter as we would not be continually packing suit-cases.

Anyway, his mind once made up, Stirling began working out the specification of his caravan. It mustn't be too large because of the varying roads we would travel on; it mustn't be too small because we wanted individual comfort; it mustn't be too heavy, because we wanted to motor fairly quickly.

Eventually we selected a model called the 'Nomad', made by the Paladin firm of Luton, and went over to see the manufacturers. Stirling startled them immediately by saying that the first requirement was that his caravan should be able to cruise comfortably at 70 m.p.h.! I'm sure they thought Stirling was a bit of a lunatic, but anyway, they humoured him, and eventually agreed to build a caravan embodying the modifications he requested.

Not for Stirling the spartan life tolerated by ordinary caravanners. He wanted all comforts—a refrigerator, hot and cold water, heating, and a shower bath—and he got them all. We even had a small metal safe welded to the chassis in which to keep starting money paid in various currencies.

The 'fridge' was an ingenious affair, worked either by electricity or by paraffin. The paraffin tank was arranged on a floating platform so that, no matter what angle the caravan assumed, the flame remained level and could even be kept on while in motion.

For hot and cold running water, an Ascot water heater was installed over the sink, at the back of the 'van, connected to a Calor gas bottle carried on the drawbar at the front. This in turn was linked to a 1-gal. water tank, situated above the axle, and inside the tank were some ex-R.A.F. submerged pumps of the type formerly fitted to Lancaster bomber wing tanks. These were connected to a battery, so that when water was required, you switched on the pump which fed water to the geyser, and then switched on the geyser, which in turn heated the water. It worked very well.

The shower was another ingenious affair, comprising a sort of square plastic enclosure embodying a waterproof container at the base, and a perforated metal top. From about two feet from the bottom a zip-fastener ran to the top; the person having the shower got inside, closed the zip to stop the water splashing out, and then his pal fed hot water from the geyser into the perforated top. When it was over, you simply undid the zip, got out, unhooked the shower attachment from the roof of the caravan, and took the entire apparatus outside to empty it.

The Moss mobile mansion, which cost in all about £785, was eventually delivered to Tring early in May, and Stirling and I worked flat out for three days, fitting curtains and all sorts of racks and wires, and loading it up with clothes and bedding and food. Our activities were watched with amused tolerance by Alfred Moss, who was dubious of some features, praised others, and was certainly doubtful whether Stirling would be able to tow the caravan along at 70 m.p.h.

A major decision which Stirling had to make in 1952 concerned his Formula 2 mount. He had contemplated remaining with the H.W.M. team which brought him such valuable experience in 1950 and 1951, but had also been approached by Leslie Johnson, proprietor of E.R.A. Ltd. Johnson had for some time been working with a brilliant young designer named David Hodkin on an entirely new Formula 2 E.R.A. to be known as the G type, powered by a modified 2-litre 6-cylinder Bristol engine. And Johnson needed a driver.

Leslie Johnson was not only a very fine driver himself; his methods of approach were startling and effective. He has a brilliant personality, and could charm anybody round to his point of view. He soon had Stirling so enthusiastic about his project that he showed no hesitation at all in signing-up to drive the E.R.A.— especially when he learnt that the team manager was to be Desmond Scannell, whom he much admired for his efficiency.

With Formula 2 racing settled, it was also decided to purchase the prototype Kieft-Norton outright from Cyril Kieft for 1952 Formula 3 racing, and to resign our directorships with the Kieft Co. Cyril agreed that as we would be planning the car's programme and running it ourselves, there was little benefit in retaining our connection with the Bridgend concern.

With the Kieft, Stirling kicked off well, winning the 500 c.c. race at Castle Combe on Easter Saturday, and that at Goodwood on Monday. But the new E.R.A. was nowhere near ready yet, and good Formula 2 races were passing by with poor Stirling a nail-biting spectator.

Furthermore, as April turned to May, Formula 2 suddenly took a stride forward in importance, for Continental race organizers, faced with the withdrawal from Formula 1 racing of the Alfa

Romeo concern, and the continued vacillation of the B.R.M. organization, whose V16 was very fast but very unreliable, suddenly found Formula 2 very attractive. Big fields were promised, with adequate British, Italian and French representation, whereas Formula 1 prospects centred on the 4½-litre Ferraris, some old and weary Lago-Talbots, and the B.R.M.

By May, even the B.R.D.C. and the *Daily Express* had swung over to Formula 2 for their big International Trophy meeting at Silverstone. Stirling entered the Kieft for the 500 c.c. race, was down to drive Jaguars in three other events, and was hoping, vainly as it turned out, that the E.R.A. would be ready for the Trophy race.

It was shortly before Silverstone that we took delivery of our special caravan, and as Stirling's object in life was to race as often as possible, he had entered for a 500 c.c. event at Brussels the day after Silverstone. That was where the caravan would face its first test.

The plan was to load the Kieft on to Stirling's Bedford lorry immediately after the 500 c.c. 'curtain-raiser' at Silverstone, when mechanic Brian Johnson would drive it down to Dover. I would follow him with the Jaguar and caravan, we would jointly catch the night ferry to Dunkirk, then drive to Brussels early in the morning.

Stirling, meanwhile, would fulfil the rest of his commitments at Silverstone, after which we had arranged with the very obliging Northants police that he would be given a lift from the circuit by a motor-cycle 'speed-cop' out to his car. This was to be parked well away from any possible traffic jams, he would dash down to London, and catch a plane to Brussels, where hotel accommodation for him was reserved. I have detailed all this to provide an insight into the amount of advance planning necessary when one goes motor racing.

In the Silverstone Formula 3 race, the Kieft let us down somewhat and Moss finished third to Stuart Lewis-Evans and Alan Brown. After the event we discovered that the handbrake was partially on, owing to the fact that a small nipple, soldered on to the end of the cable, had caught in the carrier, thus braking the car after about the eleventh lap. Not that this is to minimize the splendid driving of Lewis-Evans and Brown; it was a fine victory for the former, on an unpleasantly wet circuit, and this marked the time when people first really sat up and took notice of Stuart.

But Stirling won all three other races he was entered for, one with an XK120C Jaguar, one with a Mk. VII saloon, and one with a left-hand drive production XK120, so that in all he didn't feel too bad. It was ironic, however, that the final of the big race saw the first two places taken by H.W.M.s—the team he had left to drive the E.R.A.

As for the caravan, we were delighted with it, even though we were woken up at about 6 a.m. in the Silverstone paddock, by hearty bangs on the side, an occasional rocking, and many voices and laughter outside. It was merely a batch of early and inquisitive spectators, feeling frivolous!

We were parked next to another caravan owned by the famous *Daily Express* cartoonist Giles, and during our stay there Giles and Stirling became very great friends. More than once we went across for a meal with him and his wife, when he would tell us funny stories about the building of his caravan. It was beautifully equipped, having a bathroom, full drawing facilities and other amenities. Since that day in 1952, Giles has frequently caricatured Stirling in his cartoons around Silverstone time.

Once the Formula 3 race was over, we bundled the Kieft in the van, hitched the XK120 hardtop to the caravan, and shot off for Dover. We went via Canterbury, where our mechanic, Brian Johnson, lived. We stopped at his home for a bath and a meal, and Brian's mother gave us ten dozen eggs in a large cardboard box to take with us. We put them on top of the refrigerator.

We reached Brussels early in the morning, picked Stirling up at his hotel and then drove to the Bois de la Cambre just outside Brussels to the scene of the race. The Kieft was unloaded, we got it ready for practice, and in the general rush I regret to record that I was less efficient than I hope I have been since then—just before Stirling's heat started I inadvertently filled the fuel tank with benzol instead of methanol.

When the flag dropped, Stirling was unable to get the expected acceleration, and came round on lap 1 in about seventh place instead of the hoped-for lead. We waited anxiously to see if he would pick up any places on the second lap, but to our horror, he didn't come round at all. Nor did nine other cars, for we learnt there had been a multiple shunt, precipitated when the Dutchman Beels spun on a slippery corner; Stirling came round in the middle of the pack of cars dodging this way and that to avoid each other, and charged the straw bales hard. The poor old Kieft was completely written off.

Stirling himself was shaken but unhurt. Sadly we picked up the wreckage and stuffed it into the Bedford. I felt terrible about the whole thing, and couldn't help thinking that, if the Kieft had had methanol instead of benzol in the tank, Stirling would have been well ahead of that pile-up. Yet apart from a few choice, well chosen and very crisp words at the time, Stirling has never held that mistake against me—but then, he's not that sort of person.

The loss of the Kieft looked like putting paid to Stirling's chances of running in the second Formula 3 Grand Prix at Luxembourg, until we thought of our old friend Derek Annable, who now had a new Kieft with J.A.P. engine. If we could borrow it, and pop Stirling's double-knocker Norton unit in, then we should be able to run at Luxembourg after all.

I phoned Derek at his home in Marlow, and like the great sport he is, he immediately agreed. So it was arranged that Brian Johnson would take the Moss Kieft back to England, remove the engine, which luckily had suffered superficial damage only, and transfer it to Derek's car, after which both he and Derek would come out again to Luxembourg.

Between the Brussels and Luxembourg races, however, came the Swiss G.P., and with no hopes of the G-type E.R.A. being ready yet, Stirling was glad of the chance to drive one of John Heath's H.W.M.s. We decided that it wasn't worth dragging the caravan all the way to Berne, and planned to park it at Luxembourg, then go off to Switzerland in the Jaguar. We remained in Brussels two further days, meeting during that time a great friend named David Arkell, who was shortly to prove extremely helpful. David was the Belgian importer for Borgward cars from Germany, assembling the cars from C.K.D. units and holding distribution rights for the whole of Belgium. Then we decided to press on for Luxembourg and Berne, and so, late one evening, we hitched the caravan up to the ever willing Jaguar, and drove fifty or sixty kilometres outside Brussels in order to dodge the heavy city traffic next morning. We found a convenient lane close to the main road, parked the 'van, and spent a peaceful night.

But next morning it was like Silverstone all over again, for we were suddenly awakened by an energetic pounding on the side of the 'van, and much shouting. We thought, 'Oh blast—this must be the one morning when the farmer has decided to use this lane for his tractor or something.' But no, the callers were Alan Brown and Eric and Sheila Brandon, who were driving past *en route* to Luxembourg, spied the caravan, and thought they would come and have breakfast with us.

We soon got a meal going, and when they'd had their fill, our visitors packed into their car and drove off again, with a cheerful 'See you in Luxembourg'. Stirling and I looked at the mounting pile of washing-up and thought, 'Hang it—it can wait till later,' packed the caravan together, hitched the Jaguar up, and set off down the Namur road.

We had covered about thirty miles, and I was driving at the time, when as we descended a fairly steep hill there came a sudden sharp jolt at the back of the car. Stirling turned, and I looked in the mirror, then we both shouted, 'Crikey—the blasted 'van's broken loose!' Not only was our mobile hotel loose—it was gaining on us, so I rammed the Jaguar into second gear and accelerated hard to get out of its way. Then we slowed and gazed, utterly appalled, as the great caravan lumbered its way down.

It swayed crazily from side to side, then hit a very solid kilometre stone on the right-hand side of the road, bounced up about twenty feet in the air, and with a sickening crunch landed straddled across the middle of the road on its side, with the skylight pointing downhill. Speechless, we turned the car round and drove back, but when we got out, and saw Stirling's pyjamas hanging out of the broken skylight, with the remains of Mrs Johnson's ten dozen eggs trickling down one leg, we just sat down on the road, helpless with laughter.

As is always the case, until the accident the road had been deserted, but within a very few minutes streams of traffic were queuing on both sides, because we were completely blocking the road. But eventually a lorry equipped with dragging chains unceremoniously pulled our wrecked home to one side, and the traffic moved on.

I went back up the hill to a service station, and phoned our friend David Arkell in Brussels, who promised to arrange for the Borgward agent in the district to pick the caravan up. And so, very sorrowfully, we packed as many things as we could from inside the 'van into the small boot of the Jaguar, and set off for Luxembourg to book a hotel, before driving off to Berne.

So that washing up was never done—though it cost the best part of £700 to get out of it! After this, the idea of caravanning lost its attraction and we went back to living out of suit-cases. The caravan was so badly smashed up that when, some eight months later, we managed to get it back to England with the aid of the R.A.C., it was disposed of for £95.

Berne produced more disappointments, for after getting his H.W.M. up into third place, Stirling ran into plug trouble, and finally was flagged in by John Heath when two of the H.W.M.s broke their rear axles, and it was feared that Stirling's and Lance Macklin's might do the same.

It was at Berne that year that Mercedes-Benz ran four of their new 300SL coupés in the sports-car race. These had already shaken the racing world by finishing second and fourth in the Italian Mille Miglia, and were destined to win the Le Mans 24-hour race a month or so later.

On the evening before the race, we were having dinner in the grillroom of the Schweizerhof Restaurant at Berne—a favourite haunt of Stirling's since John Heath had introduced him to it.

Now Stirling has a very sweet tooth, and the big attraction that night was the special dessert, *banane flambé*, comprising banana liberally soaked in alcohol and 'flambéd'. While this was being served, the famous German driver, the late Rudi Caracciola, came over from the next table and had a long chat with Stirling about motor racing. Being a great admirer of Rudi's methods and his splendid racing career, Stirling was enthralled, forgetting all about his *flambé*!

We were extremely sorry when, the following day, Caracciola

had a terrible accident in the race. His 300SL went off the road and hit a tree head-on at speed. Poor Rudi, who had limped ever since 1933 when he badly broke his right thigh in a crash at Monaco, now broke his left thigh and was doomed to spend eight months on his back before recovering.

Back at Luxembourg three days later, Stirling won his heat with Annable's Kieft, but the car wasn't running too well, and sixth was the best that he could manage in the final. Indeed, the main thing I remember about Luxembourg that year is that we practically seemed to live on Stirling's favourite dish, *soufflé Grand Marnier*, which happened to be one of our hotel's specialities.

Although he doesn't drink, Stirling certainly likes alcohol in his food, and every night we would have a huge, fluffy thing looking like a mountain brought to the table! Abstainer Stirling is also very partial to things like *crêpes suzettes* and other French dishes which are cooked in wine or spirits, and though he contends that the alcohol is burned out, we often argued good-humouredly about it, my contention being that if you drink the juice of a *crêpe suzette*, you are drinking alcohol just as much as if it were from a glass.

The season was advancing rapidly but Stirling's poor luck continued. The G-type E.R.A. had still not appeared, and though he managed second place in the Eifelrennen Formula 2 race at Nurburg with a borrowed H.W.M., the Kieft shed a wheel while leading the Formula 3 race, while the Frazer-Nash he drove in the British Empire Trophy race in the Isle of Man also packed up.

I personally took this persistent ill luck very much to heart, being Stirling's manager, and the gloom was not lifted when we saw how well other drivers were doing. In particular, a young newcomer by the name of Mike Hawthorn was making a tremendous name for himself with a Formula 2 Cooper-Bristol. Of course the newspapers, who had been building Stirling up as Britain's great hope in motor racing, now created a tremendous story of rivalry between the two drivers for the B.R.D.C. Gold Star, and this didn't lift our despondency greatly, since every time the two appeared, Mike galloped away, while Stirling usually broke down.

In June Stirling was scheduled to make his first race appearance with the V16 B.R.M., he and Fangio driving two cars in the Ulster Trophy race at Dundrod in Northern Ireland. The cars were very unhappy in practice, during which something occurred which was to have a profound effect on Stirling's future attitude to B.R.M. It was found that Stirling's car was the better of the pair, and that Fangio's was suffering from severe overheating troubles. That night, therefore, B.R.M. changed the cars over without informing Moss, and although the latter willingly accepted his No. 2 role, he felt that at least he might have been told of the switchover.

When Stirling climbed into the B.R.M. on race day, he quickly spotted that it wasn't his, yet still nobody told him of the change-over. From that day onwards, he never really trusted the B.R.M. people. The full Dundrod story has already been well told in *Stirling Moss* and other books. Suffice it to say that both B.R.M.s retired, and that Stirling never drove the V16 again.

Le Mans, 1952, was as bad. Jaguars had fitted out their XK120Cs with extremely sleek and aerodynamic bodywork, but in so doing, unfortunately, brought upon themselves insuperable overheating troubles. After practice, Stirling was all for the factory flying out one of the earlier C types, but the streamliners were modified in hopes of rectifying the troubles. That these were unsuccessful is well known, and all the Jaguars went out in a cloud of steam early in the race.

While, personally, I felt very sorry for Stirling in this latest reverse, I cannot say I was sorry for myself. My job at Le Mans was to sit on the pit counter and record the individual lap times of every Jaguar for the entire twenty-four hours! Bob Berry, from the Jaguar public relations office, was to help with this monotonous task, and though the retirement of the full team put an end to the incessant watch-clicking, I felt I had already had enough of Le Mans. As it happens, that was my only visit there, and I have never felt any desire to return.

The European G.P. for Formula 2 cars at Spa came next, and our hopes centred on the G-type E.R.A., which Leslie Johnson had promised would be there. We had waited so long for this fabulous motor car, and in our minds, I am sure, had visualized a really beautiful racing car, something on the lines of, say, a Mercedes of E-type E.R.A., both of which were quite classics in appearance. Then, just before practice was due to begin, I saw a rather rough-looking green machine coming down the road, and was horrified to learn that this was the E.R.A. I wasn't watching Stirling's face closely at the time, but I think that he, too, was bitterly disappointed. Not only was the car squarish and ugly; it wasn't even a true single-seater, yet here it was, turning out for the G.P. of Europe!

Although the car embodied many unusual and clever design features, it was a really ugly vehicle, and I didn't feel at all proud that Stirling was to drive it. I may have a 'thing' about it, but I have always rigidly maintained that no car which looks fundamentally wrong has ever gone right, and vice versa. Leslie Johnson explained that its appearance was purely temporary, and that later a better-looking body would be fitted. It certainly needed one.

We could, perhaps, have forgiven the G type its ugliness had it gone well. Stirling so badly needed a good car to restore his confidence but the E.R.A. didn't help. In practice it ran poorly, and it was decided that the engine was below par. Johnson lost no time in arranging for another engine to be flown out from Bristols to Ostend, and this meant that somebody would have to be at Ostend airport at around seven-thirty next morning.

That somebody was me, and Leslie Johnson and I set off at the crack of dawn, driving two different cars as he had to remain in Ostend to transact some business, whereas I would have to get the engine to Spa as quickly as possible. Silver City flew the engine over without delay, but the Ostend Customs soon messed that up, so that after much haranguing and arguing, I didn't get back to Spa until lunchtime.

All our efforts came to naught, however, and in the race Stirling had a very lucky escape. At flagfall he made a colossal start from the back row, and was up to fifth place by means of fabulous weaving and darting, when suddenly the engine locked solid, and burst into flames. The car slid uncontrollably off the track, near Burnenville, smacking into a concrete kilometre post and wrecking the suspension and front end. A connecting rod had broken.

Stirling leapt out smartly, with only his shoe-laces burnt! Even so, it was one of his luckier escapes, for just beyond the point where the E.R.A. finished up was a great mass of barbed-wire fencing. I will never cease to be astonished at the incredible folly of organizers who permit the existence of barbed-wire fencing close to a circuit, particularly in the neighbourhood of corners. Later in this same race, the late Ken Wharton had an incredibly lucky escape when he spun on the slippery surface, his single-seater Frazer-Nash skating off backwards and careering straight towards a fence formed of a single strand of barbed wire, about three feet from the ground. With remarkable *sang-froid*, Ken ducked as the car shot underneath, but even so, his clothing was badly ripped on the wire.

The Spa crash meant, of course, no E.R.A. for the Formula 2 Grand Prix at Rheims the following Sunday, so Stirling arranged with John Heath to drive one of the H.W.M.s. We arrived at Rheims well in advance of practice, and found that Rodney Walkerley, then sports editor of *The Motor*, was there already. Rodney is a great traveller with an intimate knowledge of France acquired by motoring all over the place ever since about 1934, reporting motor races. We were all staying at the Hotel Welcome, and very soon teamed together.

He told us of a little fort called Pompel, on the outskirts of Rheims. It had been dug out of a large chalk hill on the Soissons road, and formed one of a ring of forts built for the defence of Paris in World War I. Fort Pompel has a very gruesome history, being the scene of some extremely bitter fighting during that war, having been taken and retaken by French and German forces alternately.

Rodney offered to show us this fort late one moonlit night, following an excellent dinner at one of the little-known hotel-restaurants he had discovered during which the main topic of conversation had not been motor racing, but ghosts. At Fort Pompel, so the story goes, the ghost of one of the Great War sentries still patrols with his rifle and bayonet, and although he did not turn out that night for our benefit, the atmosphere of the place in the cold moonlight was certainly very eerie.

We came back the following day and visited a tiny café near by, filled with all sorts of war souvenirs. It also contained a number of devices similar to those 'What the Butler Saw' machines adorning the piers at so many British holiday resorts. One placed 100 francs in the slot, sat on a stool, and looked through a binocular-type eye-piece, turning a handle. This flicked a series of pictures over—and what gruesome pictures they were, showing various grim scenes from the trenches during and after battles in the 1914–18 war. I remember one still, showing half a horse hanging in a tree with its entrails hanging out. Certainly I should think they were effective in bringing home to people the horrors of war, and discouraging them from having new ones.

Rodney is not only an extremely pleasant and amusing companion and an excellent guide, but also an expert on French food and wines, so that our next few days at Rheims in his company were most enjoyable. But soon the racing vans and personnel came rolling into the town, and practice began. Stirling was driving Tommy Wisdom's privately entered XK120C Jaguar in the sports-car race, as well as an H.W.M. in the Grand Prix, and it was this Jaguar which gave him his first break for a long time. He won the 50-lap race by nearly three minutes from a 4½-litre Talbot, with Jimmy Scott-Douglas third in an XK120.

The race was run on a boiling-hot day, and I recollect our amazement at Stirling's antics as he came past the pits each time. One lap he would hurtle past steering with his left arm, his right arm hanging on the side of the door, and on the next lap he would be steering with his right arm, while his left would be spread out across the back of the car.

We realized after a time that these apparently lazy attitudes were adopted in an effort to cool himself as much as the high cockpit of the XK120C would allow. When he had won the race, he couldn't even smile at this change in his fortunes, for he was fatigued beyond all measure owing to the terrific heat, and had literally to be pulled out of the car. However, a couple of bottles of Coca-Cola, a cool wash and a change of clothes bucked him up tremendously.

Even so, the Grand Prix was not to be his race. From a very good start, Stirling had to pull in with falling oil pressure. He pegged along thereafter, the engine steadily pumping hot oil all over him, and after repeated stops to replenish the oil tanks (and having most of it pumped over himself again) he finished tenth. My memories of the race are happier than his, for John Heath and Alf Francis asked me to drive Stirling's car from the garage near the Hotel Welcome up to the circuit, which I thought was a terrific honour.

I enjoyed it so much that I was hoping against hope that I'd be able to drive the H.W.M. back after the race. Unfortunately the cockpit was absolutely swimming in oil, and the car had to be towed back.

Between the Rheims meeting and the next round, the British G.P., Stirling took a change from racing cockpits and drove a Sunbeam-Talbot saloon, together with Mike Hawthorn, Leslie Johnson and others, in that extremely gruelling 2,000-mile, six-day event, the Alpine Rally. He returned, tremendously impressed by the event, the winner of one of the much-coveted Coupes des Alpes awarded to those losing no marks. Mike also won a Coupe, and finished a place ahead of Moss in the final results, the pair being ninth and tenth in their first 'Alpine'.

Stirling liked driving for the Rootes Group. Their competitions manager, Norman Garrad, is absolutely tops when it comes to team management and control in rallies, and the careful organization of the Rootes concern which was in evidence wherever they competed, coupled with their extensive service chain, which Garrad called 'the Rootes umbrella', gave Stirling a great deal of comfort.

This brings to mind an important trait in Stirling's character. He has always driven best under a strong team manager; someone who is a disciplinarian. To Stirling such a manager inspires confidence in the entire set-up, and he then can give of his very best at the wheel. In less well-controlled teams, he is apt to worry too much about the things that may go wrong, feeling less secure, and this can affect his driving.

It was around this time in 1952 that Stirling and I finally decided that our Hampstead flat was far too small for the pair of us, plus all the odds and ends we were accumulating. I found an excellent flat, much roomier, in Challoner Mansions, Kensington, and we moved down there with all our goods and chattels.

But soon the next racing round called us away from our new flat. This time it was the British Grand Prix at Silverstone, in which Stirling was to drive the G-type E.R.A. Once again the car disappointed, overheating forcing his retirement though he had never been amongst the leaders. In the Formula 3 race, however, he drove Derek Annable's Kieft again, winning after a tremendous struggle with Don Parker, which cheered him up a bit.

Then came one of those typical post-Silverstone scrambles, the Kieft being entered for a 500 c.c. race at Namur, in Belgium, the following day. Again Stirling flew over after the Silverstone meeting, and we drove down to Dover and took the ferry, then picked him up in Belgium as before. It was all trouble for nothing, though, as the Kieft's front suspension broke and put him out of the race.

Not long after this, Stirling was involved in another of those hair-raising multiple crashes which occasionally occurred in Formula 3 racing. The race was at Fairwood Common aerodrome, near Swansea; Cyril Kieft was the main force behind this meeting, being very keen to foster the 500 movement in Wales, while the *Daily Telegraph* provided backing. Stirling was driving another Kieft this time—one prepared by the works at Bridgend—but Jimmy Gregory, a namesake of mine but no relative, spun his Cooper on lap 1; a J.B.S. close behind spun in dodging him, and Stirling perforce rammed the J.B.S.; John Brown's Arnott, close behind the Kieft, ran right up the back of it and over, the final drive chain ploughing a neat furrow in Stirling's crash helmet.

So one more Kieft was unhappily wrecked. Gallant Derek Annable once more came to the rescue, and lent Stirling his car for the Prescott '500s only' hillclimb the following day. This was one of the last hillclimbs Stirling competed in, and as Derek and I also drove the car, it must have been the hardest-worked machine on the hill that day. Stirling managed second fastest time of the day, but was beaten by Les Leston in a Cooper.

The time had obviously come to 'do something' about this matter of a car for 500 c.c. racing. Derek Annable had been extremely generous in continually lending us his Kieft, but the arrangement was unsatisfactory, first because Derek was a keen driver and it was unfair to keep borrowing his vehicle, secondly because it was a production-type Kieft, which wasn't so good as our prototype, yet we naturally were not able to modify or experiment with it, as we would our own.

So one day I went down to Surbiton to see Charles Cooper, and discuss with him the possibility of Moss driving a Cooper owned, entered and prepared by the works. We eventually came to an agreement which proved satisfactory to all concerned.

This was the first major negotiation I had carried out on Stirling's behalf, for at that time, I would stress, I was still a 'manager' with a metaphoric 'L' plate on my back. Unlike many more popular professions, there is no such thing as a college for racing managers, and I was starting from scratch. At first I was more his companion and *aide-de-camp*, learning my new 'trade' as I went along, and getting to know the complex Moss character better all the time.

His first race in the works Cooper was on the new circuit at Boreham near Chelmsford, Essex, in the big international meeting sponsored by the *Daily Mail* on August Bank Holiday Saturday. 'Flying Milkman' George Wicken got into the lead, but Stirling was right at his heels, when unfortunately his goggles were broken by a stone. After that the flying grit forced him to ease up, and he finished third.

But Stirling won the sports car race in a Jaguar, then turned out with Leslie Johnson's G-type E.R.A. for the combined Formula 1 and 2 race for the *Daily Mail* International Trophy. This began in pouring rain and finished in the dry, so that Mike Hawthorn in his Formula 2 Cooper-Bristol managed to pass Gigi Villoresi's big $4\frac{1}{2}$-litre Ferrari and lead the lot!

The Italian caught him again when the track dried, but Mike was decidedly the hero of the day, with Stirling, in contrast, an 'also ran'. Yet the E.R.A. was running better this time, and was very smooth if not particularly fast, and Stirling was glad enough to finish third in the Formula 2 class to Hawthorn and Alan Brown in Cooper-Bristols.

Yet it was during this very sticky 100-miler that Moss had one of his very rare spins; this happened on the corner at the end of the straight past the new permanent pits, and was due not to error, but to chance. The G type used a Bristol gearbox mounted directly on to the engine, with a rather long, cranked gear lever coming close to the steering wheel. As Moss went into the corner with his hands at the usual 'quarter to three' position, the tail slid out, and as he quickly corrected it, his hand knocked the lever out of gear and into neutral. Power is, of course, vital for fast cornering; the E.R.A. immediately became unstable and spun in a big way.

Unknowing marshals, thrilled by Mike Hawthorn's brilliant display, shook their heads sadly as Stirling righted the car and set off again. 'Was the boy on his way out?' one could imagine them saying.

It was a great pity, but the rain at Boreham had a more far-reaching effect than the near-eclipse of a G.P. Ferrari by a Formula 2 Cooper. The *Daily Mail*, new to motor-racing sponsorship, had sunk a lot of money into the Essex circuit, but the doubtful weather kept attendance down, and their loss on the meeting was considerable.

The circuit was beautifully smooth and interesting to drive on, and could be considered as good as any airfield circuit in Britain; certainly the equal of Silverstone at that time. But it was not really suitable for a big crowd, a snag being that one of the major approach roads traversed a level crossing, and as British Railways could hardly be persuaded to alter their timetables to suit motor-racing enthusiasts, big queues of traffic, and in consequence bad tempers and dissatisfaction, developed.

Anyway, after the International Boreham, the *Daily Mail* withdrew their support from motor racing, and have never changed their minds since. As for the splendid Boreham circuit, it serves today as a private test track for the Ford Motor Co.

A few days later I was on my way to Zandvoort, Holland, driving Cooper's works van, with the 500 on a trailer behind, and Charles Cooper and his wife in the cab with me. Stirling, meanwhile, went first to Montlhéry for a successful record foray with an XK120 Jaguar, driving with Johnson, Fairman and Hadley for seven days and nights at an average of over 100 m.p.h.; then he nipped back to Goodwood to practise with a works C-type Jaguar for the first 9-hour race there, while I practised the Cooper 500 for him at Zandvoort for the Dutch G.P. meeting.

Goodwood was on a Saturday, and Zandvoort on the Sunday, which meant more rush and complicated travel arrangements for Stirling. At this time, unfortunately, the general despression assailin the Moss ménage seemed to be affecting me, and I was feeling far from well. Some weeks earlier I had contracted a foot infection which I neglected; it grew worse and worse, the foot swelling until, at Zandvoort, I could hardly walk, let alone drive a Cooper.

However, I managed to qualify the car for a second row start, and when Stirling arrived he told us of his 1952 'luck' at Goodwood—the Jaguar led the race with two hours to go, then broke a radius arm, eventually finishing fifth. Zandvoort gave him a break, for he romped away with the 500 c.c. race, winning from Wicken and Habin, but just to keep jubilation in check, the E.R.A. failed him again in the Dutch G.P. and blew up.

When I got back to England, my foot was so bad that I had first to go to hospital, and then to a specialist, who told me that the trouble was not due solely to the infection, but to my general nervous condition. The latter was brought about by the considerable strain entailed in trying to 'keep up' with Stirling and in trying to live his type of life. The trouble was to persist until, eventually, I decided to take a separate flat, so that Stirling and I could live separate lives outside our work.

I haven't said a great deal about Stirling so far, and I don't think the average reader will appreciate just how difficult a person he can be to live with. Stirling being the genius he is—and I use the word 'genius' without hesitation—he is also very demanding. Much of his success is due to the fact that he can never accept anything less than the best, and can never understand that others may not be able to achieve his standards. Stirling's best is tremendous, and his powers of energy and will-power are quite fantastic and beyond most people's comprehension.

But he is a restless sort of person, totally unable to sit down quietly. His energy is so boundless that he seems never to need to recharge himself, and in those days he just couldn't get to sleep before 2 or 3 a.m. Instead, he wanted to talk, keeping me awake all the time, discussing any subject that came to mind. The resultant shortage of sleep, coupled with an acute awareness of our current lack of racing success, was having a very adverse effect on me. Business worries of the two-man 'Stirling Moss concern' were mounting up, and while it was all right for Stirling to go off to sleep at 3 a.m. and get up around midday, as was his habit, it was not so good for me, nor for business.

Business has to be conducted with people living orthodox lives, and if I began the daily round at about lunch time, then half the day was already gone. It just wasn't practical to phone up for hotel reservations, fix plane journeys or ring people up to make any kind of arrangements in the evenings and early mornings. Business hours are business hours, and there's nothing to do about it but comply with them.

When the specialist told me I must take the weight off my foot for a minimum of six weeks—which turned out to be nearer eight—the only thing I could do was to take all my papers back to the flat at Challoner Mansions, sit by the telephone, and do what work I could from there. It was a miserable period, and I felt additionally despondent because I was unable to give companionship to Stirling just when he was needing it most. I had to miss several races, and could only learn of his progress in them from the radio, until he returned from a trip and would tell me all about it.

After Zandvoort he scored two lesser wins at Turnberry in Scotland with Formula 3 Cooper and C-type Jaguar, then went to Germany for a meeting on the very fast Grenzlandring, near the Dutch border, finishing third in the Formula 3 race to John Cooper's aerodynamic-bodied car, and Eric Brandon. Stirling had slipstreamed Eric right through the race, but when he decided it was time to nip past and snatch second place, Eric put in some masterly weaving and kept Moss behind to the finish. 'What—give you a tow all the way and then let you past?—not —— likely,' laughed Brandon afterwards, and Stirling laughed with him, admitting it was fair game.

The Italian G.P. at Monza was next, a very important race, on a circuit Stirling loved for its fast corners. How he yearned for a really fast British car, to meet the all-conquering 4-cylinder 2-litre Ferraris and the new Maserati 'six'. But Britain hadn't such a car yet, though her day was to come. It was pretty clear, however, that the E.R.A. could be counted out; it just wasn't up to it, so Stirling looked around for something else to drive. Eventually we made arrangements to drive one of Kenneth McAlpine's 2-litre Connaughts.

Stirling still had his hard-worked Morris Minor, but he didn't relish travelling in it across Europe to Milan. Now at that time, motor cars were not so readily available as now, and I was charged with the task of trying to purchase a new Ford Zephyr, a model which Stirling very much wanted, in time for the Monza trip.

I rang up the Ford Co.'s public relations officer at Dagenham, and put the question to him, but unfortunately his answer was that if Stirling Moss wanted one of his cars, then he would have to wait for it like the rest of the public. This, I felt, was a short-sighted attitude, since racing drivers who travel all over Europe are contributing materially to our national prestige, and that of the cars they are using. Both Stirling and I were disappointed that a fine company like Ford's couldn't recognize the value of this, particularly at that time, when Britain was fighting hard for international markets.

Anyway, the upshot was that Ken McAlpine sportingly lent Stirling his own Ford Zephyr. As I was still hobbling about on one foot, and couldn't accompany Stirling on the long drive to Milan, he invited Derek Annable to go with him on a holiday, as some small repayment for all the help Derek had given us.

But Monza brought Stirling one more negative result; the Connaught broke a rocker, and though this was repaired, the car retired near the end. Next it was back to the E.R.A. for the final Goodwood meeting of 1952, but unfortunately on the first lap Dennis Poore's Connaught had to take avoiding action at Madgwick Corner, and inadvertently pushed Stirling, who was close behind, into the bank. The E.R.A. was too damaged to continue, though Stirling was unhurt. Some compensation came with a win in the Formula 3 race 'after a battle as fierce as the soap powder war', as *Autosport* put it.

The season was now almost at its end, with only the Castle Combe and Charterhall meetings to come. At the Wiltshire circuit, Stirling again won the 500 c.c. race, but the ill-starred E.R.A. packed up after seven laps. In the final round up in Scotland, he was fourth with the E.R.A. to three Connaughts in the Formula 2 race, and scored 'seconds' both with Formula 3 Cooper and the Jaguar. The result of it all was his third B.R.D.C. Gold Star in three years—the only major success in a really black year for Stirling Moss.

With the racing season ended, and the tempo of existence easing somewhat, my health began to improve, and I could once again really get down to work. Inevitably the biggest problem was that of correspondence. During the racing season, we were very rarely in one place for more than a few days, and consequently the sending of any letters which needed replies had to be carefully planned so that the answers would arrive at our next port of call. Thus a letter might be sent from Luxembourg, and the reply received at Spa. If it didn't arrive until we had gone on to the next race, the letter could be lost for weeks, chasing us round Europe from hotel to hotel.

The telephone was, therefore, our main instrument of communication, though it is one I consider very unsatisfactory in many ways. Towards the end of 1952, then, I persuaded Stirling to let me open an office in William IV Street, in a room forming part of the property where his father, Alfred Moss, ran his dental practice. There I based myself, and began to form a proper administration. The business was known simply as 'Stirling Moss', but to that address thenceforth came all communications—telephone calls, callers, race regulations, fan mail and so on, and somebody—usually myself—was always there to answer queries. It meant a major improvement in Stirling's associations with the press and public.

A racing driver, particularly a successful one, is a public figure, and like a film, radio or TV star, or a famous cricketer, boxer, pianist or other public performer, gets a tremendous fan mail. The reader, examining the average morning mail that came through the letter box at 20, William IV Street, would be amazed at its contents.

'Four girl fans' from Leicester, who 'have followed Stirling's career with great interest and keep their fingers crossed for him whenever he is racing', would like autographed photos of him, please. A West Country journalist is writing an article on motoring, and would like to quote Moss's opinion on Sunday drivers (!). The mother of a twelve-year-old boy who is a staunch Moss fan would like Stirling to autograph a book she has bought him for a present. The organizers of a fête in Buckinghamshire would like Stirling to open it, and so on.

In the midst of them would be the vital entry acceptance for a Grand Prix, regulations for another, confirmation of a hotel booking, bills, receipts, a printer's proof from a cigarette firm who are advertising Stirling's approval of their product. Such were the things which had to be dealt with, besides the slight matter of motor racing practically every week-end.

With the ever-increasing correspondence, it was obvious we

needed a secretary, and at the close of the year I came to a revised arrangement with Stirling. I re-assumed the duties of Secretary to the Half-Litre Club, but at the same time maintained my manager-ship of Stirling Moss, operating in both cases from the premises at William IV Street. I took a reduced salary both from Stirling and the Club, but the two combined actually amounted to a higher salary than I received formerly. I then undertook to provide a secretary, who would work with me to administrate for both.

This joint organization worked well. Now that I was back at the helm of the Half-Litre Club, I found there was quite a lot more work to do for them in the winter, the Club now having a vigorous social side as well as ever-increasing racing activities.

At the same time, we had to consider Stirling's plans for the coming season. 1952 had not been a good year for him, particularly in the Grand Prix class, and something pretty drastic would clearly have to be done to improve matters.

We both sat down, and thought hard.

CHAPTER FOUR

1953—MORE TROUBLE

FERRARI? Maserati? Gordini? Connaught? Cooper? H.W.M.? Which should—or could—Stirling drive in 1953? The problem of his Grand Prix mount brought several lengthy discussions before minds were made up. The Kieft 500, designed and built jointly by Ray Martin, John 'Autocar' Cooper and Dean Delamont, had gone exceptionally well—why not a Formula 2 car, evolved and built by the same team?

Talks between the parties concerned followed and it was finally agreed to build a car for Stirling, using several Cooper components and a 6-cylinder Maserati engine. Late in 1952 Gonzalez had shaken Ferraris with the new 2-litre Maserati 'six' at Monza and Modena, so I wrote to the Maserati concern, asking if they were prepared to sell one of their new engines and, if so, what it would cost and when they could deliver.

Meanwhile Martin, Cooper and Delamont got down to design work, and the broad specification encompassed a tubular space frame, de Dion rear axle, wishbone and coil front suspension, Girling disc brakes at the front, and drum brakes at the rear. Thus the Moss car would be the first racing machine to employ disc braking, which until then had been tried out on a few sports cars only. At that time little was known about this new system of braking, but from tests it was obvious that they gave a tremendous rate of deceleration and did not fade under continual use as did drum brakes. On the other hand, there were snags concerning method of application and rate of wear, but even so, Stirling was a champion of the disc brake right from the word 'go'.

We waited impatiently for a reply from Maseratis, which was a long time coming. Eventually a letter came from them, saying that they were not prepared to sell us an engine, but would be happy to supply us with a complete car. We were naturally very disappointed at this, but immediately set about finding a suitable alternative. We thought hard about using a Connaught engine but it had not

yet been fully developed, however, and we finally settled for an
Alta unit, a rugged 4-cylinder twin overhead camshaft design
produced by Geoffrey Taylor at Tolworth, Surrey.

We had a new and major asset in the building of the car, and that
was Alf Francis, who had become Stirling's chief mechanic at the
close of the 1952 season. Alf had been with the H.W.M. team for
several years, and as he is a temperamental character, and rather
difficult to get on with, it was not surprising that he and John
Heath, who was of a similar disposition, should come into conflict
occasionally. When Alf at last decided to leave, Stirling saw his
opportunity to get a first-rate mechanic, and immediately engaged
him.

We then set about finding an assistant for Alf. I remember that
we placed advertisements in the 'Sits. Vac.' columns of *The Motor*,
The Autocar and *Autosport*, and received over a hundred replies
within a very few days. We sat down every evening in the flat at
Challoner Mansions, sifting through the letters, and eventually
selected the most promising eight.

We then interviewed the eight applicants, and finally engaged,
as Alf's junior mechanic, a young man named Tony Robinson.
Today Tony is my chief mechanic, and is a tremendous worker
and enthusiast. So much so that in joining us in 1953 he gave up a
job bringing him about £18 a week, to become a junior racing
mechanic at a salary of around £7 weekly, which was all Stirling
could offer then in his capacity as private entrant.

With the car on the way, a lesser problem waiting to be solved
was that of a vehicle to transport it around Europe. Stirling accordingly went to see Sir William Rootes, with whom he had become
well acquainted, and persuaded him to loan a left-hand drive
Commer chassis on a long-term arrangement. Sir William also
agreed to have a body built on the chassis to Stirling's specification.

Then came irony. After we had placed a firm order for an Alta
2-litre engine, and made all plans to adapt it to the special chassis,
another letter arrived from Maserati. 'As we did not wish to purchase a complete car,' it said, 'they would now be prepared to
supply us with the engine alone.' The price they quoted was well
within our budget, and one which we would certainly have
accepted, had the first letter been in the same vein. It was too late

now, however, and we had to press on with the Cooper-Alta, as our car was to be called. Snags galore were arising in its construction, moreover, which meant much hard work and many late nights for Martin, Francis and Co., down at Ray Martin's new garage at Merton Abbey.

Besides the Cooper-Alta, we also had the Cooper-Norton, for Stirling still intended to indulge in Formula 3 racing. The car was to be looked after by Alf Francis and Tony Robinson, but in the early months, while everyone was concentrating on the new Formula 2 machine, the Cooper got short shrift. Alf and Tony only ever looked after the Cooper on sufferance; neither of them had much time for it, nor did they really understand it, for though both are exceptionally good engineers and mechanics, the single-cylindered, chain-driven 500 requires specialist knowledge which they did not seem interested in acquiring. The Cooper-Alta was to keep them busy enough, heaven knows!

One problem after another reared itself over this design, and completion was alarmingly delayed, and in the end it was only after a tremendous amount of overtime and considerable shortage of temper that the car reached Goodwood just in time for its first race on Easter Monday.

It was unpainted, it hadn't the correct exhaust system nor the right springs, and altogether it was a very unhappy Stirling who took the car out for its first race, while Alf Francis and Tony Robinson were practically asleep on their feet. This was one instance when I can say I was glad not to be present; I was busy organizing the Brands Hatch meeting on the same day.

The car ran poorly, and Stirling drove it in only one race, scratching from two others. After Goodwood it was brought back to Ray Martin, and we started to correct some of the many faults revealed, besides getting a coat of green paint on it. But no amount of green paint could make that car behave itself. It was awkward from the word 'go'. The suspension and steering were far from right, the handling was most tricky, while the engine did not give enough power for Moss to hold his rivals, despite all his efforts in the cockpit.

The car also proved heavier than anticipated, and stressed the point which I have made a guiding principle ever since; namely, that if you are going to design and build a car, you must allow not only the time for design and construction, but also a development period. The Cooper-Alta was designed and built in four months, after which it should have had at least a three-month development period.

Instead, it had to be taken straight to a race meeting, and raced thereafter as often as possible. At every meeting faults manifested themselves which should have been traced during development. These faults were then rectified in readiness for the next race, with no time at all for steady development. I think we all rather hoped that the Cooper-Alta would turn out an immediate success, as had Ray Martin's swing axle Kieft; but the Formula 2 car was far more complicated and there was no second miracle.

Its second race, after the Goodwood débâcle, was the *Daily Express* Silverstone, by which time we had managed to get some of the bugs out of the design. Stirling had a busy day planned, for besides the Formula 2 International Trophy race in two heats and a final, he was down to drive the Cooper-Norton in the Formula 3 race and a works Jaguar in the sports-car event.

Owing to the amount of work I had on hand, I was unable to get to Silverstone until first practice was in progress, and I remember speaking to a marshal on arrival, asking what the commotion was on the other side of the circuit. He answered, 'Someone's turned a Jaguar over at Abbey Curve.' It didn't occur to me in any way whatsoever that the 'somebody' might be Stirling. He didn't do that sort of thing!

I was horrified, then, to learn that in fact it *was* Stirling's car which had overturned. I raced across the circuit and reached the medical tent just as the ambulance arrived with Stirling. He wasn't seriously hurt, but badly shaken, and he told me his greatest fear had been that the Jaguar would catch fire while he was trapped beneath it.

What had happened was that, while drifting out of Abbey Curve, the wheels went on to some loose gravel on the outside of the corner; the back broke away and the Jag went off sideways to the infield. Unluckily, just at that point the farmer had ploughed up the land close to the track verge, the car dug its wheels in and turned over on top of Stirling. He had instinctively ducked under the cockpit on the passenger side as it rolled, and as it finished up on its back he was trapped within.

Even then, the engine was still running; he quickly groped for the ignition switch and turned it off, but he was frightened stiff that the fuel might drain from the tank on to the hot exhaust and catch fire. Fortunately it didn't. Stirling's crash helmet was split centrally and you could get four fingers through it, just above the centre of the skull. Without it he would have been very seriously injured.

After careful examination, the doctor told Stirling that he was fit to drive, though he took it easy for the rest of that day. We gave Sally Weston the key to the flat and she drove down to Kensington, collected his other crash helmet and brought it back to Buckingham, where we were staying.

Just as the crashed airman traditionally gets back into the air as soon as possible to restore his nerve, so Stirling resolved to drive the Jaguar in the actual race. It was only superficially damaged, but he took it easy on the Saturday. He gave the Formula 3 race a miss, but won the Touring Car event with a Mk. VII Jaguar. In the International Trophy, the Cooper-Alta ran quite encouragingly in its heat, Stirling finishing second to de Graffenried's Maserati. In the final he had to stop to refuel the rather small tank when lying sixth, dropping back to ninth in the final placings.

The sequel to Stirling's unhappy week-end came when we got back to Challoner Mansions, and found the front door slightly ajar. We rushed in, to find that, whilst we had been busy at Silverstone, some of the local criminal types had made a night call at the flat, to the detriment of our wardrobes.

Eight suits were missing, and the thieves took two suit-cases as well to carry them in. We phoned the local C.I.D., who quickly sent an inspector round. 'Yes,' he said after we had told our tale of woe, 'we heard there was a character in Hammersmith Broadway on Saturday night, selling suits at £2 a time.' I only wish we'd been able to buy them at that price!

In an atmosphere of tension and waning morale, Stirling, Alf and Tony struggled on with the Cooper-Alta, but it was a losing battle. At Crystal Palace the car came fifth, at the Eifelrennen sixth, at Rouen eighth and last. And at Rheims the clutch disintegrated while the car was pounding down the straight from La

Garenne to Thillois, Moss being very lucky that only one flying remnant caught him, making a rather nasty gash in his shin.

So far 1953 was going as badly for Stirling Moss as 1952, and we now realized that no amount of concentration on the Cooper-Alta would improve matters. Stirling decided not to drive the thing any more, and as I had already negotiated his entry for the German G.P. four weeks hence, we had to scramble round very quickly to find an alternative mount—something in which we could use the Alta engine.

There was only one answer—a Cooper—so down to Surbiton we went, to discuss things with Charles and John Cooper. To their credit, they never said 'we told you so' when we explained the shortcomings of the 'improved' Cooper-Alta, but agreed to let us build the Alta unit into a Mk. II Cooper Formula 2 chassis down at their works.

As the clutch had flown to pieces, the quickest solution to the transmission problem was to fit a Wilson preselector gearbox which required no clutch as one drove off on the selector bands. Work began in earnest less than three weeks before the German race, so that the job was done in an even bigger rush than the first Cooper-Alta, in order to get to Nurburg in time for practice.

The work was more straightforward, however, and we had the help of several of Cooper's staff to speed the task. But there *were* snags, and a colossal one reared itself late on the evening that car and crew were due to leave for Dover. Starting the engine for a final check-up, Alf Francis discovered a large crack on the timing gear casing at the front of the engine, through which oil was pouring out. Alf switched off.

Everybody's face dropped, and there was a general air of gloom and despondency, with some good healthy swear words flying around. Then Tony Robinson, who is extremely cheerful and doesn't believe in wasting words, chimed in: 'Well, come on. Let's get the engine out and get it done.' While they were tearing the Alta engine out of the chassis, I phoned John Heath at Walton-on-Thames, and persuaded him to leave his bed and dig out a timing cover from his H.W.M. spares. This then had to be modified, and after tremendous trouble and all-night work, the car was completed and ready for shipment the next morning.

Meantime, I had had to practically break everybody's heart at the Dover ferry offices, getting a suitable shipping transfer. There were only two cross-Channel ferries capable of taking a vehicle as large as the Commer transporter, and as it was the height of the season, space was very hard to find for a private car, let alone a great lorry. But somehow they managed it, and when the Cooper had been loaded on the transporter, and Alf and Tony were just about to leave, John Cooper shouted cheerfully across to them, 'Tell Stirling to try this one in practice, and if he doesn't like it, we'll build him another one for the race'!

Well, this time all the tear and rush was well worth it, for the car ran extremely well despite being completely untried, finishing sixth behind the works Ferraris and Maseratis, being the first British car home. And if sixth place in a Grand Prix seems little enough to exult over, it should be remembered that Stirling had not scored a higher position than that in a major race since his H.W.M. days.

Incidentally, there was some excitement and speculation before the race over the fact that Stirling's entry was given in some quarters as a 'Cooper-Jaguar'. Well, there is no smoke without fire, and it was true that we had entertained ideas of using one of the experimental 2-litre, 4-cylinder Jaguar XK100 engines in the Cooper. The first of these units had been built several years ago, before the XK120 appeared in 1949, and had been used successfully by Goldie Gardner in his streamlined M.G. to break 2-litre-class records.

We had heard all sorts of figures about the engine's power, and because of Stirling's close association with the Jaguar team, and with Sir William Lyons, we felt there might be a chance of trying the XK100 in the Cooper. This, however, proved impossible.

We certainly never entered the car as a Cooper-Jaguar, and I can only think that rumours circulated, as rumours will, and the local German press got hold of them. Of course, it is generally accepted in the motor-racing world that there is no such thing as a secret! News of the most confidential decisions seems to get on the grapevine within ten minutes of being decided, and it all reminds me of that useful saying which I have employed many times when someone is trying to draw information out of me: 'It's not me who can't keep a secret; it's the people I tell.'

The second Cooper-Alta was certainly better than the first, being lighter and having the benefits of prior development in its chassis and suspension. Even so, the engine's power was insufficient to cope with the Ferraris and Maseratis, and the hunt began to find more brake horsepower.

After a pleasing little run at Sables d'Olonne, where Moss finished third, S.U. fuel injection was experimented with. This brought more speed, but complications with it; however, Alf Francis persevered, and the next step was to use nitromethane fuel.

This was the then highly controversial 'liquid dynamite', used by the Americans in their 'hot rods' with remarkable effect. It is extremely unpleasant stuff to use, but yielded such a marked increase in power that it could hardly be ignored despite its expense.

One day I went down to Goodwood with Charles Cooper, for some 'nitro' tests with the works Cooper 500. We met Beveridge Rowntree, one of the chemists of Shell-Mex and B.P. Ltd., unloaded the Cooper, and poured some nitromethane into the tank. It smelt horrible.

Both Charlie and I did several laps each with the car, the object being to get the carburation right so that Stirling could race it later on without time-wasting experimentation. Now we didn't notice it at the time, but Charles Cooper had been taking some interested sniffs at the nitro when it was put into the tank, and later, when driving the car, the fumes apparently affected him.

He began to act in a strange, remote manner, and by the time we were having lunch in a little café in Chichester had become extremely vague. He kept saying: 'What day is it?' 'What are we doing here?' and, pulling out a couple of cheques which he had in his pocket, 'What are these doing in my pocket?'

His son John had won the Formula 3 race at Avus, in Germany, the previous day, and when one of us mentioned this, and congratulated Charles, he said, 'John?—John who?' 'John Cooper—your son,' we answered. 'My son?' said poor Charles, looking hopelessly bewildered.

At first we had thought he was playing the fool, but it was soon clear that he wasn't, and that he was far from well. We went back to the circuit, packed the car on the trailer behind the works van, and drove back. And every now and then Charlie would ask: 'What's going on? What am I doing here?' and so on. We had arranged to call at Francis Beart's tuning premises in Byfleet on the way home, and I was not certain of the route. 'Now Charlie— where is Beart's place? Come on, try to remember,' I said, but it was no use; Charlie couldn't.

I found it on my own, and when we got back to Surbiton we had to help poor old Charles Cooper out of the van, for he was not at all himself. The nitromethane fumes had, in fact, induced what is known as 'temporary amnesia'. Charlie got over it in time, though to this day he can remember little of that day at Goodwood.

When nitromethane became more easily available there was considerable concern amongst race organizers. Unlike ordinary fuels, which require oxygen to 'combust', nitromethane produces oxygen within itself, and therefore needs no air for combustion to take place. Thus any fire involving 'nitro' is very difficult to put out, especially as it burns with an almost invisible flame. We of the Half-Litre Club were very concerned, as organizers, at the special problems thus imposed in the event of accidents.

Nitromethane was, additionally, very expensive, and prices of as much as £10 per gallon were spoken of. I do not think this figure was by any means accurate, but as Stirling Moss had his fuel supplied by Shell on an experimental basis, I never did learn an accurate price for the stuff. A further snag of nitromethane is the unpleasant 'tear gas' effect its exhaust gases have on those in the close vicinity. With 'nitro' burners on the starting grid, it was not an uncommon sight to see other drivers sitting in their cars with tears streaming down their cheeks.

But there was no denying its effect on performance. The Cooper-Alta, as raced by Stirling in the 1953 Italian G.P. when fitted with S.U. fuel injection, gave a fantastic 198 b.h.p. on nitromethane— and the highly successful 2-litre Ferraris and Maseratis weren't exceeding 200 b.h.p. themselves. Yet the S.U. injection system was not altogether ideal in this application, having originally been designed for aircraft engines, which run at more or less constant throttle openings, and not being responsive enough for the constant acceleration and deceleration of a racing-car engine. Yet the car was extremely quick at Monza, and quite shattered those accustomed to the normal pace of a Cooper. The limitations of the fuel injection, and of the Cooper's cornering, as compared with that of the Ferraris and Maseratis, meant that Stirling lost on the corners most of what he gained on the straights, but he got a great kick out of repeatedly passing Mike Hawthorn's Ferrari. He knew full well that Mike would pass him again as they got to the next corner, but he would tail the Ferrari as closely as possible, and as soon as the finishing straight came up, Stirling gave the Cooper its head and caught the Ferrari up, passing in front of the grandstand to the mixed surprise and admiration of the crowd, and to the satisfaction of his own ego, if not of Mike's!

He also had similar fun with de Graffenried and Bonetto, but the pace was too much for the Cooper's tyres, which repeatedly flung treads and brought Moss to the pits for wheel-changes. Despite all his brilliant driving, therefore, Stirling only managed to finish thirteenth.

But he managed one victory at least with the nitro-burning Cooper-Alta—at Crystal Palace, the week-end following Monza. He won both heat and final of the London Trophy race for Formula 2 cars, heading Tony Rolt's Connaught and Horace Gould's Cooper-Bristol. This helped to lift the Moss gloom awhile, although considering the hopes with which the season had started and all the hard work with the two Cooper-Altas, it had been another disappointing year for us.

I was heavily concerned with that meeting at Crystal Palace, for it had been organized by the Half-Litre Club, being the second meeting we had staged there in 1953, when the circuit was re-opened by the London County Council. The British Automobile Racing Club had organized the first post-war Palace meeting on Whit Monday, 1953, but we of the Half-Litre Club were also keen to promote racing on a course right in the heart of London, and our first effort was on 11 July. It was very successful, as was the September meeting, proving to our satisfaction that the Club organization could cope not only with a very full Brands Hatch season and the Silverstone 100-mile race meeting, but also take in a third circuit.

With the additional work entailed in these meetings, on top of my normal secretarial work with the Half-Litre Club and with

Stirling Moss, it looked as if my own short career as an amateur racing driver was virtually over. However, one opportunity arose in 1953 for a drive, which I grabbed without hesitation. This was at the Great Auclum hillclimb, held in August on a splendid little quarter-mile course near Reading, organized by the Hants and Berks Club.

I was entered with a J.B.S. '500' owned by Dick Richards, and as soon as I knew I had one car to drive, I took steps to find another, and persuaded Charles Cooper to lend me the works 1100 c.c. Cooper-J.A.P. twin. He stipulated that the car should be shared with Stuart Lewis-Evans, who also wanted to have a crack at Great Auclum.

This suited me down to the ground, because Stuart had a transporter which would not only take his 500 but the 1100 as well, and we happily shared the driving and maintenance of the car. In the Formula 3 class, Stuart was fastest with his Cooper, and I was second in the J.B.S., and just couldn't do anything about approaching his time.

But in the 1100 c.c. class we shared the same car, so rivalry was very keen. On the first runs, I made the fastest time of the day so far, breaking Eric Brandon's old hill record of 22·20 sec. with 22·07. Then came Stuart's turn, and he beat my time by one-fifth of a second. In the second runs, it was Stuart's turn to go first with the Cooper-J.A.P., but this time he only did 22·24 sec.; this looked easier to beat, and in my run I managed 21·70, which pleased me no end, as you can imagine, standing as F.T.D. and a new record.

But there was a 'but'. In the regulations it was laid down that there would be two runs in each class, but if time permitted, third runs would be included, these counting in the official results. Well, the entry was not too large, the meeting was well up to schedule, and it was a nice day, so naturally the organizers said 'let's have a third run'.

This time, then, it became my turn again to drive first, and I set off, determined somehow to carve a fifth off somewhere, to try and keep F.T.D. But half-way down the first part of the hill, before one hits the banking which is such an attraction at Great Auclum, one of the plugs oiled, and the Cooper became a single-cylinder. This was a blow I could not remedy, and my time was well down. We put a new plug in, and Stuart took over, rocketing off the line to clock a record 21·47 sec.

So that was that, though I wasn't really disheartened at being second in two classes to a driver of Stuart's calibre. But there was another class, exclusive to Hants and Berks. M.C. members, and just before the start I had gone to the Club Secretary and checked on who had paid their 'subs', and found that Stuart had not. So I immediately joined the Club myself, paid my sub., and won the Cup for the fastest time by a member. I told Stuart about this, and he laughed and said, 'I'll let you have that one.'

Stirling's 1953 season ended very suddenly with an accident at Castle Combe, which could have had nastier consequences than it did. Feeling perhaps that the Cooper-Alta would not be at its best on the very sinuous 1·8 mile course near Chippenham, he decided instead to use an 1100 c.c. Cooper-J.A.P. in the 20-lap Formula 2 race.

That he had made a mistake soon became apparent, as first Salvadori's Connaught and then Gerard's Cooper-Bristol passed him. With the Cooper-Alta he could have held both. Tony Rolt in Rob Walker's Connaught was the next to challenge Stirling, but unfortunately the wheels of the two cars contacted momentarily while braking for Quarry Corner, and in a trice the tiny Cooper had rolled over.

Stirling was flung out on to his shoulder, but picked himself up, staggered across to a straw bale, and then collapsed, while Tony Rolt immediately pulled off course and rushed to his aid, together with the ambulance men at the corner.

A broken arm and bruised shoulder proved to be the main injuries, and Stirling was swiftly removed to hospital at Chippenham. There they put him in plaster, and the next day, Sunday, he was driven home to Tring. I was spending the week-end there, and as usual we shared Stirling's room. When we went to bed that night, he was clearly in great pain, and couldn't sleep.

His father gave him what light sedatives he had in the house, but they did not help very much. All I could do was to talk as much as possible to try and keep his mind occupied, but he wasn't really interested in talking; he was just in agony. I got damp flannels and bathed his brow periodically through the night, but neither of us got any proper rest, and I resolved that we would visit a specialist first thing in the morning.

Now a good manager must have an answer to every sort of situation which arises, and fortunately in this case I had one. At St Thomas's Hospital I had a friend named Dr Philippe Bauwens, who is the Director of Physical Research there, has done much research work on polio, and on the various conditions affecting the bones and muscles.

I had first met Philippe on Paddington Station, one day early in the war, when it was the habit of civilians to give lifts to servicemen owing to the acute shortage of taxis and petrol. He gave me a lift to a London Forces Club where I was staying for the night, and *en route* we had a drink and formed an acquaintance which has existed to today, and which, I hope, will continue for a long time.

I took Stirling along to see Dr Bauwens at St Thomas's and he decided that the plaster probably had not been set as comfortably as might have been, and had the shoulder X-rayed. This done, and the plates examined, St Thomas's utilized an entirely new form of treatment, removed the plaster altogether, and supported the arm in a sling. Stirling was then subjected to a series of remedial exercises which allowed the bone to knit back quite naturally without plaster support.

This immediately relieved the pain, the bone mended well, and no complications ensued, although Stirling was unable to drive for five or six weeks, giving him ample time to ruminate on the past season, and on the approaching one.

CHAPTER FIVE

TO MERCEDES, MASERATIS AND 'THE MONTE'

WE WERE now entering into the most critical stage in Stirling's racing career. 1954 was to bring a new Formula 1 into force, permitting unsupercharged cars of up to 2½ litres, and supercharged cars up to 750 c.c. It was known that Ferrari, Maserati and Gordini, also various British constructors, would build to the new rulings, and further, that the mighty Mercedes-Benz firm of Germany were to re-enter Grand Prix racing under the new Formula.

One British driver, Roy Salvadori, had already fixed up to drive one of the new 6-cylinder Maseratis, called the 250F, which was being acquired by Syd Greene of the Gilby Engineering Co. Ltd. But what was Stirling to drive, if he was to drive anything? The way he felt after his 1952 and 1953 seasons, it wouldn't have taken a great deal for him to decide to chuck it altogether, give up motor racing, and take up something else as a profession. Prospects of joining any of the established foreign teams were small, while the British cars were an unknown quantity. If Stirling was to drive, he wanted something to give him a real chance to win this time.

Well, it wasn't just his problem. I was his manager, and had to do something about finding him a suitable wheel. So I sent a telegram, unknown to Stirling, to Rudolf Uhlenhaut of Mercedes-Benz, asking if he was prepared to meet me if I flew over to Germany. Back came his reply promptly, saying Yes, he would, so I arranged to fly across one Sunday afternoon, and wired Uhlenhaut: 'Arriving Stuttgart Sunday evening; staying Park Hotel. Will you join me for dinner, 8 p.m.?'

I got to the Park Hotel on time, had a bath and went down to wait in the lounge, and a few minutes after eight o'clock Rudi Uhlenhaut appeared. I had never actually met him before, but I recognized his face immediately, from photographs which had been published. He is a charming person, speaks excellent English, and although he was unable to dine with me that night owing to a previous engagement, he remained for over an hour for a drink and chat.

He wasted little time in getting down to the subject. 'What do you want?' he asked. I told him that I wanted a place for Stirling in the Mercedes team. 'I think he is a very fine driver,' I said, 'with the sort of temperament which would suit your team; I hear you are coming back to racing, and I believe his case would be very well worth considering.'

Uhlenhaut answered that, while he agreed with much that I said, it wasn't for him to decide who joined the team. He would, however, arrange for me to see Director Neubauer, the famous team manager, tomorrow morning. I would receive a telephone call at my hotel, telling me what time I should go along to see him.

I went to bed that night feeling very excited, and wondering what hopes there were for Stirling to get a place in a really first-class team. And with that bland and, I suppose, typically British assurance that nothing could possibly happen before midday on Monday, I stayed awake quite late, reading and anticipating a leisurely rising the next day before Uhlenhaut's call came through.

I didn't know the Germans then, nor just how efficient their famous 'efficiency' was. Promptly at 8 a.m. next morning the telephone rang; it was from Daimler-Benz, to say that the directors would see me at a quarter to nine! I had no time to marvel at this example of Teutonic thoroughness, but by a mad scramble just managed to get to the Unterturkheim works in time, and was ushered in to see the great Alfred Neubauer.

Apart from his imposing corporation and general vastness, I was particularly impressed by Neubauer's great turnip watch, placed prominently on his enormous desk, facing him. He constantly referred to this watch; his entire daily routine centred upon it, and he worked with machine-like precision, never wasting a minute of his day.

Through his interpreter, Fräulein Bauer, Neubauer asked what he could do for me, and I repeated my story. He considered awhile, then answered that he, too, considered Stirling was a very fine driver—in a sports car. But he did not think he had had anything like sufficient experience of Grand Prix cars.

Somewhat taken aback, I pointed out that, although Mercedes-Benz were to have Fangio driving for them, the rest of the team, I understood, were to be Germans, and though I realized this was desirable to a German marque, I did not think that any of them were as good as Stirling or, for that matter, any other of the regular European Grand Prix drivers.

I expected a storm at this, but Neubauer seemed inclined to agree, so I pressed on, saying, 'If only you will give Stirling a test in one of your cars, you would soon see whether he is good enough to drive for you or not.'

Yes, said Neubauer, he felt that that would be the thing to do in normal circumstances, but unfortunately Mercedes already had drivers under contract to them, and it was his duty to see that they practised constantly for the coming season. Two cars only were available for practice, these being 300SL competition sports machines formerly used in the 1953 Mexican Road race, while only one racing car was in existence at that stage, and this, too, was in continuous use.

Furthermore, he said, if Moss were to undergo a test, and proved unsatisfactory, that would mean so many kilometres of training lost to drivers already signed up. And while Mercedes-Benz were hoping to build Grand Prix cars which would be so superior to their opponents that they would not need the very finest drivers, they were determined that every possible kilometre of practice would be driven by the German members of the team.

On that basis, he felt unable to offer Stirling a place with Mercedes, he said, and after a discussion lasting over two hours he said he considered the best thing I could do for Stirling was to get him a drive in one of the other teams; then, if he did particularly well, Mercedes would consider him for the following season.

We bade each other farewell, and I returned to my hotel, in a turmoil of emotions—disappointment at the negative result, resentment at being told Stirling needed more experience in a Grand Prix car, when I knew just how well he could drive one, and surprise that a renowned talent spotter like Neubauer would not recognize Moss's ability.

Yet it was reasonable, I told myself in the end. If their drivers are all signed up, why should they complicate things by trying out others? And it was true, Stirling had never driven a topline Grand Prix machine up to that time, yet so far as the 1954 $2\frac{1}{2}$-litre cars were concerned, nobody else had either. Anyway, Mercedes had the finest driver of all—Fangio—so all they had to do was to make sure his car kept in one piece, and he was bound to win most of the races and the Championship.

I told Stirling all about it when I got back to London. He was pleased at my efforts on his behalf, but naturally disappointed at the Mercedes reply. So we dismissed it from our minds and discussed other possibilities, but before any decisions were reached he had to leave for the United States to drive a Sunbeam-Talbot in the Great American Mountain Rally, after which he was going down to Nassau for a much-needed holiday. This was to be Stirling's first visit to the Bahamas, and he found he liked Nassau enormously, beginning an association with the island which eventually led to his taking up residence there.

Before he left for London Airport and the Transatlantic plane, he turned to me and said: 'Well, Ken, I don't know what we can do right now. I'll just leave it entirely to you. See if you can sign me up with Connaughts or someone—or try Syd Greene and see if he's prepared to get a second Maserati and let me team up with Roy. I don't mind, as long as you fix up something.' And hearing these words, I realized that right then the Moss morale was at rock bottom, and that it wouldn't have taken much to make him throw the towel in.

We knew Syd Greene well, of course, Stirling having driven his 2-litre Frazer-Nash on occasions, and winning the 1952 British Empire Trophy race in the Isle of Man with it. So I phoned Syd up, and at his invitation went to his house in North London and talked the problem over. To buy one 250F Maserati was a big enough financial undertaking, and although I think Syd Greene, in his heart of hearts, would very much have liked to team Stirling with Roy Salvadori, he was not prepared to say Yes or No, just like that! He wanted to think over it first.

One big problem was that of fuel and oil contracts, for whereas his contract was with the Esso Petroleum Co., ours was with Shell-Mex and B.P. Ltd. Having long enjoyed the support of Bryan

Turle and the Shell people, we were reluctant to change over, and doubtless Syd had the same fidelity to Esso.

Time dragged by, and although Syd Greene still could not reach a decision, we now had it fixed in our minds that, if Stirling was to get a real chance in Grand Prix racing, he'd have to drive Italian—either Maserati or Ferrari. Although Connaughts were then on their way up, and Tony Vandervell was up to something at his Acton works, the Italian cars were well in the ascendancy at that time, and offered the best chances of success, apart from whatever Mercedes-Benz might produce.

It was during the liqueurs and cigar stage of the B.R.D.C. annual dinner of 1953 that we came to a decision. Alfred Moss, Bryan Turle and I had a long talk about the situation, after which I went across to Syd Greene's table for a quiet word with him. I asked if he could say, then and there, whether he would be able to run two Maseratis or not. He answered that he still could not say, as there were so many points to tie up, so I said, 'All right, Syd, we'll have to leave it.'

Returning to our table, I said to Alfred Moss, 'It's no good—we'll have to make up our own minds now, and do something definite.' And so fed up with the general indecision were we, that on a sudden impulse both agreed that the best step was for me to go to Italy—not next week, not in three or four days, but as soon as possible—tomorrow—to pursue the question of a car for Stirling, either by joining a team, or our buying one outright.

The prospect of some real action at last was exhilarating, and next morning I caught a plane to Milan, then took a train down to Modena, the home both of Ferrari and Maserati, two of the greatest names in motor racing.

Which should I approach first—the 'prancing horse' of Ferrari, or the 'trident' of Maserati? Having booked in at the Albergo Reale, the focal point for the racing fraternity in Modena, I stood in the middle of the town and pondered the question. Well, there was one quick way of making one's mind up!—I reached in my pocket for a coin. Heads I go to Ferrari, tails I go to Maserati.

It came up tails, so off I went down the road, to the premises of Officine Alfieri Maserati S.p.a. On reaching the factory in the Via Ciro Menotti, I sent my card in with the gate-keeper, and after a few minutes was motioned into an office to meet Omer Orsi, son of Count Adolfo Orsi, the proprietor.

There was no real language difficulty. Maseratis had a considerable export side to their business in machine tools, particularly milling machines, and because of the many communications they had to make in the English language, they kept a resident interpreter there.

Following the usual preliminaries, Omer Orsi asked what he could do for me and 'Mister Moss', and I answered, without hesitation, that I wanted a drive for him in the works team. His answer came equally quickly. They regretted they could not consider this; the Maserati team for 1954 was already formed, and they felt it was perfectly satisfactory for their requirements. I stressed that Fangio would be unable to drive for them once Mercedes-Benz were racing, that they would obviously need someone as good as possible, and that if they didn't take the opportunity quickly, Moss would drive elsewhere.

This, I regret to say, failed to impress Orsi, who remained unmoved. Yet what else could I expect, no matter how fervently I believed in Stirling's skill? There were plenty of drivers to pick from in those days, and the rise to stardom of Fangio had produced a spate of Argentinian talent which suited Maseratis rather well. Orsi was doing great business with the Argentine Government at that time, which probably influenced his choice, and his 1954 drivers included Fangio for the early part of the season until his Mercedes contract came into force, Onofre Marimon and Roberto Mieres, both from Argentina and both excellent drivers.

Omer Orsi then told me that they had laid down six 250F chassis. Of these, three were destined for the works team, the fourth was for training and reserve, the fifth had been sold to Sydney Greene for Salvadori to drive, while the future of the sixth was still undecided. He then took me all over the racing department and erecting shop, where I saw the new cars taking shape. Three were due to make their début in the Argentine Grand Prix on 17 January, 1954, and these were well advanced. They looked simply magnificent, and with my old belief that 'things which look right are right', I felt sure they would go as well as they looked.

I decided then and there that we would purchase the sixth car. How it would be paid for I did not know, for we had made no clear arrangements over finance when I left England. But I felt most strongly that this was the car for Stirling to drive, and took the plunge. The Italians are fantastic business people; from the moment I entered the factory until the drawing up and signing of the contract, there was no suggestion of stopping for a drink or meal or anything. It was almost one o'clock in the morning when we had finished, and only then did we go out to eat.

The purchase price of the Maserati was nine million lire, and I arranged to send a deposit to them as soon as possible. With the document in my pocket, and a welcome meal consumed, I returned to the Albergo Reale and telephoned Alfred Moss. By then it was well past two o'clock in the morning, but I just had to speak to him. When he came through, I said, 'Good morning, Alfred; I've just bought a Maserati.'

It wasn't a particularly clear line, and I didn't go into financial details, otherwise I think I might have spoilt his night's rest. As it was, I think he was rather shattered at the news, but like the good father and supporter that he is, his reaction was, 'Well, that should help Stirling along—we'll discuss it all when you get back,' and with the happy thought that at least he was going to support my action, I went to bed.

I flew home again next morning and drove down to Tring, where the problem of paying for the Maserati was then tackled. The manner in which it was solved speaks well for the unity and generosity of the Moss family, for all of them—Alfred and Aileen, and Stirling's sister Pat—contributed from their own savings to make the car available to him.

This having so happily been settled, all felt it was time that Stirling himself should be told about the Maserati he was going to drive. And we thought we might as well have a bit of fun in the telling. He was on the *Queen Mary* at the time, returning from his Nassau holiday, so we sent him a telegram which simply said: 'Watch out for ship's newspaper announcements. Don't argue. Signed, Dad, Ken and family.'

This, it seemed, had hardly been transmitted through the Post Office when the phone rang at Tring, and the operator announced that a Mr Moss was trying to reach us from the *Queen Mary*, which was then in mid-Atlantic. Stirling's curiosity had obviously overcome his powers of patience. Eventually the call came through, and I remember that the conversation went something like this.

'Hallo, hallo.'

In the remote, crackly distance came a faint 'Hallo, hallo' in answer.

'Is that you, Stirling?'

'Hallo, hallo,' even fainter.

'Halloooo-oo-oo-o, Stirlingggg-gg-g?'

'Hallo,' hallo,' getting more desperate.

This rather narrow conversation went on for about three minutes, during which all we could gather was that the *Queen Mary* was in the middle of a gale, and that Stirling couldn't make out anything at all of what we were saying.

He gave it up as a bad job. When he arrived at Southampton he was met by a flood of reporters, for I had by then issued a detailed announcement that Stirling Moss was to drive an Italian Maserati for the 1954 season. When the ship docked, Stirling was besieged by pressmen, all out for the inside story for their papers. 'What do you think of the Maserati?', 'What is it like to drive the car?', 'How did it all happen?' and so on. I am afraid Stirling had to give some very evasive answers.

Only when he got to London did he get the news in all its details. He was very anxious to know what colour I had specified, and what the pedal positions would be. I was able to satisfy him on both these points. When drawing up the contract with Orsi, it had been agreed that the car would be painted in Moss's particular shade of green, which we ourselves would supply; also that it would have a red band around the nose to signify that it was an Italian-built car. As to the pedals, I had insisted that the accelerator pedal be positioned on the right, and not central, as is the normal Italian practice.

This business of pedal position is something about which Stirling has strong opinions. On British cars of all types, almost without exception, the placing of the three control pedals is consistent: the accelerator is on the right, next to it comes the brake, and on the left is the clutch pedal.

On their Grand Prix and competition sports cars, however, the Italians have constantly favoured a central position for the accelerator, with the clutch to its left, and the brake to the right, the idea being chiefly to facilitate 'heeling and toeing'. Years of practice with a right-hand accelerator makes most British drivers prefer their own position, however, and the confusion arising when they transfer to a car with the 'Italian' pedal positions can sometimes lead to disaster.

Stirling once tried a car with central accelerator—a Ferrari—and automatically pressed the accelerator instead of the footbrake when approaching a corner, nearly meeting disaster. The habits of years are not easily overcome, and although other drivers have adapted themselves to a central throttle, Stirling never could.

So the major problem of finding a mount for the 1954 season was settled at last, and we now had merely to wait patiently until Maseratis could get down to assembly of the car. As the year turned, we felt further assured that we had done wisely in buying the Maserati, when Fangio won the Argentine G.P. in January with the first of the 250Fs. We had hoped to have the car ready in time for the Pau G.P. in April, but this proved impossible, so the *Daily Express* Silverstone meeting a few weeks later became our target. But before that day there were quite a few other things to keep us busy and interested in life.

Looming up large ahead of us was the Monte Carlo Rally. Stirling was once again to share a Sunbeam-Talbot with Desmond Scannell and John Cooper of *The Autocar*, and I was going down to Monte Carlo in order to assist during the final section. As I had to visit Maseratis at Modena on various items of business, including payment of the deposit on the 250F, we agreed it was a good idea if I made an extended journey out to Monte Carlo via Switzerland and Modena. I was to use a Hillman Minx which I had acquired by then, and was to take out with me an experimental radiator and several cans of Stirling's chosen shade of green paint for the Maserati.

I took with me Ron Smith, who had now been helping me with the Half-Litre Club for two years or so, while a friend of Ron named Reg Meekings also came along. I was very keen on motoring whenever possible in those days, and planned that we would drive to Modena via Switzerland, then go to Monte Carlo, check up on arrangements for Stirling, and then drive up across France to Dunkirk, and put Reg and Ron down by the cross-Channel ferry. After that I would turn round and drive back to Monte and take up my position on the Mountain circuit, as prearranged, and wait for the Rootes team to come through.

The weather looked grim from the start, and as we crossed France we kept hearing reports of heavy snow and bad conditions ahead. It was bitterly cold, and as we neared the Swiss frontier we ran into a veritable blizzard and had to ease our pace, the Minx's heaters and wipers going full blast to combat the flying snow.

We arrived at Pontarlier, a little place on the French-Swiss border, in the dead of night, and rushed out of the snow into the Douane hut to have our passports stamped. In the back of the Hillman we had the radiator, the green paint, and all sorts of bits and pieces for the Maserati, with no paperwork at all, so we were a little bit concerned.

To our relief, the gendarme apparently decided it was far too cold outside to bother about inspecting the car, and simply stamped our passports and said 'O.K.'. Out we went, and I was about to let the clutch in when suddenly the door of the hut opened, and the gendarme yelled 'Attendez!' 'Hullo' we thought, 'this is it—now he's decided to examine the car after all.'

But it was nothing like that. The gendarme was simply a student of the English, he explained, and had we some English papers for him to read, so that he could improve his tongue? We had no newspapers, but as it happened, in the boot of the Hillman were a pile of children's comics, such as *Beano*, *Film Fun*, *Adventure* and so on, which we hastily gathered up and handed to him, saying they were very good English newspapers, and we hoped he would enjoy them.

As we passed through Switzerland next day, I thought we would have a look at the famous Bremgarten circuit, scene of the Swiss G.P. since 1934, and rated by Stirling and many others as one of the very finest in Europe. The course is situated outside Berne, and it was deep in snow, making it difficult to pick out where the actual circuit was. Eventually we found it, and started pounding round, until I suddenly 'lost' the car well and truly on the packed snow, and we ended up in a nine-foot snowdrift. It took us hours to dig the Minx out, and Gregory's name was 'Mud' to his two companions!

Weather conditions were bad well into Italy, and our original schedule was thoroughly sabotaged. By the time we reached Milan the roads were atrocious. Tremendous blizzards had raged in northern Italy, and the snow then partially thawed, leaving a layer of thick slush on the roads. Countless heavy lorries had left their double tracks in the slush, which had then frozen solid overnight, leaving the roads like miniature mountain ranges, with treacherous ruts each side, for mile after mile.

Of course the wheel tracks of the Minx were much narrower than the twin channels left by the lorries, so that we were driving all the time with the back of the car weaving from side to side as the wheels caught in one rut or the other. It was quite the most hilarious, frightening and worrying journey I had ever undertaken in my life. Wheelgrip, of course, was very limited, and for every ten miles covered, the speedometer trip registered almost double.

Soon we were running into long columns of traffic, all creeping along, and I well remember crossing one bridge on the Via Emilia, which is the main road down to Modena, Bologna and Rome. There was a long line of traffic in both directions, all of it stationary owing to a shunt between two vehicles farther up the road. After a while this cleared, but when the time came to get moving, I let the clutch in on the Hillman, which just stayed still while the rear wheels spun uselessly. Ron and Reg got out to give the Minx a shove, and suddenly it started forward. I shouted desperately, 'Come on, you two—I can't wait for you,' but there was no response. Eventually I managed a hasty look back, and there were the pair of them, flat on their faces on the icy road, which was incredibly slippery, having been polished by passing vehicles until it was like a glass table top.

Eventually we got going again, then stopped at a little café by the road and had some black coffee; by now it was past midnight, and we were hours behind schedule. Resuming the journey, I grew more accustomed to the conditions and pressed on until, at one stage, we were doing some 45 to 50 m.p.h. We had just passed three lorries which we had followed for about seven miles, and the back of the car was repeatedly slewing from left to right, then from right to left as it struggled with the icy ruts.

Suddenly the tail of the Minx came round, but instead of right-ing itself as before it just kept on sliding, and I couldn't control it. I suddenly yelled out, 'It's no good—I've lost it,' and the car careered along the road for 400 yards or so, spinning like a top the whole way. We ended up on the other side of the road, facing back the way we had come; three shaken people, fortunately quite un-hurt. By the time we got going those three lorries had gone by again!

At last we got into Modena, but too late, of course, to call on Maseratis until the morrow, so we made our way to the hotel and tumbled thankfully into bed. We made our call next day, then set off immediately for Monte Carlo, this time taking the Genoa *autostrada* after Piancenza, then the coast road up through San Remo and across the frontier to Monte Carlo.

For some reason which I never could fathom, Stirling Moss, Desmond Scannell and John A. Cooper, the trio who did so well in the previous year's 'Monte', decided to start from Athens in 1954. Once again their car was a Sunbeam-Talbot 90, entered by the Rootes organization, and before the actual Rally, in common with all the other teams, they had made an advance 'recce' over part of of the route, in particular the 165 miles between Gap and Monaco itself, which was to constitute the all-important Speed-Regularity Test.

This was divided into four sections, and constituted a veritable 'battle of the stop watches'. Competitors were required to main-tain speeds of between 45 and 65 k.p.h., having to estimate their speed in advance, and then being required to maintain it through-out the four sections.

Section 1 was over fairly flat and easy terrain, but Section 2 was over the Col des Leques, a very twisty and steep mountain section, covered, of course, in snow and ice, and these conditions had to be taken into account when estimating the average speed. The higher the average selected, the higher the marking, but on the other hand, penalties for failing to maintain one's chosen average were severe, and could quickly eliminate from the results any entry which made a serious over-assessment of their possible average speed.

Obviously advance information of conditions on the Col des Leques would be extremely valuable to the competing cars, so it had been arranged before the Rally that my Hillman, and also a Humber Hawk driven by Ron Clayton, a photographer, were fitted with radio-telephone transmitter-receiver equipment by the Pye concern of Cambridge.

On the night before the Speed-Regularity Test was to take place, I drove out from Monte Carlo along the route, taking particular note of conditions on the Col des Leques and elsewhere. Next day I took up station in the Minx just outside Gap control, and Ronnie Clayton positioned himself on the far side of the Col des Leques section, the scheme being that I would pass on information regarding conditions on the Col to the crews as the Rootes cars came through, to assist them in assessing their potential average speeds. Then, as each car entered the Test I would notify Clayton over the radio-telephone.

As each car passed Clayton's Humber Hawk, they would then tell him if they had over- or under-estimated their speed, and this information could then be radio-phoned back for me to notify the next car. As Stirling's was the last, he should have the benefits of all the preceding cars' experience passed on to him, thus having a good chance of completing the Test with high markings.

But things didn't work out that way. Team manager Norman Garrad, who, as I have said, is very widely experienced and knows every wrinkle of the rallying game, had studied the regulations and decided that our scheme to help the team would come under the heading of 'outside assistance' and as such might entail disqualification.

Consequently, when the first car came up, it neither stopped for me at Gap, nor for Clayton beyond the Col des Leques. Nor did any of the other Rootes entries, until Stirling's Sunbeam-Talbot 90, which had had a terrible run from Athens, hove into view. They unloaded every bit of spare luggage and piled it into the Minx to lighten their own car, while I told them of the road conditions as I knew them.

Unfortunately, when I had crossed the Col eight hours earlier the ice on the road was mixed with grit, and this grit, being ingrained into the ice, gave quite good traction on the corners. But by the time Stirling, who was one of the later starters in the Test, came through, he found the corners very polished and slippery after the passage of numerous earlier cars. Thus their speed assessment was a bit too high, and despite Stirling making the best time of all over the Col des Leques, they lost quite a few penalty marks, and only finished fifteenth in the final results.

This was a pity, and I believe that had the team stopped, as originally planned, to pick up and pass on information, they would have been placed higher. But Sunbeam-Talbot won the team prize, anyway, while the Moss-Scannell-Cooper car was the highest-placed Rootes finisher, and won the Athens starting award.

But it was not a happy rally for the Sunbeam-Talbot team. After making a magnificent effort in the Speed-Regularity Test, Leslie Johnson, who had John Cutts and Norman Garrad in his '90' with him, suffered an attack of coronary thrombosis which left him a very sick man. He went doggedly on to Monte Carlo, and was taken into the British Hospital there, subsequently being brought back to London. Poor Leslie never really recovered, and was never to resume the very active existence he formerly led.

After the Monte Carlo Rally, Stirling decided it was a good opportunity for us to go back to Modena in the hard-worked Minx, so that he could get his first glimpse of the car he was going to drive and also see the people at Maseratis. He met the Orsis, father and son, and also their export manager Sergio Toumaniantz and others. Stirling asked innumerable questions about the cars, collected a lot of blueprints, and we drove back to Milan that evening. The next day we set off again for home.

We arrived home on 30 January, and the next night Stirling had one of his periodic illnesses, which seemed to arise after undue stress and strain. He suffered swollen glands and felt dizzy and generally out of sorts. Today we are used to this trouble of his, and whenever the symptoms appear, he is packed off to bed for two or three days.

Once over this little indisposition, Stirling was soon up and about, preparing for what was to prove probably the most important season in his entire racing career. He made careful study of the racing calendar, selecting suitable events and drawing up a provisional programme.

It was obvious that, with the Maserati to look after, Alf Francis and Tony Robinson would have little time to devote to the rather specialized preparation and tuning of a Formula 3 car. Stirling decided, therefore, to give up being a private entrant, and signed up with Francis Beart of Byfleet to drive his lightened and always very well prepared Beart-Cooper, powered, of course, by the inevitable Norton twin overhead camshaft engine.

Francis Beart is a very easy person to get on with, and in temperament he and Stirling suited each other well. Beart is extremely methodical, takes immense pride in his work, and knows the Norton engine through and through, after many years of motorcycle racing and tuning. He is quiet and unexcitable, likes to be left alone to get on with the job, and altogether gave Stirling the confidence he needed.

In March, Stirling went out to Sebring, to score a remarkable victory over the bigger Lancias, Ferraris, and Aston Martins in the Florida 12-hour sports-car race, driving Briggs Cunningham's 1500 c.c. OSCA, with Bill Lloyd as co-driver. With his season starting so well, was the bad luck of 1952 and 1953 to leave Stirling at last?

Soon came welcome news from Italy that the Maserati would be ready well before Silverstone, so that Stirling could safely make an entry for the Bordeaux Grand Prix on 9 May. Alf Francis had been over at Modena for weeks, watching over the car as it was assembled, so we all felt confident that it would be in good fettle.

Then, as the Bordeaux date drew nearer, I began to notice in Stirling a peculiar new quality, one of concern. I think he was realizing that the eleventh hour was approaching; he had tried so hard, for so long, with so little return in Grand Prix racing, that to himself he was wondering just how he would fare, now he was to face the proven champions of Grand Prix racing in a car of equal potency. Was he, in fact, the man for the job?

In my own mind, I knew full well that he was, and so did his father and his supporters, but it was less difficult for us—we weren't driving the car. Formerly Stirling had always been at the wheel of a car which was inferior to the best, and if things didn't go right, there was always the consolation that 'he did jolly well considering the car he was driving'. Now he was to have a car as good as the rest, and if he didn't do well, people would be saying, 'Well, there you are—you put Moss in a decent car, and he's just not capable of making the grade.' This was the sort of argument we sensed a hyper-sensitive person like Moss was building up within himself, although we knew that once he got going his confidence would return in full measure.

Nevertheless, the period immediately preceding the G.P. of Bordeaux was unpleasantly tense, and often the atmosphere between us reminded me of an extremely hot, sultry day, when tempers are apt to flare up at the slightest provocation. I was, in fact, more than pleased when news arrived that Alf Francis and Tony Robinson were on their way from Italy with the car, and Stirling left for Bordeaux.

I didn't go with him, but I gathered that the car looked a perfect dream in its shimmering green paint, when taken out of the Commer van, and that it went as well as it looked, making Stirling a very happy man. Faced by a three-car works team of 4-cylinder Ferraris, he sensibly treated the race as a try-out, kept a strict revs. limit, and despite a pit stop to change from Dunlop to Pirelli tyres, which at that time handled better under wet conditions, finished fourth behind Gonzalez, Manson and Trintignant, all in Ferraris.

After that, Moss obviously felt more satisfied in his own mind as to his capabilities, and life with him became easier. In fact, he could hardly wait for the next race, which was the *Daily Express* Silverstone, just six days later.

Like Roy Salvadori, but opposed to several other drivers, Stirling likes Silverstone, not only because of the circuit, which suits his driving, but for the pleasantness of our stay there. Since racing first started at Silverstone in 1948, we had put up at a place called The Rectory, in the village of Wicken. This offered good value, and was pleasingly quiet, but it grew more and more popular, and the local padre seemingly decided that here was an opportunity to supplement his stipend, and turned his rather large rectory into a mammoth boarding house.

The charges rose, and the value lessened until after one particular meeting we decided to call it a day. This was largely due to a surcharge of ten shillings per head for drinks, and as none of us had any drinks we queried this with the Vicar. His answer was, 'Well, in my house we don't charge anybody individually for drinks; we just put as much drink as is necessary on the sideboard, and put ten shillings on everyone's bill.'

Although this meant poor value for us, I've no doubt it worked out well for others who made full use of the contents of the sideboard, but the upshot was that we decided to find new lodgings for the future. Thanks to Sally Weston, we found a new address which proved to be so excellent that we have stayed there ever since. This is the Castle House, at Buckingham. It is a beautiful old building, with parts originating from a Norman castle, hence the name, and the owner is John Bristow-Bull, who has become a very close friend of ours.

By profession a courier, John looks after us, prepares all the food, does the cleaning, waits on us at table, and generally keeps us content. We sit, eat and sleep amidst priceless antiques, in a house steeped in history. The room Stirling sleeps in is known as the Catherine of Aragon room, that lady having used it when she stayed at the House for a considerable time during the reign of Henry VIII. My room, which I still use regularly today, has a genuine four-poster bed, and in sleeping there I achieved one ambition of my life—to sleep in a four-poster bed!

It was at Castle House that we made a film for Pathé called *A Day in the Life of Stirling Moss*. It provided a wonderful setting, particularly as the film, which formed part of a Pathé Pictorial, was in colour. All the classic beauty of the house, inside and out, was fully exploited, and the closing scene showed Stirling retiring for the night in the Catherine of Aragon bed.

But let's get back to the Silverstone of May 1954, and the excitement of the new Maserati. The International Trophy was divided this time into two heats and a final, and Stirling came third in Heat 1 behind Gonzalez (Ferrari) and Bira, who drove a most spirited race in another Maserati, having quite a tussle with Stirling.

But Stirling was holding his effort back for the Final, and when this got going, he left Bira way behind, and fought a great duel with Behra's Gordini, passing it into second place behind Gonzalez. Then, with ten laps to go, the Maserati's de Dion tube broke at Club Corner, and Moss walked in. This looked like 1952–53 luck all over again, but he wasn't downhearted, for the car had gone well until then, and he was confident that it would do well in the future.

After winning the 500 c.c. race in Francis Beart's Cooper, by 23 sec. from Les Leston, Stirling met another rebuff in the Saloon car race, when a jammed starter on his Mk. VII Jaguar made an anticlimax of his usually brilliant Le Mans start. He got away last but one, and spent the rest of the race climbing back to third place, behind two other Mk. VIIs. I took part in the same race, driving a very different sort of car, a Standard Ten prepared by Dennis Done, who drove a similar model.

In an excess of zeal, I had warmed the engine up too much before the start, and my efforts to do a 'Moss-style' Le Mans getaway were spoilt by a vapour lock, due to the fact that the fuel line to the carburettor ran close to the cylinder head and got too hot. As a result I went off spitting and spluttering, and didn't get full power until I reached Copse Corner. After a few laps I remember catching a glimpse in the mirror of a Mk. VII Jaguar breathing down my neck at Becketts; it was on me, and whanging past before I could think about who was driving. It was Stirling making up time after his bad start.

The rest of my race consisted of a struggle with D. O'M. Taylor in another Standard. We were never more than three or four feet apart, repeatedly swapping places for lap after lap, and having tremendous fun. Meanwhile Dennis Done, who had made a brilliant start, was about half a lap ahead, and finished third in his class behind a young dental student from Cheshire called Tony Brooks in a 3-cylinder D.K.W. and Alan Foster's Morris Minor.

Immediately after Silverstone we sent a cable to Maseratis, notifying them of the de Dion tube breakage. Their spares service was tremendous, and by the following Wednesday I was at London airport, collecting the replacement tube which they sent by air. The price was a mere £6. Meantime, Alf Francis had repaired the original tube, so that we now had one in reserve.

Two weeks later came a new race at a new circuit, the B.A.R.C. *Daily Telegraph* Aintree '200' at Mrs Topham's new 3-mile course which followed the outline of her famous Grand National track at Aintree, outside Liverpool. Right from this inaugural meeting, Aintree has proved a remarkably lucky track for Stirling, who has won nearly every race he has driven on that circuit. 29 May, 1954, was very dark and depressing, with a lot of rain about, but Stirling drove impeccably, and won the '200' race with considerable ease—his first outright victory in the Maserati—and also won the Formula 3 event in the Beart-Cooper.

It was around this time, in between racing, that Stirling and I took part in a film on motor-race marshalling, which Shell-Mex were producing in collaboration with the B.R.D.C. Stirling's main task was to spin a car round at a corner for the benefit of the cameras, and the spin had to be staged pretty accurately. The car used was the unsuccessful Cooper-Alta No. 1, which had been on loan for some while to the Ferodo concern for brake testing, as was agreed when we gained their support in 1953.

The engine had been taken from the No. 2 Cooper-Alta (this having been sold, minus engine and gearbox, to Eric Brandon), and replaced in the original car, and now that the darned thing didn't have to race any more, it behaved very well and ran reliably!

In the first part of the film, Alan Brown and I were the principal performers, Alan in a Cooper-Bristol and myself in the Cooper-Alta. In one particular scene we had to depict cars passing each other so that the flag boys could get into action, and on one lap I arrived at Copse Corner far too fast, missed a gear, and spun the car well and truly. If only the cameras had been there at that particular moment, Stirling need never have bothered to come to Silverstone at all!

Then Alan Brown had to stage a fire, bringing his car in with smoke pouring from the bonnet, when a crowd of inexperienced and over-enthusiastic marshals were supposed to put the fire out. The marshals, who were real actors working to Equity rulings, did their job a bit too well, and poor Alan had to endure the sight of six or seven fire extinguishers being emptied all over his engine. It took him two days to get it clean again!

In Stirling's spin scene, the car had not only to spin, but then to turn over. They didn't expect him to perform this part of the manœuvre as well, but staged it by turning the car over on its side, then cunningly getting it back on its wheels. This whole procedure was filmed, and then reversed, after which further 'doctoring' produced quite a realistic accident.

Meanwhile the Half-Litre Club was going from strength to strength, and the latest development was the extension of Brands Hatch. An extra quarter of a mile was added to the original 'kidney bean' shape, by running a new stretch up what was known as Druid's Hill, with a tightish bend at the top, running down and joining up with Bottom Straight. The course was now reversed from anti-clockwise to the more normal clockwise direction, which meant that the painted starting grid now faced the wrong way.

The 'new look' Brands Hatch was inaugurated at Easter with a mixed meeting, and proved extremely popular, both with the public and the drivers. Significant was the ban on the use of nitromethane and other oxygen-bearing fuels, the Half-Litre Club having decided to impose this measure by a majority vote at its Annual General Meeting.

There was also a change in our London Office at 20, William IV Street. Ron Smith had been giving invaluable help for a considerable time on a voluntary basis, and he now decided to join me as a full-time, fully paid assistant. What with the filing and documentation of the Stirling Moss side of things, and all the Half-Litre Club business being conducted there, the office was becoming a somewhat crowded hive of industry and obviously something would have to be done soon about finding further accommodation. This couldn't be tackled in the middle of the racing season, however, and had to be put off to a quieter period.

CHAPTER SIX

STIRLING VINDICATED

STIRLING having come through a particularly tense period, it now seemed it was my turn to be 'under the weather', and I began to feel the combined stress of living and working with him to such an extent that I suffered a slight nervous breakdown. As I have already written, Stirling is possessed of ceaseless energy. I will never know how he does it, but he can be active both mentally and physically for hours and hours, goes reluctantly to bed, and in remarkably few hours has recharged his energy, and is once again bounding zestfully around. I just couldn't keep up with his pace.

The strain manifested itself in the form of a rather serious skin rash, so I went to see a man I had known for a long time, Hugh Wallace, a dermatologist at St Thomas's Hospital. Without more ado he packed me off to the annexe of St Thomas's, down at Goldalming in Surrey.

There I was given a sort of negative 'shock' treatment, which involved taking a considerable number of sedatives and more or less staying asleep for almost a fortnight, virtually cleansing one's mind completely of all its troubles and worries. Hugh Wallace's advice then was that I should give up living at Challoner Mansions in company with Stirling, and take a flat of my own, in order, he said, to give my mind an occasional rest from work, and enable me to really relax now and then.

He was right, of course; as Stirling's companion and manager, I was living, eating, drinking and sleeping motor racing, twenty-four hours a day. There was no relaxing. If I went to the Steering Wheel for a drink, the talk was inevitably about motor racing; I loved the subject, yes; it was my job and my life, but it was impossible to get away from it.

In order that I could keep fairly normal hours, and follow fairly normal business routine, I had moved some time earlier into a second bedroom at Challoner Mansions, leaving Stirling to get up later and retire in the early hours of the morning, as was his preference.

Then one night came the episode which finally decided me to take Hugh Wallace's advice and take a separate flat. I was in bed and asleep after a particularly hard day, when at about two o'clock in the morning Stirling came in. He clumped into the kitchen, which was next to my bedroom, and barged into tables and things, making sufficient noise so that I could not possibly go on sleeping. Then he poked his head round the door, and said, 'Ken, are you awake?'

I said, 'Yes, I'm awake.'

And he said, 'Will you get me a tube of toothpaste in the morning?'!

Next morning I went out and began enquiring for a flat, and was able to find one with the same landlords, only four hundred yards away in a block called Barton Court—near enough for convenience, but far enough to ensure myself a little peace.

It was, of course, thoughtlessness on Stirling's part; he can be thoughtless to others, and on many occasions he has hurt his father and mother, and quite a few other people. But it is a human failing which in his case can largely be excused, simply because of the mode of life he has to lead.

When you are somebody like Stirling Moss, constantly in the public eye, it is rather like standing on top of a very tall pillar, with thousands of howling, hungry wolves below, waiting for you to fall off so that they can devour you. That is the price of being famous. At all times your behaviour has to be impeccable, for a celebrity does not possess the right to do the little things in life which are indiscreet. The moment you do so, the news reaches the papers, your behaviour is criticized, and the 'wolves' howl in triumph.

As a result, people like Stirling are constantly on their guard, ever watchful that they do and say the right things. Is it surprising, then, that he should relax his rigid codes a little, and 'let off steam' amongst his closest friends? It is thoughtlessness, yes, but it is also his relief valve, and this is one of the problems which a manager must understand thoroughly if he is to succeed.

Anyway, back to motor racing. After Aintree, Stirling drove the Maserati in the Grand Prix of Rome, over a new and very fast circuit at Castel Fusano. In this race, performing before the eyes of the Maserati team personnel, Stirling's reputation with them went up considerably. They were most impressed by his drive, and almost as disappointed as he was that final drive failure forced him to retire.

His 250F could not match the pace of the works car driven by Onofre Marimon, the talented young Argentinian and protégé of Fangio and Gonzalez, but he held second place determinedly without over-stressing the car, leaving Luigi Musso and Sergio Mantovani in works Maseratis way behind. It was on lap 52, with only eight rounds to go, that the final drive went, and Stirling ground to a stop near the finishing line.

As soon as Marimon had taken the chequered flag, Stirling pushed the crippled Maserati over the line, thus qualifying as a finisher, being credited with sixth place. This is an old practice with Moss, and visitors to the Dundrod T.T. will well remember seeing him waiting near the line with a disabled Jaguar on at least two occasions, ready to cross as soon as the winner came round.

Then he finished third behind Fangio's works Maserati and Trintignant's Ferrari in the Belgian Grand Prix at Spa—a World Championship event. Stirling rates the Spa-Francorchamps circuit very highly indeed; it is very, very fast, and is a real 'driver's circuit', counteracting any advantage which a good car with a not-so-good driver might have elsewhere. It possesses every type of corner, from the very slow Malmedy hairpin to the extremely fast Stavelot Curve coming after the Masta Straight. As this is one of the fastest stretches on any circuit, anywhere, permitting speeds of over 180 m.p.h., the driver using it to the full has to know what he is doing.

That Fangio, driving his last race for Officine Maserati before joining Mercedes-Benz, should have won was to be expected; the Argentinian master was incomparable at Spa, but it was exciting that already at this time Moss was being compared with him. Fangio won his race with his front suspension partially collapsed, whereas Stirling took third in a privately owned and much slower Maserati, and that despite two stops for oil, so that their achievements that day were certainly comparable.

Next up on the Calendar was the French G.P. at Rheims, the race in which Mercedes were to make a sensational return to racing, with Fangio and Kling taking the first two places. We were dubious about racing at Rheims, realizing that our private 250F would not be able to match the official Maseratis, let alone the Mercedes; it was a question of saving our engine, for the only way to go fast at Rheims was to go flat out—there was no question of second-saving on the corners, as at Spa or other circuits.

As a replacement engine, if ours blew up, would cost something between £1500 and £2000, Stirling decided to let the French G.P. go by, and instead the car was sent down to the Modena factory for a thorough overhaul in preparation for the next event, the British G.P. at Silverstone. Then came an unusual request from Maseratis. Would Signor Moss consent to lending his car to them, so that Villoresi could drive it in the Grand Prix? They undertook to recondition the car throughout after the race, and would see that he had it back, brought up to latest works specification, in good time for the British G.P.

Having himself renounced the opportunity of driving in the Grand Prix, Stirling was reluctant at first to agree, but in the end he was made to see the advantages, and thus the Moss 250F appeared on the starting line at Rheims after all, looking strange in a hasty coat of red paint, and with Luigi Villoresi, the silvery-haired veteran, in the cockpit. It took fifth place in the race despite a misfiring engine for much of the distance.

Came the British Grand Prix, on which we all set tremendous hopes for Stirling, particularly as Maseratis had prepared the car so well, and had additionally guaranteed replacement of the engine if it blew up. It was wonderful to see the green 'Maser' on the front row of the grid alongside Fangio's Mercedes and two works Ferraris (Gonzalez and Hawthorn). The race was full of surprises, and showed what a magnificent driver Froilan Gonzalez—once the 'wild man'—had become.

He made a tremendous start, and nobody saw him after that, though Fangio tried desperately hard in the unwieldy aerodynamic Merc, which was not suited to the Silverstone swerves, especially when it began to rain. Stirling became embroiled in a monumental battle with Mike Hawthorn, and when, at the chosen moment, Alf Francis gave Moss the 'get him' signal, Stirling discomfited Mike by outpacing him, leaving him farther and farther behind. Then he passed Fangio's Merc, and looked nicely secure in second place when the gremlins got to work. With only nine laps to go the rear drive failed, and Moss's gallant race was over.

So Mike Hawthorn took second place after all—and frankly admitted he was lucky to get it and Stirling '—— unlucky to lose it'. Now the press had made a big splash about the Hawthorn-Moss rivalry, both before and after the race, speaking, in the way the press do, of the tremendous battle between these two widely differing personalities.

Yet contrary to what most people apparently thought, the pair were close friends in many ways. Of course, Mike was a totally different character to Stirling; he was a chap who enjoyed his beer and his pipe, whereas Stirling enjoyed neither. Mike was an extrovert and lived an extrovert life; Stirling, on the other hand, was more an introvert, and never tended to that hearty over-exuberance to which Mike was prone, particularly at post-race parties!

Putting the two characters in another setting, I always have thought that, had they been old enough for service during the Hitler War, both would have joined the R.A.F. But whereas Mike would have made a fighter pilot, blazing away through the skies, gunning at anything that came his way, the real 'blood and thunder', devil-may-care, hair-in-the-wind 'First of the Few' type, Stirling would have been the coldly calculating, precision-minded type to be found in Bomber Command; he would have made a splendid 'Pathfinder' character. He is much more the exact scientist than dear old Mike ever was; he is the purist, the professional, the man who exerts every single ounce of everything he's got, all the time. Stirling may not feel well, or may not feel like driving; the car or something else may be wrong, but he will always make the maximum effort, because he is a professional, and feels he has a duty both to the public and himself to fulfil.

Mike was more the type of person who drove as the will took him. If he felt well, he would drive well, but if he felt awful, he would sometimes drive awfully. He had no dedication to motor racing; he drove because he liked driving, because he loved the sport of motor racing with all its glamour. It satisfied a craving for excitement, and in many ways satisfied his extrovert way of life.

Differing thus as chalk from cheese, they were nevertheless good friends, and despite all the publicized rivalry, there was never a scrap of enmity or animosity between them. If anything, they were like the gladiators of old; friends before and friends during the fight, even though they might try a few tricks during a race to put each other in a compromising position. Certainly they enjoyed a bit of lighthearted baiting of each other, particularly before a race, when each would try to demoralize the other.

'They've given me an old banger—only got 260 on the brake,' Mike might say, and Stirling, having made best practice times, would rejoin, 'Mine's a bit down on power—Bertocchi says the engine's none too good.' Then each would give the other a look as if to say, 'Who's kidding whom?'

On the track, too, they were adepts at trying to take each other into a corner a wee bit fast, though both were too good at the game to get into any sort of danger. The lay reader may be horrified at such things, but the confidence each had in the other's ability permitted them to try such things, and the same applies to all the real Grand Prix drivers. Each knows the other's ability, and can trust him not to do anything silly, which is why Grand Prix racing, practised by the finest class of racing driver of all, is so much safer than sports-car racing, in which many more drivers, of lesser ability, in cars of widely varying size and capabilities, compete on the same circuit.

Grand Prix drivers are the élite of racing men, and I am sure that Stirling will agree with me when I contend that driving in a Grand Prix today is considerably safer than driving on the London–Brighton road at the week-end.

At around this time, I note from a study of the motoring magazines of the period, Stirling's face was appearing regularly over a glass of Lucozade in a series of advertisments. It was my duty and pleasure to negotiate these with a man named Bagnall Harvey, who amongst other things was Denis Compton's manager.

I don't know why it is, for I've had no training in it, but the negotiation of contracts is something I really revel in. To most people, such a task may seem as dull as ditchwater, but I have always found it one of the most enjoyable of the many facets of management. To me, the negotiation of a contract is like the painting of a picture to an artist. As you never sign a contract unless it suits you, and the other party never signs unless it suits them, there is an overall satisfaction about the whole business. Stirling, for his part, specified what he required, and then left the whole thing to me, and I must say I always got a kick out of it.

Now there are some people who snort at advertisements featuring celebrities, declaring that they have merely sold their names and couldn't care less about the products they are supposed to be praising. This may be so with some, but it certainly isn't with Stirling Moss, who has never allowed his name to be associated with anything he did not genuinely approve of.

Thus the name of Moss does not appear in 'alliance' with dozens of diverse products, and there is a second reason for this. I do not believe in taking out lots of advertising contracts and getting small fees for each. Better, I consider, to keep the name exclusive, not only to satisfy Stirling's principles, but also to impart a certain scarcity value which lends dignity and sincerity.

I think Stirling's first advertising contract was with Craven A, and the famous 'When I do smoke, I'm choosey' feature made a tremendous impact on the public. The contract was signed by Stirling himself before I became his manager, and his fee was very modest, but it certainly caught on, and must have been an advertiser's dream. Although the series ended in 1952, many still seem to remember the 'message' of the ad. and frequently, when Stirling is invited to dinner, the host or hostess produces a box of Craven A especially for him. Wherever he goes, in fact, it is not long before somebody produces a packet of Craven A and pointedly offers Stirling one. Let me stress, therefore, that Stirling *does* smoke Craven A, though I must also place on record that he is a very moderate smoker. Five or six a day satisfy him, but he really enjoys them.

Stirling next drove his Maserati in the Grand Prix at Caen, a place better known as a key point in the Allied offensive in Normandy in 1944. Alfred and Aileen Moss and I had arranged to fly over with an old friend of ours, Peter Ayles, chief instructor of the Herts. and Essex Aero Club, in a four-seater Miles Messenger, but unluckily the weather grounded us, and we missed the race.

This was a pity, because Stirling drove very well and had a great tussle with Maurice Trintignant in a works Ferrari. Now 'Trint' is one of those unobtrusive drivers who can all too easily be discounted in a gathering of Grand Prix stars, but he is a shrewd tactician, has immense experience and very great skill which he used to full effect at Caen when the rain came down. Stirling's tyres were definitely inferior in the wet to the Ferrari's Pirellis, and his hard-won lead was inexorably worn down by 'Trint', and in the end the Ferrari won by 3 sec., with Behra's Gordini third.

We were both busy on the August Bank Holiday week-end, for while Moss was driving in the European Grand Prix at Nurburgring on the Sunday, I was heavily occupied with the Half-Litre Club's International meeting at Brands Hatch on the Monday. And just to emphasize the advantages of modern transport, and the energy of Stirling, he was driving there too!

The Maserati lasted only a single lap at Nurburg, which might make the race seem hardly worthy of mention. But it was, in fact, outstandingly important in Moss's career, since it marked the end of his independent status as a Grand Prix driver. Coming less than six months after both Mercedes-Benz and Maserati had declined his services, this was gratifying, to say the least.

In practice with the green Maser, Stirling was fastest of all on the Friday, and third fastest on Saturday to a Mercedes and a Ferrari, gaining a place in the front row of the grid. That his private Maserati should be faster than three of the Mercedes, all but one of the Ferraris, and every works Maserati, was a pretty shattering performance, and in combination with his feats elsewhere, it decided Officine Maserati to offer Moss a place in the works team without further delay. Thus came recognition at last of his remarkable ability.

It did not immediately mean that his green 250F was put to rest, but it did mean immediate relief from that anxiety which every independent driver knows so well—the keeping of his car in one piece. An 'independent' has a tough time, in face of works opposition, because he must respect rev. limits in order to preserve his engine—miss a gear, hold on to second or third a bit too long and let the revs. go too high, and the result can be a wrecked engine, a bill of anything up to £2000, loss of *primes de départ* in the next race, and other expensive complications.

Works backing means emancipation from all these worries, and while a works driver is hardly encouraged to exceed rev. limits, if he *does* make a mistake and blows his engine up, he will have to face an angry proprietor and team manager, but not the heavy repair bills.

When driving his green Maserati, Stirling did not simply respect the revs. limit advised by the works; he willed himself to drive at least 200 r.p.m. below it, in order to make sure that his engine didn't break. Yet he could equal, and even better, the performances of the works Maseratis under such circumstances. With full works backing, therefore, it could be expected that he would be able to offer a real challenge to the opposing Ferraris and Mercedes.

Maserati accepted full responsibility for the mechanical reliability of the car, and made the entry under their name, while Stirling got a certain percentage of income. Maserati took the balance and also agreed to cover some previous expenses we had incurred—an excellent arrangement altogether.

Then the whole happy situation at Nurburg was changed through grim circumstance. The popular young team driver Onofre Marimon, who had won at Rome, crashed during the Saturday training period, and was killed. As a result Orsi, who was on a business trip in Argentina, wired instructions to withdraw the official Maserati team. Stirling's car, though now painted red, remained his property, however, so it was reverted to private entry status, as was Roberto Mieres's car, but Villoresi's Maserati did not start.

In the upshot, it made little difference, for our Maserati ran a big end on the second lap when lying third, causing a piston to collapse, and one more race was run. But any despondency at this failure was dispelled by the comforting knowledge that we now had full works backing. Even better, Officine Maserati had also consented to Stirling retaining Alf Francis and Tony Robinson to maintain his car, thus continuing a very successful association.

On the day after the European G.P. at Nurburgring, we of the Half-Litre Club had our August Bank Holiday Monday meeting at Brands Hatch. Once again it was sponsored by the *Daily Telegraph* and had attracted a crowd of some 40,000 spectators. I have always enjoyed the Bank Holiday Brands meetings and the organization of them. They were quite tricky to put on, because we aimed to introduce as much variety as possible into the programme in order to keep the public interest high. There were fifteen races, which meant careful and accurate timing throughout the programme as well as an 11 a.m. start.

In common with one or two other drivers, Stirling Moss competed at Brands, despite being at Nurburg the day before. Now many people will think this a tremendous feat, but in actual fact it is comparatively simple. Nurburgring is only five or six hours by road from Dunkirk, and the most popular boat with the motor-racing crowd, encumbered by racing transporters, is the Dover–Dunkirk night ferry, which leaves Dunkirk at about 1 a.m. Thus one can compete at Nurburg, have a comfortable drive back, allowing time for possible customs delays, and get on board at Dunkirk in good time for the one o'clock departure. If one is wise, a cabin has been reserved weeks beforehand, and you simply wash, go to bed, and wake up next morning in Dover. Then the car or van is taken off the boat, and off you go to Brands Hatch or whatever meeting you have entered, with a comfortable margin of time.

Stirling's race was the 5th *Daily Telegraph* International Trophy, which was split into four 10-lap heats and a 40-lap final. In his heat Stirling, who was driving Francis Beart's modified Cooper-Norton, met unexpected opposition from Charles Headland in a Martin-Headland, largely built by Ray Martin.

Now Charlie was notoriously a 'wild man' at the wheel, spinning off much too often, and having a hectic career before he finally decided to give up racing. But at Brands Hatch that day he drove one of his best races ever, and when Stirling came up from the back row, not having practised at all, Headland kept his head and his line, and though passed three times at Paddock Bend by Stirling, he retook the lead every time and won by a few yards.

And in the final, Stirling met further opposition from another driver then on his way up to the top of the Formula 3 tree—Jim Russell of Downton Market, Norfolk. Jim kept his red Cooper out in front to the end, leading Moss home by just over 6 sec.

It was at this time that the Club began negotiating to effect a change of name. I and many members of the Committee had long felt that the title Half-Litre Club was not synonymous with the increasing classes of racing we were promoting. We had come into existence through 500 c.c. racing and still retained a predominant interest in it, but by 1954 were also introducing sports car and

Formule Libre races to increase the variety and interest at Brands Hatch.

Our outlook had, in fact, broadened considerably, and we now sought a new name more indicative of that outlook. Many Formula 3 exponents were against the proposed change, however, considering that their class of racing would suffer, and that the whole nature of the Club would change. Today Formula 3 has, in fact, waned considerably in popularity, but this, I believe, can be attributed to a stagnation of design and other factors, but not to the Club's action in 1954.

Certainly it was not our intention then to reduce the influence of Formula 3, and we were able to persuade members that if the Club did not, in fact, change its name, its expansion would be impeded. That the name Half-Litre Club had its limitations became particularly apparent when we were negotiating for the use of the Crystal Palace circuit.

The L.C.C. were not impressed by our title; it didn't sound important enough, and did not suggest a major National Club, which was the sort of body they preferred to have to run meetings on their circuit. The upshot was an extraordinary general meeting of the Club at the R.A.C., where the decision was reached to change our name to the British Racing and Sports Car Club, which inevitably came to be abbreviated to the B.R.S.C.C. Incidentally, the use of the word 'British' in the new title meant obtaining the sanction and approval of the Board of Trade, which rather delayed its official adoption, so that it was not until September 1954 that we finally shed our old name.

This, I feel, is the opportunity to give a toot on the trumpet on behalf of the Half-Litre Club, *née* the 500 Club, and today the B.R.S.C.C. It began in 1946, and by 1954 had grown from a specialists' affair to one of the 'big three' in British motor clubs, alongside the B.R.D.C. and the B.A.R.C. It raised 500 c.c. racing from home-built to International status as Formula 3, and produced many of the finest of British post-war drivers, including Stirling Moss, Peter Collins, Stuart Lewis-Evans, Ivor Bueb, Harry Schell, Jim Russell, Graham Hill and Cliff Allison. By 1954 the Club had so expanded that from running meetings at Brands Hatch exclusively, we were also promoting events at Silverstone,

Crystal Palace, Brough (Yorks.), Cadwell Park (Lincs.) and Oulton Park (Cheshire). The infant had, in fact, grown to robust maturity.

After the German G.P., Stirling was firmly established as a top-line Formula 1 driver. He won the Gold Cup race at Oulton Park a week later, also the Formule Libre event, both in a works Maserati, as well as the Formula 3 race with the Beart-Cooper. Three races, three wins! But his luck didn't hold out for the next race, which was the Pescara G.P. on that very long and 'hairy' road circuit in Italy. Stirling was enthralled by it; 15·8 miles round, starting at sea level on the Adriatic coast, and running inland into the foothills of the Abruzzi mountains, it had everything: fast sections, twisty ones, steep gradients and every variety of corner.

Stirling pulled away from the start, but four laps later, when well ahead of Bira and Musso, an oil pipe broke and he retired. The Swiss G.P. ended in the same way, for all oil pressure departed after twenty-one laps, when he had 'kept pace' with Fangio's Mercedes and worried team manager Neubauer considerably. Would his 'Continental luck' never change?

The Italian Grand Prix at Monza a fortnight later brought the cruellest blow yet. I went to Italy to see the race, and the memory of it is with me still. I had never been to Monza, and I found the fantastic atmosphere, the mad-keen Italian crowds and everything about the place completely intoxicating.

The line-up was tremendous. All the great names were there, for this was Italy's and perhaps the world's greatest classic. The crowd came in tens and hundreds of thousands to see Mercedes-Benz, Ferrari, Maserati and Gordini do battle, with a new British contender in Tony Vandervell's Vanwall Special to bring the first serious splash of green to a classic Grand Prix race for a long time.

Two of the greatest among the drivers, Ascari and Villoresi, looked like being absentees as they had signed-up to drive the new G.P. Lancia at the beginning of 1954, and still the car was not ready. The partisan crowd were overjoyed when their idols appeared after all, Ascari making a temporary return to the Ferrari outfit, and Villoresi driving one of the works Maseratis.

There was some slight disruption, in fact, over the arrival of Gigi Villoresi in the team. He was without doubt a superb driver

in his day, and being an Italian one perhaps couldn't blame
Maseratis for looking upon him as their leading hope. Much more
attention was devoted to his car in practice than to Stirling's; and
Alf Francis became extremely touchy when after the second session
the Maserati mechanics began removing the tyres from Moss's car
to refit them on Villoresi's. It was all smoothed over in the end, and
in any case, the outstanding fact was that Stirling had made the
fastest lap of all the *Maseratisti*, third quickest of all the cars, and
would thus take a front row start together with Fangio's Mercedes
and Ascari's Ferrari.

Before the start I saw a new, almost frightening Stirling Moss;
Moss the ice-cool scientist, applying his mind wholly to the task
ahead and completely shutting everything else out. Now the
Monza starting grid is wildly chaotic before flagfall, with mechanics and officials rushing to and fro, shouting at each other, and
police desperately trying to control everything; the crowds in the
stands are adding to the din, and the excitement and tension are
almost unbearable.

Amidst all this, Stirling was sitting in the Maserati, while I sat
on one of the rear wheels, chatting to him about anything I could
think of, in an effort to keep his mind at ease. He listened, but said
little, and then I saw him look at his watch, which indicated that
there were exactly $1\frac{1}{2}$ minutes to go.

He began to button his helmet up, then put his gloves on, and
the person I had been talking to, who knew me as his manager, his
friend and confidant, was suddenly a stranger. He became ice
cold, and it was as if he suddenly erased everything from his mind
save the job ahead; his eyes saw nothing but the strip of track in
front, the starter taking up his position, the mechanics around the
car, the rev. counter, the gear lever and the steering wheel. I had
been obliterated from his mind, and as I got up, wished him good
luck, and walked away, I knew very well that he neither recognized
nor heard me; his mind was completely on the race ahead.

What a race it was! And what a carve-up from the start! First
Kling led, then spun off. Then Fangio took over until Ascari
screamed past, at which a tremendous roar went up from the
crowds all round the course. Behind there was a glorious mix-up
between Gonzalez, Hawthorn, Villoresi and Kling, but all the

time Stirling sat imperturbably on their tails, playing the waiting game in expectation that the more excitable of those around him would tax their cars beyond mechanical endurance, and 'stretch the elastic' to breaking point.

Gonzalez was the first to go, then Kling's run ended in the straw bales. Moss lay a smooth third to Ascari and Fangio, then Villoresi took the revs. up and passed him, taking Fangio as well. But it was too much for the Maserati, and Gigi went out with a burst engine. Then came the big thrill for us in the Moss camp—Stirling passed Fangio, and then nosed up to Ascari's tail.

Can you imagine our excitement when Stirling tore past the pits, leading Ascari and Fangio? Two of the greatest names in racing, and he had passed them both! Ascari fought back determinedly, re-took the lead, but over-extended his engine, the Ferrari coasting in to retire a lap later.

Soon it was clear that Stirling was pulling away from Fangio. With 20 laps to go, he led the Mercedes by no less than 15 sec., 5 laps later he was over 20 sec. ahead—and Neubauer was looking very worried. *Now* did he think Stirling needed more experience before driving a Grand Prix car, I wondered.

The sight of Fangio making 'I can't go any faster' signals to Neubauer was something I shall never forget. But it was too good to last, and with 12 laps to go, Stirling rushed in for more oil, overshooting the pit somewhat in his haste. A lap or so later and he came to a stop out on the circuit, his engine seized. The oil pipe leading from the oil radiator to the tank had broken, and most of his fresh oil was pumped out on the circuit. We were almost sick with the disappointment of it, but Stirling never loses his head, and was still determined to finish.

He pushed that disabled Maserati almost half a mile to the line, then waited until Fangio brought an exhausted Mercedes home to an extremely lucky victory. Then Stirling gave his car a heave, and was classified in tenth place. Tenth place, after all that; after outpacing Villoresi, Ascari, Fangio and the rest, before thousands and thousands of Italians!

But there was no mood of black despair in the Moss camp. The much-talked-of 'jinx' or 'gremlin' had got him once again, but at least the world now knew what kind of driver he was. No longer was he a boy who played with 500s, but one of the top Grand Prix drivers, destined to form the spearhead, in conjunction with Mike Hawthorn and Peter Collins, of Great Britain's attack on the Continental stronghold of motor racing.

Those two stalwarts were also prominent at Monza on that unforgettable day, Mike being second for Ferrari, and Peter seventh in the British Vanwall Special. I wonder if Tony Vandervell had any inkling then that in the none too distant future his cars would come back to Monza, and win the same *Gran Premio d'Italia* for Great Britain, and that Stirling Moss would play his part in the victory?

That momentous 1954 season was not over yet. Stirling won the Goodwood Trophy race for Formula 1 cars at the B.A.R.C.'s Autumn Goodwood meeting, and had a drive in a car new to him, the Lister-Bristol, which was usually driven by the illustrious Archie Scott-Brown. Although finding that the marked oversteer which Archie preferred took some getting used to, Stirling fought a tremendous duel with Roy Salvadori's 2-litre sports Maserati and failed by only one-fifth of a second to beat him to the chequered flag.

Then Moss went to Aintree, where the racing was now reversed to run in the more orthodox clockwise direction, and there he repeated his Oulton Park performance by scoring three wins in three races. With the Maserati carrying his favourite No. 7, he won the Formula 1 and Formule Libre races, and with the Beart-Cooper he won the 500 c.c. event. This, by the way, was to prove Stirling's last Formula 3 race.

We next went over to Montlhéry for the Coupe du Salon meeting, where Stirling drove Peter Bell's 1½-litre sports Connaught. After a run of serious Grands Prix, this was a delightfully casual meeting, and we all thoroughly enjoyed ourselves. Stirling won the 1½-litre class with the Connaught, but the memorable thing about this meeting was the party which succeeded it.

Our little party, which comprised Stirling, myself, Dennis Done, Peter Bell, and George Boyle, Bell's chief mechanic, went to a nightclub in Montmartre called La Nouvelle Eve. This place was less known for its food and drink than for its fantastic floor-show. We sat there, regaled by bottle after bottle of champagne, thoroughly enjoying ourselves, and though Stirling didn't join in the champagne session, he was in just as good form as any of us.

Another pleasure of Paris is, of course, that of eating, and 'Jabby' Crombac, one of the real characters in French motor racing, introduced us to a pleasant little restaurant called La Delice de St André, where the menu was limited, but out of this world. Their speciality was a sort of shrimp pancake, which fairly bubbled with shrimps, butter and fresh eggs, followed by wild mountain strawberries with lashings of fresh cream served from a two-gallon bowl on a Do It Yourself basis.

Barcelona and the final Grand Prix in the World Championship series, that of Spain, was far less cheerful. Stirling practised with a works Maserati having a central throttle position, did just what he always feared with this arrangement—pressed the wrong pedals at the crucial moment, and crashed on the first practice day, fortunately with no injuries.

In the race, he scrapped with Fangio's Mercedes while Ascari in the new Lancia, making its début, disputed the lead with Schell's Maserati and Hawthorn's Ferrari, the eventual winner. But Stirling's race ended with piston trouble after he had covered twenty-one laps. It was a poor finish to the most vital racing season in Stirling's career, but his more outstanding performances were to receive pleasing acknowledgement.

At the close of the year he was awarded his fourth B.R.D.C. Gold Star, and was also voted Driver of the Year by the Guild of Motoring Writers, for which he was presented with a beautiful plaque, upon which was mounted a metallic cast of his hand, set in a rather beautiful wooden frame.

By November the usual rumours were flying about, concerning which drivers would drive what cars. We of the Moss *équipe* were not wholly certain whom Stirling would drive for, although it looked as though he would continue his successful relationship with Maseratis. Whatever materialized, one thing was comforting—he was in a much happier frame of mind than in 1953; there was no uncertainty and indecision, and if needs be, we had the green 250F Maserati to fall back on.

It was in November that the bombshell came. Stirling had

arranged to make a longish trip to the United States. He had been engaged by Rootes to drive a Sunbeam-Talbot in the Great American Mountain Rally, and decided that, while he was over there, he would make an extended tour of the States before the start of the Rally.

On November 4, the day he was due to leave England, we were both at his flat doing the final packing when a telegram arrived. It read: 'CABLE WHETHER STIRLING MOSS BOUND FOR 1955 STOP. OUR INQUIRY WITHOUT COMMITMENT—DAIMLER-BENZ.'

Stirling looked at me. I am certain that inwardly he was gratified to receive such a valuation of his worth by Mercedes, but all he said was, 'Tell them "Sorry, nothing doing"—I'm contracted to Shell.' At this stage we had a two-year contract with Shell-Mex and B.P., running from 1 January, 1954 to 31 December, 1955, and having always enjoyed the most friendly and co-operative relationship with them, Stirling was not anxious to make the change which would be necessary if he drove for Daimler-Benz.

My feelings were rather different. By now I had acquired more experience as his manager, and believed in seizing opportunities when they arose. Having tried hard but unsuccessfully to get Stirling into the Mercedes team in 1954, I felt that now *they* were making the overtures, the chance should not be wasted. If the fuel contract problem could only be circumvented in some way, and Stirling could join the Mercedes team, then, I felt, his education as a Grand Prix driver could be completed, and he would have, at last, the chance of driving a first-class car backed by a vast organization with matchless experience in the racing world.

I saw Stirling off at London Airport that evening, and 'sat on' his instructions to wire a refusal to Mercedes, deciding, instead, to consider the matter with a little more calmness in quieter surroundings. Stirling packing for a long trip is pretty disturbing, and the flat was like a whirlwind most of that day!

In the end I talked to Alfred Moss about it, and between us we decided to ignore Stirling's instructions, agreeing that nothing would be lost—in fact, much might be gained—if I were to fly over to Stuttgart and meet Neubauer. 'Talk big, Ken,' advised Alfred. 'If Stirling isn't keen to drive for them, there's only one thing to do. Just ask for so much money that it will frighten them.

If they are prepared to pay it, then it will be worth considering, and if they aren't, then it gives you a let-out.'

Armed with this advice, I wired Herr Neubauer, saying that Moss himself was now in America, but that I was prepared to negotiate on his behalf. A meeting in Stuttgart was arranged, and off I went. In the plane my thoughts dwelt entirely on the coming meeting. I have already mentioned my love of negotiation, and now I looked forward to seeing Neubauer again. I would negotiate on big terms, I told myself, on the grounds that my driver was fully capable of handling one of their cars, and was just the man they needed to support Fangio.

But I had a shock coming. When I got to Stuttgart and was shown into Neubauer's office, we exchanged pleasantries for five or ten minutes, then, through Miss Bauer, his usual interpreter, we discussed the past season, Stirling's successes and his failures. And let me here say that, although I thought I knew most details of Stirling's career, it was soon clear that Neubauer knew even more.

With customary Teutonic thoroughness, Daimler-Benz had kept records of all his lap times in every race, and comparative times of all the other drivers; they knew the power output figures of all the rival cars, and their ultimate performance; nothing was left to chance memory when it could be recorded on paper and carefully assimilated.

It was the same when we got down to discussing the proposed contract. There was no question of 'negotiating' with Neubauer; he rattled off a string of facts stating what Daimler-Benz would do, and left me gasping. The amount Daimler-Benz were prepared to pay, and the requirements of the contract, thoroughly sabotaged my own much debated proposals. They were so startling in contrast with other contracts I had made for Stirling in the past that in truth I could only sit and gasp, and certainly would not have had the audacity to suggest that he should be paid more. I just sat and listened to what I was told, knowing full well that when it came to it, Stirling would have to agree, and that he would be very foolish if he didn't.

When the question of sports-car races arose—for Mercedes-Benz were to contest all Sports Car Championship events with the new 300SLR—I was able to get Neubauer to agree on pairing Fangio and Moss together. I told him of Stirling's admiration for Fangio, and of how I felt such an arrangement would be desirable, and the Mercedes team manager concurred.

The major problem which perforce remained unsolved then was that of the contract with the oil companies. Mercedes were signed up with Castrol for their oil supplies, while Stirling had his contract with Shell & B.P. Ltd. We had to postpone this problem, but otherwise saw eye to eye in every part of the agreement. I stressed that Stirling would not consider signing any agreement without first trying the car. Neubauer, for his part, didn't even require Moss to try it; he just wanted him to sign up.

The following day I traced Stirling to the Rootes office in New York, and told him the news. His initial response was definitely cold. 'I told you I don't want to drive for Mercedes—why do you bother to negotiate with them?' he said.

Then I told him the details of the contract, of the fee they were prepared to pay, that they would leave him free to drive his Maserati in non-championship races, and finally, that they had agreed he and Fangio could be paired together at Le Mans, and any other sports-car races requiring two drivers per car.

For a few seconds there was silence on the line, then Stirling said, 'But what about Shell?' I said: 'I don't know. We'll have to see Brian Turle and ask him if anything can be done—but at least agree to try the car—they will lay tests on at Hockenheim.' Eventually he agreed to do so and we made arrangements for his flight to Germany.

I am not at liberty to state the sum Mercedes-Benz offered for Stirling to join them in 1955, but I note from his personal diary for 22 November he wrote: 'Up early, called on Jaguars, then to Rootes, where Ken called and told me of the fantastic Merc. offer. Wow!'

Alfred Moss and I met Stirling at London Airport on Friday morning, 3 December, Stirling having flown in from New York on a Pan-American Stratocruiser. As his flight had a stop-over point at London Airport, and then went on to Frankfurt, we had reserved places on the same plane.

The British publicity agents for Daimler-Benz at that time were

Downtons of Fleet Street, and Jerry Ames, who was in charge of the Mercedes-Benz account, was naturally keen to exploit the publicity of the Moss tests as much as possible. He had arranged quite a 'scoop' with the magazine *Picture Post*, who were sending one of their star photographers named Bert Hardy, and a feature writer, Trevor Philpots, to Germany to cover the story.

So we all flew to Frankfurt, where we were met by Neubauer and various Daimler-Benz officials. It was all most impressively arranged, with a string of Mercedes cars outside to take us to the track. There was some discreet selection, to get the right people together in the cars, and it was seen that the two *Picture Post* representatives were in one car by themselves.

When we set off, all the cars save one headed for Hockenheim, the other, containing Hardy, Philpots and all their gear, drove off in the opposite direction. They were, in fact, neatly kidnapped! Naturally they were both furious about the whole thing, but Neubauer, it seems, had decided that he didn't want the press around initially.

We all had some lunch, and then got down to serious matters at Hockenheim, by which time the *Picture Post* photographers were allowed back again. Hockenheim is 4·8 miles long, and very fast, so it was arranged that Stirling would drive three cars, a 220A saloon, a 300SL, then the Grand Prix car. Rudolf Uhlenhaut, the Mercedes technical wizard, and driver Karl Kling were present, as well as various executives from Unterturkheim, while the vast Neubauer was in the forefront, armed with his famous watches.

The track was wet at first, but by the time Stirling climbed into the Formula 1 car it was almost dry. As he came by on his first lap he gave the O.K. signal, and eventually he got down to a lap time of 2 min. 15 sec., about 128 m.p.h. A little later, when the course was drier still, Karl Kling equalled this time.

But Stirling was not immediately at home with the Merc., and while Kling was circulating he told me he thought it a very difficult car to drive; it was 'flighty', inclined to oversteer, and much more sensitive to handle than the Maserati, though the power, he said, was 'fantastic'.

Naturally we were all very anxious to know what his decision would be, and after a short discussion with Alfred Moss and myself, he said he felt he could master the car and would accept the Mercedes offer, assuming the problem with the fuel companies could be solved.

During the Hockenheim tests a telegram arrived for Neubauer. It was from Commendatore Orsi of Maseratis, who had got wind of Stirling's activities, and it more or less said, 'Hands off Moss—he is under contract to us.' The Germans quickly showed us the telegram, but we were able to reassure them, and explain that there was obviously a misunderstanding.

After the 1954 Italian G.P., which Stirling so very nearly won, Orsi had asked him if he would drive for Maserati in 1955. Now Stirling at that time expected that he would, and probably said something like 'I hope so'. No agreement was reached either verbally or in writing, however, nor was Stirling under any obligation to give them first option.

One can understand Orsi's anxiety. Stirling was an admirable No. 1 in the Maserati team, ever ready to 'have a go' at Fangio, as the Italian G.P. had shown. If he now joined the same team as Fangio, then the opposition to Maserati would be doubled. It was hard, but that is the way of things; those able to offer the best car usually get the best drivers.

For crossing the last hurdle before signing-up, we were immeasurably grateful to Shell-Mex and B.P., and their competitions manager Bryan Turle, whose understanding and friendly relationship finally made it possible for Moss to join Mercedes. When we put our case to Bryan, he made it clear at once that he did not wish to stand in the way of Stirling's career, and unhesitatingly released him for the 1955 season from his Shell commitments.

So, by December 1954, the racing world learned that it was to be *Stirling Moss* (*Mercedes-Benz*) for the coming season.

CHAPTER SEVEN

WORK AND PLEASURE

BY NOW Stirling Moss's interests had expanded at such a rate that it became necessary to form a limited company. Following discussions with our accountant Len Gould and our solicitor, Felix Nabarro, Stirling Moss Ltd. came into being at the close of 1954, with Alfred Moss as Chairman, Stirling as Managing Director, and myself as director and secretary.

That company has existed ever since, and has been entirely responsible for all Stirling's racing activities and business affairs. There is a belief in some quarters that the limited company was formed to reduce payment of income tax, but this is just silly, and people who believe such a thing have little knowledge of the income-tax laws of this country. Whether you operate as a company or as an individual you still pay tax, and very often you pay more as a limited company than as an individual.

One of the main reasons that Stirling Moss Ltd. was formed was because, while he was having to travel all over the world, business on his behalf still had to be transacted from the home base. As an individual he was the only person who could sign necessary documents, whereas with a company arrangements could be made with the other directors to sign on behalf of the Company. Thus business procedure could continue without delays while Stirling was on the other side of the world.

The Christmas holiday brought both work and pleasure. Rather daringly, the B.R.S.C.C. were putting on a race meeting at Brands Hatch on Boxing Day. This was an idea I had conceived in the midsummer of 1954. We were always looking for innovations which would enhance the reputation of the Club, and since there was motor racing on every other holiday during the year, I argued, why shouldn't there be racing on Boxing Day? We broached the subject with John Hall, Managing Director of Brands Hatch Circuit Ltd., and he was more than delighted to have a shot at it, even though the chances of bad weather were greater.

We put out plenty of publicity for the meeting, which was to be a festive affair with a roast ox, Father Christmas, and so on, as 'side-shows' and secured an excellent entry despite its being the off-season. Getting this meeting organized kept me busy before Christmas, and I was glad to leave town on 24 December and make my way down to Tring, where I was to spend Christmas with the Moss family.

Christmas with the Mosses, which I have had the pleasure of sharing on several occasions in the past few years, is a gay and happy affair. A mammoth Christmas tree was always installed in the games room, and in the evening Alfred and I would decorate the tree, fixing fairy lights and generally jazzing it up. The others would be busy wrapping up presents, and the completed parcels were hung on the tree, or put in the tub in readiness for the next day.

Christmas Eve would be spent watching the television, with plenty of good-natured chaff and leg-pulling amongst the company; Stirling came in for a fair amount that year, having joined Mercedes-Benz, and it was good to see him in lighthearted mood again for he was now looking forward to his first race for Mercedes-Benz, the Argentine G.P. on 16 January.

On Christmas Day Stirling and I got up late, and that year, I remember, his sister Pat lent me a pony to go out riding, so that I could work up an appetite. I make no claim to be a rider, but like to try most things once. We rode out of the farm together, Pat on a very intelligent pony called Marcus, who had been very successful in gymkhanas, and I on a smallish, rather old pony which, I believe, had been taken out of retirement.

We trotted down the road and through a gate into a field, when Pat suddenly dug her heels into Marcus and came flashing past me, whereupon my pony took the bit between his teeth and tore after her. I hung on like grim death but after half a mile or so the saddle started to slip under the pony's belly; I just managed to pull it to a halt before I fell right off the thing.

Pat rushed up in fits of laughter, tightened the saddle girth, and we were off again. Making our way homeward, our path went downhill between two cabbage fields, covered in snow and quite brittle with frost. Suddenly my pony went mad again, and began to rush along flat out, and nothing I could do would make it stop—

it was just as if the throttle was stuck wide open, and there were no brakes!

Suddenly Pat dashed past me, calling, 'I'll go ahead and open the gate.' But the faster Pat went, the faster my pony decided to go, and I could see the gate getting closer and closer. As it loomed up, I decided discretion was the better part of valour, jumped off and landed in the middle of the frozen cabbages! Once again Pat dissolved into fits of laughter, and when the story was retold to the family on our return, I came in for much teasing about my horsemanship.

Next came Christmas dinner, always a hearty affair, after which we settled down in the guest room with sherry and cigars or cigarettes, surrounded by chocolates, crystallized fruits and other 'goodies'. Then followed the distribution of Christmas presents, after which the guests would depart to their various quarters, replete physically and in spirit, to indulge in a quiet *siesta* before Christmas tea and the evening's television.

Boxing Day was more active, and Stirling, Alfred and I made our way down to Brands Hatch in the morning. The weather was excellent for December racing—cold but bright, and, above all, dry. The crowd was large, the entry list long and interesting. The programme included races for Formula 3, sports cars and Formule Libre racing cars, plus a demonstration by Stirling Moss, the new Mercedes-Benz recruit, in one of the gull-wing doored, fuel-injection 300SL coupés.

Don Beauman, an excellent driver, won the Formule Libre race in his 2-litre Connaught, from hillclimb expert Tony Marsh in a Cooper-J.A.P. and Horace Gould (Cooper-Bristol). Ivor Bueb won the Senior Formula 3 race from Stuart Lewis-Evans, both in Coopers, and Syd Creamer won the Junior event. The sports-car race brought victory for John Coombs in a Connaught-engined Lotus, followed by the late David Blakely's Emperor-H.R.G. The spectators—and there were nearly 40,000 of them, which was remarkable for a traditionally 'sit-about' holiday—enjoyed it all, while the appearance of Father Christmas, the smell of the roasting ox, and the nip in the air, left them in no doubt as to *which* holiday it was.

Stirling played the part of Father Christmas. We hired a Santa

Claus outfit from Bermans, the theatrical costumiers of Irving Street, then padded Stirling out with pillows, put on the huge white beard and whiskers, the big black boots and black belt, and there he was; nicely in time to start the Senior Formula 3 race for the Christmas Trophy.

The final signing of the agreement between Mercedes-Benz and Stirling Moss was effected in January, and as he was due to leave with the works party for the Argentine G.P. Felix Nabarro and I decided to go across to Stuttgart and clear up the final points of his contract, and see Stirling off at the same time. We spent a morning's work with the Daimler-Benz solicitors at the factory, then we all went to Stuttgart airport.

I believe there were about twenty-four people in the Mercedes party travelling to Buenos Aires, and at roughly £500 per person for the flight, that amounts to around £12,000 for air fares alone. Although their South American flight did not normally stop at Stuttgart, K.L.M. needed little persuasion to stop there this time, to pick the party up. And Neubauer, knowing how things invariably crop up to make somebody late, insured against this by organizing a luncheon party, which started some two and a half hours before the plane was due to take off.

Nabarro and I joined this lunch before taking our plane back to London, and I met Stirling's team mates, Karl Kling and Hans Herrmann. This pair differed widely. Kling was a rather intense, grey-haired figure. He was a driver who missed greatness largely because of his age; he had been with Daimler-Benz before the Hitler War, but not as a Grand Prix driver. By the time the war ended, he was a bit too old for the game of Grand Prix racing, and found himself faced by many brilliant youngsters. He put up some splendid performances in Mercedes 300SL sports cars, proving that he had toughness of physique, while none will ever attempt to deny his courage. But although he struggled very hard, I feel he hadn't the speed of reaction or flair to make a star Grand Prix driver, and he could not make headway against people like Fangio or Moss. This, I believe, he found rather galling since he was the only German driver in the team apart from Hans Herrmann, and felt keenly that his compatriots were looking to him for good performances in their beloved 'silver arrows'.

Hans Herrmann, on the other hand, laboured under no delusions; he was just a young chap who had done well in sports-car racing, mostly with Porsches, and who liked a good time. He was gay, debonair, very fond of the opposite sex, and an able, but not brilliant, driver. In private life, he owned two night clubs in Stuttgart. As the youngest member of the Mercedes-Benz team—he was a few months younger than Stirling—the Germans had a particular affection for Hans, and while he had not so far achieved much in Formula 1 racing, he was a useful team member.

I also met the team's official racing photographer. Mercedes never did things by halves, and this expert accompanied the team on all their races in order to record the victories they hoped for—and usually managed to achieve. He showed me his special camera case, fitted out to carry all his extensive equipment, and it was a photographer's dream. There were at least three Leicas, and every sort of lens, filter, and other kind of camera fitting one could think of—literally thousands of pounds' worth of equipment, all craftily clipped in place in the beautifully lined case. I am sure that man's eyes hardly ever left his case while he travelled from race to race!

Our plane left a few minutes before the Mercedes party took off for Buenos Aires, so we bade Stirling farewell and departed. We had to make a change at Frankfurt to catch a London plane, and when we landed there, and walked into the reception room, I was horrified to learn from a Pan-American official that there was a 'panic' on at Stuttgart. Mercedes-Benz had omitted to tell me that Stirling needed an Argentine visa, and this created a tremendous problem, since officially K.L.M. were not allowed to accept a passenger on the Buenos Aires flight unless he or she had a visa.

I phoned through and arranged to call at the Foreign Office immediately I got into London, to ask them to contact the British Consul in Buenos Aires. When I reached town, I also got in touch with the British Consul at Rio de Janeiro, which was one stop before Buenos Aires, while at the same time the Daimler-Benz management contacted the German Consulates in those two cities. In fact, there were so many strings being pulled while the plane was crossing the South Atlantic that by the time Stirling reached Buenos Aires he had the easiest passage into the country of all, just sailing through Customs and the rest!

There was an amusing incident on the plane which Stirling told me about later on. Neubauer, of course, is a huge man, weighing abound 20 or 21 stone, with a vast frame and massive shoulders and corporation. About an hour after take-off he wished 'to spend a penny', so lumbered along to the back of the plane to the little room which plane designers grudgingly squeeze into their designs.

When he got there he found he could not get through the door, either forwards or sideways! In the end Stirling and Hans Herrmann were enlisted to help, and they turned him sideways and literally forced him through the door. And then they had to get him out again by grabbing his arm and pulling like fury until he popped out like a cork from a champagne bottle!

Stirling's first race for the 'three-pointed star', the Argentine G.P., was remarkable for several things, not least of them the appalling heat, which largely controlled the result of the contest. It was run over one of numerous possible layouts at the Buenos Aires Autodrome, and I remember how impressed we were to meet one of the Mercedes 'Boffins' at the Hockenheim tests. He had a detailed plan of the Autodrome, with full information of every bend and curve, and by some wizardry on the slide rule was able to predict the potential lap times of the Mercs. on the circuit several weeks before they got there. What is more astonishing is that his estimated times came within a fifth of a second of the correct ones!

It was interesting, too, to learn how much trouble Mercs. would go to, to get their drivers really comfortable in their cars, and to meet their individual wishes. When the cars went out for practice, Stirling found one or two things not quite to his liking, and technical chief Rudolf Uhlenhaut promptly set about modifications. This doesn't mean that their drivers were pampered, but simply that Mercedes realized how vitally important it is for a driver to have things 'just so', in order to give of his best.

Now Stirling prefers the back of his seat inclined at an angle of 17 degrees; he likes firm support round the hips, but less about the legs, so that he can have freedom of movement. The back of the seat firmly supports his back, and seated thus, with his arms outstretched, his hands rest naturally on the wheel in the 'quarter to three' position. His vision is just over the top of the screen, straight forward over the bonnet on to the road.

Another Moss preference is for a very light brake pedal. Some drivers like a hard pedal requiring plenty of pressure, but Stirling is extremely light and springy on his feet; were he of the opposite sex I would say he had 'ballet feet', and so he likes a lighter, more sensitive, pedal. At Buenos Aires he found the Mercedes brake pedal far too heavy, and spoke to Uhlenhaut about it.

As a result, between the first and second day's practice, the Merc. engineers procured a servo brake unit from a Chevrolet Saloon, and adapted it to Moss's Grand Prix car, giving the sensitive control he favoured. He also had the three-spoked steering wheel he preferred, and, as a result of these efforts by Mercedes, rapidly adapted himself to the car, and began to put in some fast lap times.

Typifying his level-headedness, he did not attempt to go very fast just in order to impress, but took a third-row position on the grid, although only 1 sec. slower than Fangio, ½ sec. slower than Kling, and ·3 sec. faster than Herrmann. In the race he fastened on to Fangio, while Lancia and Ferrari went out in front, fighting for the lead. The heat was appalling, with a temperature of 104° Fahrenheit, and much more than that on the circuit. Racing-car cockpits were like ovens. One after another drivers began to wilt, Gonzalez, Farina, Schell, Herrmann and Castellotti all coming in for relief, but 'tough man' Fangio just went on and on and on.

Stirling hung on awhile, but was virtually all in; then a vapour lock developed in his car and he came to a stop on a corner. Somehow he clambered out and dropped on to the grass to rest, at which several ambulance men rushed up, assuming he had collapsed, whipped him on to a stretcher, thrust him in an ambulance, and tore off to hospital. Stirling protested that he was all right but he didn't speak their language and they didn't speak his, and the ambulance was almost into Buenos Aires before they were persuaded to return him to the Autodrome!

The Mercedes pit had no idea what had happened to him and were amazed but delighted when he turned up in the ambulance. They thrust him into Hans Herrmann's car, which had also been driven by Kling, and he went on to finish fourth. Fangio won after a magnificent demonstration of physical endurance, driving without relief and making only one stop for fuel and refreshment. In contrast, the second-place Ferrari had been driven by three different drivers, while at one stage of the race another Ferrari which was perfect mechanically stood at its pit, drivers either suffering heat stroke or being out in other cars!

When Stirling finished, black with grime and soaked in perspiration, he was introduced to ex-President Peron. As he approached, he tried to wipe his hands and bow, and Peron said 'Allow me' and handed him his handkerchief. Stirling thought so much of this that he used it only to clean his hands sufficiently for a handshake, and has kept the handkerchief ever since as a souvenir.

A fortnight later Mercedes ran in the Buenos Aires City G.P., which was a Formule Libre race on an even twistier layout of the Autodrome. The Germans put 3-litre engines into their cars, but Ferrari had the same idea, and Farina managed to head Fangio, Moss and Kling off in the first heat. In the second heat, Stirling had his first exercise at following in Fangio's wheelmarks—the pair running nose to tail for 28 of the 30 laps, until Fangio signalled Stirling past.

Stirling thus had the pleasure of receiving the chequered flag of victory on his second race with Mercedes, although in the overall G.P. result, decided by adding up the times of the two heats, he was placed second to Fangio, also sharing fastest lap with Farina's Ferrari.

When Stirling went back to Stuttgart he had the pleasure of collecting a Mercedes-Benz 220A for his private use, it being the pleasant habit of Daimler-Benz to supply their drivers with a private car. There was, of course, method in this apparent generosity, for Mercedes desired their drivers to appear at all race meetings and public places in a car of their manufacture, and the acceptance of a personal car was, in fact, part of their contract.

It was stipulated that the drivers would keep their cars clean, and perfectly maintained; they didn't expect the driver to pay for this, and were quite prepared to meet the cost themselves, provided they could be sure of their men appearing smartly on 'parade'. When Stirling collected his 220A, finished in British green at his request, he was delighted to find not only that it had been fitted with his favourite three-spoked steering wheel, but had also been tuned by Uhlenhaut's department to impart some extra performance.

It was not very long after Stirling's return from South America that he was travelling again, this time accompanied by me. We were bound first for New York, then Nassau in the Bahamas, where we were to take a holiday, and then Sebring for the 12-hour race, where Stirling had arranged to drive an Austin-Healey with Lance Macklin.

The trip was one of overwhelming importance in my life, for ever since I was about eight I had cherished a tremendous desire to visit America. I think the New York skyscrapers were the original attraction, but later on it became the thought of flying across the Atlantic. Aircraft have always fascinated me, and I enjoy few things more than flying, either as passenger or pilot.

Stirling had insisted that I take a holiday. Work had been getting pretty hectic, and the relatively quiet period between the Argentine *Temporada* and the start of the European season was the obvious time to snatch a week or two's leisure. Even so, there would be plenty to do at Sebring, where I had agreed with Donald Healey to act as team manager for the Austin-Healey effort.

We crossed to New York in a Pan-American Boeing Stratocruiser, a wonderful lady of the skies, extremely comfortable and particularly liked by the Atlantic travelling population, mainly because of its two-floor construction. Passengers sat on the upper deck in very comfortable reclining seats, and if you fancied a drink, or a stretch, you descended a small stairway into a lower cabin containing a bar. Naturally this bar was very popular, quickly filling to capacity until it became, in effect, a miniature club. I found the idea of taking a gin and tonic, standing at the bar over mid-Atlantic, particularly appealing!

From New York we caught another flight down to Miami, Florida, then headed east towards the Atlantic and Nassau, capital of the Bahama Isles, and fabulous as a holiday resort. Set in the north of New Providence Island, Nassau was in its high season when we arrived. Winters there are delightfully warm to us, but cool by Bahamian summer standards, and between December and April American holiday-makers flock to Nassau.

It is a British island, having a Governor representative of the Monarchy, and assisted by a legislative and executive council, and there is a distinctly nineteenth-century 'English Colonial' atmosphere. But the mighty dollar is much in evidence today, and there are two currencies, the Bahamian pound, carrying the same value as the pound sterling, and the U.S. dollar. Nassau might well be termed America's Monte Carlo, for it is only a four-hour flight from New York and is *the place* to go for Americans in quest of pleasure.

The main town of Nassau is quite small, and is based around Bay Street. We were staying at the British Colonial Hotel, one of the biggest on the island, costing £8 or £9 per day for full board; expensive, yes, but offering such incredible luxury that we felt on balance it was worth it. Certainly if I were a very rich man, I would be more than happy to stay there every year.

Apart from the British residing on the island, there is a considerable coloured population, and the place is rich in tradition, having been alternately a British and a Spanish possession, and the haunt of smugglers and pirates in days gone by.

The holidaymaker is offered numerous diversions, with aquatic sport naturally a favourite. The sea is wonderfully clear, and you can go out in glass-bottomed boats and view the ocean bed, down to depths of fifty feet and more, with crystal clarity. Water skiing, spear-fishing, skin-diving and deep-sea fishing are amongst the attractions, and Stirling's favourite was water skiing.

We both found our previous experience with snow-skiing in Switzerland useful on water skis, and I was soon proficient enough to enjoy the full thrill and exhilaration of skimming across the water at some 25 or 30 m.p.h. behind a motor-boat. Stirling became a very accomplished water skier, and it remains today one of his favourite sports.

The Bahamas sun is very strong, and because of the pleasant sea breezes which temper its heat, one does not realize how fierce it is until too late; we learned very quickly to take all precautions against sunburn. Surprisingly, we suffered most when waterskiing, since the sun's rays were reflected directly from the water on to our legs, and the backs of our knees became painfully sore until they acquired a harder cuticle.

We had, need I say, a tremendous time. We would get up at between nine and ten o'clock each morning, have a fairly light breakfast, then go out to the beach for some skiing or fishing. Lunch would be taken in front of the hotel, cafeteria-style; mountains of food were available for the eating, and you simply helped yourself to whatever you wanted—bowls of lobsters and shrimps, eggs, chicken, tunny fish—anything and everything.

After lunch came more recreation—usually skiing or deep-sea fishing, which we found an excellent sport. There was ample variety of fish to catch, the best of the lot being the tunny fish or tuna, known out there as the 'chicken of the sea'. It is a tough, aggressive fish, dark blue in colour, and should you catch one on your rod, it has the habit of staying quiet until you have brought it almost up to the transom of the boat. Then suddenly it goes mad, makes a dart for the bottom of the ocean, and goes down like a plummet, taking your line with it. Altogether it takes quite a long time to bring in a big tuna.

Shark and barracuda are frequent catches, and the barracuda is a really fierce customer, ever ready to fight. The swimmer who meets a barracuda finds it difficult to get away from him; whatever direction you take, he always faces you, ready for a direct attack. If you swim towards the barracuda, it will draw back, but always with its nose facing you; if you swim sideways, he swims sideways too, and if you swim backwards, he swims towards you. Yet it is said by the islanders that the barracuda never directly attacks a human unless he is shedding blood, either from his person or from a fish he is carrying.

In the evening we would change for dinner, always an elegant and fairly prolonged affair, after which we would go into town and look at the Nassau night life. This mainly centred on personal parties, for there is much society life on the island, and many of the British residents have beautiful homes and naturally enjoy giving parties and meeting people. We attended several of these, but there are also two or three cinemas showing British films, as well as numerous night clubs featuring particular varieties of native dancing and cabaret.

At some there was general dancing as well as cabaret, and one native club called the Silver Slipper was popular with many of the whites. Now amongst the many coloured customers there were the usual trouble-makers, whom the proprietors would not admit to the dance floor. This undesirable element took to having their drinks outside, and then tossing the empty bottles over the front façade, so that they landed on the dancers inside!

The proprietors countered this by stretching a huge net above the open dance floor to catch the bottles. Unfortunately, as more and more bottles were caught by the net, occasionally one would strike another, both smashing to smithereens and showering the people below with broken glass. The natives got over that by dancing with their hats on!

Nassau is famous for its calypsos, which are improvised for almost any occasion. We also went to a most novel exhibition featuring the only flock of pink flamingoes in the world. These picturesque birds had been trained assiduously by their native keeper, and he put them through a most impressive drilling, in which they turned left, turned right, halted, quick-marched and so on with real soldierly precision. Quite fantastic, as were so many things in Nassau.

By the end of our holiday, we had both acquired deep tans and felt fighting fit. Sebring was our next port of call, and we flew from Nassau's Windsor airport to Miami and then motored 150 miles or so to the circuit. Stirling had been there before, of course, but I was a newcomer, and found America's premier road-racing circuit a considerable eye-opener.

Most of the United States is so slick, so up-to-date, so rich in amenities, that one is amazed at the comparative isolation and primitive nature of the Sebring circuit, on which the annual 12-hour race, counting for the World Sports Car Championship, is held. Sebring itself (they pronounce it 'See-bring', by the way) is a peculiar place; it is a small village in the heart of Florida's crocodile swamp country. Earlier in American history the region was inhabited mainly by Indians, and between Miami and Sebring is a large stretch of water called Lake Okachobee, after the Okachobee Indians who lived in the locality.

The principal industry today in the area seems to be orange- and grapefruit-growing, with miles and miles and miles of unfenced groves lining the roads. The aroma given off is pleasant and powerful, and one thing I shall always remember about Sebring is that orange smell late at night and first thing in the morning.

Sebring is a small American town with American small-town inhabitants; I don't mean this disparagingly, but it is the sort of place where Ed the café proprietor, Joe the policeman, and Al the fire-engine driver are all friends at the Lodge; something like *Peyton Place*, in fact, though without the drama and intrigue encountered in that fictional American 'small-town'!

There are only two hotels in the town, and as a result nearly everyone stays at motels which have sprung up all along the highway running through Sebring. The nearest airports are Miami, West Palm Beach, Palm Beach and Tampa, and all four mean a car journey of over 100 miles to get to Sebring.

So abundant are the oranges and citrus fruits, and so abundant, too, is petrol out there, that practically every filling station in Florida invites you to drink as much chilled fresh orange or grapefruit juice as you want—providing you buy your petrol from them. You don't have to give a tip for this; it is simply a 'come hither' arrangement to boost petrol sales.

The Sebring circuit itself is primitive in comparison with any European racing venue. It comprises a vast, desolate, disused ex-Army air base. The lap distance is 5·2 miles, and the surface, of concrete and tarmac, is nothing wonderful. The course is hard on brakes because of the number of long, fast straights and slow corners, it is bad on tyres, and spectator amenities are limited. On the other hand, I don't suppose it is any worse than Silverstone or any other British airfield circuit as they were in the beginning, before stands were built, the road resurfaced and so on.

The organization was below par, too, by European standards, and I was mildly shattered to see the chief pit marshal driving up and down in front of the pits in his J2 Allard, both during practice and the race, regardless of whether competing cars were coming in or going out. And during the night spell of the actual race, one of the senior marshals, wishing to get to another point on the course, drove his Mk. VII Jaguar round the circuit in the reverse direction!

The Austin-Healey 100S which Stirling and Lance Macklin were to drive came direct from the works, being shipped over from Southampton to New York on the *Queen Mary*, Lance Macklin travelling with it. He then drove it from New York down to Sebring, unfortunately incurring a speeding offence *en route*, where he was fined 45 dollars—roughly £15—on the spot!

We were staying at one of the larger hotels on the outskirts of Sebring, a place called Harder Hall, and Lance joined us there. Harder Hall is principally a golfing centre, but that week the motor-racing fraternity had taken over *en masse*. Amongst the interesting people we met were Chuck Daigh, today a senior member of Lance Reventlow's very successful Scarab venture, the Marquis de Portago, Porfirio Rubirosa—that enterprising Dominican—Phil Hill and Carroll Shelby.

Donald Healey came to Sebring as well, and the performance of his car, virtually a standard 100S model, shook the Americans considerably. After making his usual 'first off the mark' Le Mans start, Stirling and his co-driver Lance Macklin sped on, meeting no trouble, and finishing sixth in most august company.

Near the starting line at Sebring was a raised wooden platform with a ramp at each end; this was so that the winning car could be driven up there after the race, but it was used during the 12 hours by the race commentator, who was a character straight out of a soap-box opera. He wore a ten-gallon Stetson hat, and the sort of figured leather jerkin that Flint McCullough would wear in *Wagon Train*, rawhide pants with chaps on, and high-heeled cowboy boots. The only thing he didn't have was a pair of six-shooters!

Comic though he looked, this commentator knew his stuff. Speaking in that delightful American free and easy manner, his commentary was certainly informal, but also informative, and I should like to see some British commentators adopting a similar style to get their information over to the public—I don't mean the cowboy uniform, though—just the free and easy manner!

My opinion of the race organization went down still further when a squabble arose over the number of laps covered by the first and second finishers. Protests flew left and right and the Hawthorn/Walters Jaguar victory became an anti-climax, until it was officially confirmed eight days later by the A.A.A. Had the official lap scorers kept an accurate chart this could have been avoided; as it was, they referred to the Jaguar and Ferrari charts, and based their verdict on a careful perusal of them.

After the leisure of Nassau and the whirl of Sebring, Stirling and I flew north to New York, to spend two days there before sailing home. Now while we were at Nassau, Stirling had met a girl named Nancy, and I a girl named Marianne, both of whom lived in New York. So we arranged to meet them again when we got to New York and have a party. The result was the most hilarious and hectic two days I have ever known. We didn't need a hotel because Bob Said lent us his flat in Manhattan, but as things worked out, we never went to bed from the moment we arrived to the moment we boarded the *Queen Mary* for the return voyage to Southampton.

I was vastly impressed by New York as a city, although I don't think I should like to live there. Here in London, there at least appears to be some sanity and reason in things, and although many of us keep trying to cram twenty-five hours of work into a twenty-four-hour day, we are not as bad as the New Yorkers, who try to squeeze in another twelve hours' play as well. When the Americans work, they work hard, and when they play, they play hard. Consequently I cannot for the life of me think how they ever get any sleep!

We had arranged to see *The Pajama Game* with Nancy and Marianne, but unfortunately this was preceded by a jaunt round town which included visits to the El Morocco, a little bar called The Embers where the blind pianist George Shearing played, and one or two other night clubs, ending up at the Stork Club. Not surprisingly, during this round we had one or two drinks, and when we got to The Stork the proprietor recognized Stirling, whom he had seen down at Sebring, and sent down a bottle of champagne.

Now Stirling doesn't drink champagne, or for that matter anything alcoholic, which left the two girls and myself. As we had only ten minutes or so before the theatre started, that champagne had to be knocked back pretty quickly. By the time we got into a taxi I was definitely feeling a bit 'off', and when we had reached the theatre I felt extremely sleepy.

We had to pay ten dollars for each ticket, theatre tickets in New York being like gold dust, and virtually impossible to obtain without paying a premium. I regret to say that, such was the effect of the champagne upon me, and also on Marianne, that neither of us saw the show at all, having slept through the entire performance.

More champagne flowed when we left New York on the *Queen Mary*, for Bob Said brought a bottle along; Nancy and Marianne also came to see us off, and we were feeling rather sorry that our American trip was over. Eventually the girls left as the last gangplank was about to be lowered.

Amongst the passengers on the boat was Lord Essendon, who was probably better known to racing enthusiasts as the Hon. Brian Lewis, a very fine driver in pre-war days. We quickly became acquainted with him, and were also fortunate in being put on the Purser's table. Stirling and I were travelling cabin class, and here again we were lucky, for it happened that there were more cabin-class passengers on this voyage than cabins. Thus we were allocated a first-class cabin instead, at cabin-class prices.

These transatlantic Cunard liners undoubtedly provide the most luxurious and comfortable form of travel one could ever wish for. 'Thy wish is my command' rather sums up the service on the Cunarders, and we were thoroughly spoiled. We would get up at about eleven o'clock in the morning, when the steward would bring whatever we wanted for breakfast in bed, as well as copies of the ship's newspaper, which was printed on board. Then we would go down to the gymnasium and have a 'work-out', before looking into the swimming pool for a swim. This was terrific fun, as the liner was rolling quite steeply in the following sea, giving a slow and almost graceful movement; result, we found ourselves swimming in about nine feet of water one minute, and in about two feet the next.

After a swim came lunch, and after lunch we would go to the ship's cinema, which showed a new film every day. Stirling is extremely keen on films, and seldom missed a new showing. Then came tea, followed perhaps by another swim, a gym. work-out or a book, until dinner. And after dinner we would either join in a game of housey-housey or 'horse racing', which is quite an exciting way of having a small gamble.

From about 10.30 every evening there would be dancing in the upper ballroom until midnight, after which everybody went two decks down to the lower ballroom, where dancing continued until there was nobody left. This was often four or five o'clock in the morning, when Stirling and I would retire to our cabin to consume hot chocolate and turkey sandwiches before going to bed.

Incidentally we had complete freedom of choice on the menu for all meals on the *Queen* while for the last dinner of all, before putting in at Southampton, the chef really puts himself out and everyone is invited to hand in his or her particular menu for the table. So ended a perfect holiday.

But it ended with some sad news, for as we disembarked at Southampton we learned that John A. Cooper, sports editor of *The Autocar* and a great friend of ours, had been killed in a road accident. John had played a great part in designing the successful 'swing axle' Kieft 500, besides being a confidant of Stirling's, to whom he could always turn to discuss technical problems; they also had similar tastes in music, and were very close friends.

Once home, I was soon embroiled in business again. The B.R.S.C.C. had their usual round of meetings at Brands Hatch, Crystal Palace and other circuits, with a new, major one looming up in midsummer at Oulton Park. There were regs. to draw up and send out, and various other Club matters to attend to, as well as a fine accumulation of correspondence to deal with on behalf of Stirling Moss.

Early in April, the British Racing Drivers' Club staged the British Empire Trophy for sports cars at Oulton Park. It was a race I shall never forget. I volunteered to act as a marshal, and had been given the task of observer at the Knickerbrook post. The race was split up into three separate heats for cars of various capacities with a Final to decide the outright placings, and racing was rendered difficult by persistent rain, which made the track very treacherous.

I was standing next to one of the medical officers, Dr Sutton, and several marshals, including Peter Wilson, outside the B.B.C. commentary hut. Inside the hut were Robin Richards and his wife, and behind was parked the B.B.C.'s special Austin taxi containing the radio transmitter equipment. Three cars were coming down the straight during Heat 3, Peter Blond's C type and Bob Berry's very fast XK120, both making a bid to pass Irishman Joe Kelly's C type, Blond on the left and Berry on the right.

Kelly's car was nudged by one of the other Jaguars, went out of control and shot off-course, straight at our group. I was absolutely mesmerized as the Jag careered on to the grass. Instead of slowing, it seemed actually to accelerate, and one can only assume that Kelly had his foot pressed hard on the brake pedal, and was skidding with all four wheels locked on the road, so that when he hit the wet grass the adhesion became less and in fact the car did accelerate, straight at us.

I have often wondered how people react under emergency, and on this occasion I remember being absolutely rooted to the ground, until my brain somehow got a message through to my frozen limbs, saying, 'YOU'VE GOT TO MOVE.' I started running like hell away from the car, only to be clouted suddenly from behind with great impact, and bowled over. I picked myself up, to find that the Jag. had hit the B.B.C. box a few feet away; Robin and Mrs. Richards had leaped out in the nick of time, and the blow I received was from a flying piece of debris.

But poor Dr Sutton, who had been standing next to me, was caught by the Jaguar and had one ankle severed, while others in the group were cut and bruised. Doc Sutton was in a bad way, and later had to have his other foot amputated. I was lucky to suffer only a severe cut in the right leg, some bruises and shock, and was glad to be relieved by another observer. I made a report, and then went back to the hotel, had a hot bath, and went to bed, feeling very stiff.

The Easter Goodwood came a week later, and Stirling drove his 250F Maserati without success, something being amiss with the roadholding. We had decided that, despite his engagement by Mercedes-Benz, Stirling would keep the Maserati, with Alf Francis and Tony Robinson 'on the roll' to look after it. The plan was that we would engage other drivers when Stirling's Mercedes commitments kept him away, and after he had taken fourth place at Bordeaux, then retired from the *Daily Express* Silverstone, the car was prepared for the Monaco G.P., where it was to be driven by Lance Macklin, a team mate of Stirling's in the old H.W.M. days. Lance was a skilled driver, though he hadn't anything like the fighting power of Stirling.

Lance proved a bit of a disappointment, being slower than anticipated, and failing to qualify the car for Monaco. Johnny Claes drove it in the Belgian G.P., but retired, and Lance again drove in the British G.P. at Aintree, finishing eighth after wasting a lot of time spinning off.

Others who drove the Moss Maserati—which incidentally was painted grey in an effort to drive away the gremlins seemingly afflicting it!—were Bob Gerard, who won with it at Charterhall; Peter Walker, who had only two laps in it at Zandvoort before retiring with hub trouble; Les Leston, John Fitch and Mike Hawthorn.

Mike Hawthorn's drive in the Maserati was at Crystal Palace on Whit Monday. As there was some doubt about Stirling being able to get there, he being engaged with tests in Germany, we entered the car without nominating a driver. It was agreed that I would try to qualify the car, and that if I put up a sufficiently fast lap, I should drive in the race.

Well, I had no delusions about my ability as a driver, and whilst I was keen to have a go, I was not optimistic of my chances. I reasoned that it would be better to have a driver who would do the Maserati full justice. Suddenly I thought of Mike Hawthorn. As he was free at Whitsun, it seemed a fine opportunity to secure his services, at the same time scotching those silly rumours about a feud between Moss and Hawthorn. So I offered him the car.

Mike accepted cheerfully. I think the idea of driving a car entered by Stirling Moss Ltd. tickled his sense of humour. He liked the car, and drove it splendidly. He won both his heat and the final of the International Trophy, and broke the lap record by over 2 sec. Moreover, Stirling watched him do it, having got back in time from Germany!

The Maserati's last race of 1955 was in the Italian G.P.—the event which Stirling so nearly won the previous year. Now Stirling was in a Mercedes, and the 250F was handled by that very likeable American, John Fitch, who brought it home ninth—a place higher than poor Stirling took after his 1954 ill fortune!

How different were the circumstances for Stirling in 1955! With the Daimler-Benz organization behind him, he no longer knew the agony of losing a race which seemed within his grasp. He had his disappointments, true, but they were more than made up for by his successes.

Without a doubt, the greatest drive of Stirling Moss's career was in the 1955 Mille Miglia, which he won at record speed, aided by Denis Jenkinson in the passenger's seat. Neubauer had already said, before the start of the 1954 season, that he considered Moss an excellent sports-car driver, and the 1955 Mille Miglia surely bore out his opinion. Stirling could never quite match the ultimate skill of Juan Manuel Fangio in a Grand Prix car, but in a sports car, even in 1955, I contend, he was superior to the great Argentinian.

The Mille Miglia, Italy's world-famous 1000-mile race over public roads from Brescia to Rome and back to Brescia, has always been a sports-car race, of course, and the carrying of a passenger was optional. Stirling decided he wanted one, in order to act as a sort of navigator, to signal details of the course immediately ahead. He asked me if I wished to go with him, but I relinquished the chance, frankly because I hadn't sufficient courage to face some 1,000 miles of road racing at speeds which at times would exceed 175 m.p.h., and felt I might let him down at some highly crucial moment.

But Stirling was very fortunate in getting the services instead of Denis Jenkinson, the bearded Continental Correspondent of *Motor Sport* and at one time the passenger to World Sidecar Racing Champion Eric Oliver. 'Jenks' was virtually devoid of nerves, and in fact viewed the prospect of accompanying Stirling with considerable relish; he is very competent and serious-minded, well able to log all necessary information and feed it to Stirling as they tore along.

They put in a prodigious mileage, practising over the entire course, learning the difficult sections while Jenks made numerous detailed notes on a sort of endless notebook which they called the 'toilet roll'. During this period of training, Stirling met with two mishaps. The first occurred when he and Jenks encountered a flock of sheep being driven down a road; as the Merc. approached, one sheep began to stray on to the road, and instead of leaving Stirling to cope with the situation, the shepherd threw his pole at the sheep, which promptly bolted across the road. As a result, Stirling left the road and badly damaged his car.

Stirling telephoned team chief Neubauer at the Brescia headquarters and told him of the incident. Neubauer told them to make their way back as best they could, and when eventually they arrived, Neubauer asked, 'Was the Jeep badly damaged?' Stirling answered, 'Oh, it's dead,' and Neubauer retorted: 'Dead? How can a Jeep be dead?'! 'Not Jeep—sheep!' said Stirling and Jenks in chorus.

The second incident was when an army lorry—carrying a load of unexploded bombs!—suddenly turned off the main road without warning, just as Stirling came by in a training 300SL. Apparently the driver was on an unauthorized route, visiting his girl friend or something, and the police dealt with him pretty severely. The 300SL was practically wrecked but miraculously Stirling and Jenks stepped out unhurt.

As a result of these accidents, one German newspaper of anti-British sentiments lamented the fact that one of Germany's beautiful and magnificent Mercedes-Benz 'constructions' should be entrusted to a dolt of an Englishman like Moss, who seemed able only to wreck the cars by hitting sheep and lorries with them. I often wonder how the editor of that paper must have felt when he got the news—and had to publish it big—that the Mille Miglia had been won by a Mercedes driven by that same 'dolt'.

I will not dwell on the actual race; Denis Jenkinson wrote a detailed account of it which has become something of a classic of race reporting. Suffice to say that Stirling Moss in the 3-litre 300SLR had scored a victory equally as meritorious as that of the late Dick Seaman in the 1938 German G.P., also with a Mercedes-Benz.

After averaging 97·9 m.p.h. in a race lasting ten hours and four minutes, and then withstanding the victory felicitations, one might expect a man to creep to his hotel, have a bath, perhaps a quick meal, and then go thankfully to bed. But not Stirling! He was so wound up emotionally that he left Brescia at around midnight in his green 220A Mercedes, and drove all the way to the works at Stuttgart. They hardly expected to see the Mille Miglia winner so soon, but Moss lunched with some of the directors, and said he was glad to have won, to make up for crashing two cars in practice!

After that came the Monaco G.P. where the Mercedes fortunes changed. Fangio led, with Stirling following closely, but they retired, one after the other, and with Herrmann having crashed in practice and his 'stand-in', André Simon, also retiring, the German team was right out of it. The result was an unexpected Ferrari victory which, frankly, was a good thing for motor racing, as complete monopoly is never popular.

There was fun during practice. While Stirling was taking the Mercedes round, he noticed a rather attractive girl watching from a window just beyond the Station hairpin. Now a driver needs to give every scrap of attention to his driving on the tight 2-mile round-the-houses circuit at Monte Carlo, but Stirling found time to pick this girl out each lap, and gave her a friendly wave. Next time round she waved back. During the next few laps, Stirling tried to convey by sign language that he would like to meet her there after practice.

She must have got the message right, because they did meet after practice, and she turned out to be a young Dutch governess, who was looking after a family living in Monte Carlo. Stirling arranged to see her that evening, and they eventually ended up at a night club called the Ali Baba.

They danced together, then Stirling found a note on their table which read, 'Der Moss must in der bed be, mitout mein frau— Neubauer.' Stirling grinned, then looked around, spotted a familiar bearded figure lurking in a corner, and knew where the note came from—Jenks, who knew all about Mercedes discipline.

I joined the Moss family at Monaco to watch the race, and we stayed at the Bristol, which is on the course itself, on the back stretch returning from the Gasworks hairpin, behind the harbour leg. We never needed an alarm clock on practice days! Our room had a balcony overlooking the circuit, and the first bark of the racing cars as they came out at 6 a.m. woke us up. As they came past, below us, they were just changing into third for the Ste Dévote right-hander, providing an unusual reveille!

We watched the race from the balcony, and after seeing Stirling take the lead when Fangio retired, noticed with apprehension the increasing trail of smoke behind his car. Then he, too, failed to come round, and as we were looking across towards the Tunnel and the Chicane, hoping to see the Merc. come through, we saw instead Ascari in the red Lancia burst into view in the lead, only to miss the turn down the harbour road. I saw a brief flash of red as it went over the edge, and then a cloud of spray and steam as it plunged into the harbour waters. Had Ascari been trapped in the cockpit, he would have drowned, but he bobbed up on the surface, swam strongly for the nearest boat, and was brought safe and sound to land.

A few days later Alberto Ascari was killed at Monza, when driving a few laps in Eugenio Castellotti's 3-litre sports Ferrari. He wasn't practising for a race, but simply 'getting his hand in' again after the Monaco drama. The circumstances of his accident are shrouded in mystery even today, but his death brought major changes to the Italian motor-racing picture. The Lancia team, of which he was No. 1, was disbanded, and the cars, 2½-litre V8s with numerous ingenious features, were handed over to the Scuderia Ferrari, who modified them in various ways and raced them until the end of 1957.

Nineteen hundred and fifty-five was altogether a season of tragedy, but no race in the history of motor racing was more tragic than Le Mans that year. Stirling was co-driving one of the 300SLR Mercedes with Fangio, as had been agreed with Neubauer, and together they were waging a tremendous battle with Mike Hawthorn's D-type Jaguar.

I was not with Stirling at Le Mans, but was listening to radio reports of the race. Like every other listener, I shall never forget the numbing effect as the news of the accident grew worse. Levegh's Mercedes had gone into the crowd opposite the pits, inflicting terrible carnage, and as the day wore on, Le Mans became a grim No. 1 news item, instead of just another motor race.

Quite enough has been said and written about the disaster, and far too many commercial interests were so busy trying to safeguard themselves that many people were put to considerable embarrassment. I know that many tried to blame Mike Hawthorn for it, and that he vigorously denied it, but there was never any open admission that the course was too narrow at so important a point past the pits. Nevertheless, the fact that regulations were subsequently framed concerning the entry to the pit area on other circuits, and that Le Mans itself was drastically modified, certainly suggests that the circuit itself contributed to the accident.

The horror of Le Mans cast a gloom over motor racing which

was not to lift for a considerable period. Many races were cancelled, but the Dutch G.P. was courageously run a week later, Stirling playing 'follow my leader' to Fangio from start to finish, Mercedes finishing first and second.

They performed a similar act at Aintree in the British G.P., but this time Stirling led Fangio home by a few feet. It has often been suggested that this race was 'fixed' in order to give a British driver victory on his home ground. Well, no race of the Mercedes team was ever 'fixed'—that is, beyond being run according to the set principles of team management. Whether there was a tacit under-standing between Fangio and Neubauer that Moss should win, I do not know; certainly Fangio was far too much a sportsman ever to spoil Stirling's victory by telling him so, if there was.

But this I do feel strongly. Had Moss and Fangio been fighting each other, instead of driving as team mates, I believe Stirling would have won anyway; he knows every yard of the Aintree cir-cuit, and could consistently lap faster than Fangio; not by any appreciable margin, of course, but just a fractional part of a second. Furthermore, Stirling was in tremendous form both physically and morally that day, and was thoroughly revelling in the drive, whereas to Fangio it was probably just one more race.

After the British G.P. the Moss family, Stirling and I all dashed back to Tring, as they were entertaining several of the Mercedes-Benz team to lunch the next day. It was wonderful to see these famous figures at Tring—the vast Neubauer, press officer Artur Keser, Karl Kling, Rudi Uhlenhaut, and others. Having recorded a 1—2—3—4 victory the day before, everyone was in great spirits, and after lunch we went on a tour of White Cloud Farm, with the Mercedes-Benz photographer 'firing' off his camera at practically everything he saw. We tried to persuade Alfred Neubauer to sit on one of Pat's horses—it was a big one, which could have stood his 21 stone—but the Merc. team manager wasn't having any! 'Nein, nein'—he only liked his horses under the bonnet of a racing car, he explained!

The Stuttgart team were all back in the British Isles two months later, for the T.T. at Dundrod. This was the 'Golden Jubilee' T.T., which was first run fifty years before, and as a World Cham-pionship event was vitally important to Mercedes, who were behind

Ferrari and Jaguar at that stage of the season. There was a tremendous entry, with Ferrari, Maserati, Mercedes, Aston Martin and Jaguar works cars all bidding for outright victory.

Once again Stirling proved his superiority over his team mates in sports-car racing; he set the pace, and left them way behind, becoming involved in a monumental battle with Mike Hawthorn and Desmond Titterington, sharing the lone works Jaguar.

Stirling, relieved for a few laps by the American John Fitch, won a magnificent victory by a lap from Fangio; the Jaguar broke down after the most valiant of drives by Hawthorn and Titterington, which drew the immense admiration of the Mercedes personnel from Neubauer downwards. The race result brought Mercedes dead level with Jaguar in the Championship placings, both now having 16 points, and only 3 points behind Ferrari, making the final round, the Targa Florio, the vital decider.

After winning the Oulton Park Gold Cup again with a Maserati, one week after the T.T., Stirling went on a holiday in the Mediterranean with his friend from Maidstone, David Haynes. They chartered a boat from Cannes harbour, and lived aboard, spending their time skin-diving, swimming and lazing about. Stirling knew the Targa Florio was ahead but wanted to get right away from motor racing for a while. I think the triple deaths in the T.T. of Jim Mayers, Bill Smith and Richard Mainwaring, following on the Le Mans disaster and one or two other fatalities in that calamitous season, rather sickened him of the sport awhile. He told me that, whatever happened, nobody was to be told where he was.

He had not been gone more than a few days, when my bedside phone rang one morning. It was a call from Mercedes-Benz. Neubauer wanted Mr Moss to be in Sicily for the Targa Florio by such and such a date, and would I please tell him? They also needed two more drivers, one as co-driver for Moss, the other to share with Fitch. Could I select them, please—they didn't mind who they were, so long as they were good men whom Moss himself would recommend; and they would be happy to leave all arrangements with me. . . .

This was a fantastic turn of events—requested by the august Mercedes Company to appoint two drivers to handle their cars in a classic sports-car race! I put in a call to Stirling right away, and luckily got him without undue delay. I gave him the news, and we discussed who the drivers would be. Both of us agreed that if Peter Collins could be freed from his other commitments he would make an excellent co-driver to Stirling. As to the second man, there were several choices, but we finally settled on Desmond Titterington, the young Ulsterman, who had driven so brilliantly in the T.T. with Mike Hawthorn in the works Jaguar.

I contacted Peter Collins at Kidderminster, and he was extremely keen to drive, provided David Brown would waive the terms of his contract with the Aston Martin team. This Mr Brown agreed to do, and Neubauer sent him a personal wire, thanking him for the concession. Desmond Titterington also agreed to drive. His performance at Dundrod had obviously impressed others besides ourselves, for the following day he had a wire from Ugolini, of Scuderia Ferrari, offering him a drive with a Ferrari in the Targa Florio.

I next arranged to meet Collins and Titterington to finalize schedules and so on. We met at the Park Lane Hotel one evening, where I gave them their plane tickets to Sicily, at the same time passing on their instructions from Mercedes-Benz.

Well, Stirling and Peter proved an admirable team over the unique Madonie mountain circuit, winning by over four minutes, despite Stirling losing about nine minutes in going off the road. The 300SLR bounced off a bank, shot straight over a ledge and finished up in a field about ten feet below. In next to no time a dismayed Stirling was surrounded by cut-throat Sicilians, but they looked far more ferocious than they were. They joined forces with a will in getting the Merc. out, but the field was very muddy, and Stirling had to creep along, rear wheels wildly spinning until he could find a more or less level spot to drive out.

With about forty Sicilians all heaving like mad, he eventually got back on to the circuit, and drove back to the pits, having boiled most of the radiator water away. Peter Collins then took over, and in an epic drive closed up on the Fangio/Kling Mercedes, now leading, and the Castellotti/Manzon Ferrari. He lost about a minute after hitting a wall, but simply went faster on to the next lap before handing back to Stirling.

They won at record speed, followed by the Fangio/Kling Merc.,

Castellotti and Titterington/Fitch in the third Mercedes. The up-shot was that the World Sports Car Championship fell to Germany by one point, while, had there been an individual Sports Car Champion, Stirling would have become it, having won the Mille Miglia, the T.T. and the Targa.

The amount of equipment Mercedes took to Sicily showed how seriously they took the race. They brought six transporters, a total of twelve cars for training exclusive of the actual race machines, about forty mechanics, and installed mobile short-wave radio stations at several different points on the course!

Many thousands of words have been written describing the legendary Targa Florio circuit, with the stress laid on the mountains, the precipices, the bandits and the general 'wild and woolly' nature of the place. The course is 45 miles long, which alone makes it unique, and in all there are over 800 corners and only one long straight.

I, too, had read these accounts, but could never visualize the place properly until I went out to Sicily four years later for the 1959 Syracuse G.P., when I was able to drive over some of the roads. Some of them are verily cart tracks, frighteningly narrow, with no end to the corners, while the surrounding countryside is barren and forbidding. As for the bandits, I saw none, but they are there, without a doubt, although nowadays I think they must have a private treaty with the organizers, for not since the '20s has any trouble been reported!

But I do like the story about the driver who was practising in a private car, and suddenly found himself being shot at when out in the wilder regions of the circuit. He put in an excellent time for the rest of the lap, getting out of range of the bullets, and when he got back to Palermo, he complained strongly to the organizers. By devious means, the officials got in touch with the bandits in their mountain fastness, requesting them to refrain from shooting at Targa Florio competitors, please. Back came the reply, 'A thousand apologies—we thought it was a police car!'

Not long after their Targa Florio victory, Daimler-Benz held a big reception at Stuttgart, attended by all the drivers. As Mercedes had scored a fantastic triple success, winning the World Drivers Championship for Fangio, the Sports Car Championship and the

European Rally Championship, it will be appreciated that there was a very large gathering.

Now it was known already that Mercedes were to withdraw from Grand Prix racing at the end of 1955, this having been announced just after the Dutch G.P. They would, however, continue in sports-car racing, they said, supporting the Mille Miglia, Le Mans, the Nurburgring 1000 Kilometres race, probably Sebring and the Carrera Pan-Americana in 1956; so it looked as if Stirling would continue to drive sports cars for them in 1956, but would have to find a new Grand Prix mount.

The reception opened with a cocktail party, followed by a film, then Artur Keser, Mercedes press officer, stepped on to a stage and addressed the gathering in German. Stirling was sitting next to an English-speaking German journalist who suddenly turned to him and said, 'Do you understand what he is saying?'

'No, I don't,' Stirling said.

'Well,' said the man, 'he has just told us that Mercedes-Benz have decided to withdraw completely from all racing—no Grands Prix, no sports cars, no nothing.'

So that was the end of a magnificent experience for Stirling with the greatest exponents of motor racing the world has known. He had benefited immensely from it; he had for the first time enjoyed the true peace of mind induced by driving in a team knowing that no effort had been spared to ensure efficiency; he had been provided with an instrument worthy of his skill, enabling him to win three classic sports-car races, and the British Grand Prix; he had learned much of value in driving methods from Fangio, particularly in fast cornering; and he had come out of it all financially much better off.

I, too, gained from the association. I learned much on the organizational side from Neubauer, with whom I formed a friendship maintained to this day; whenever I go to Germany, I take him a gift of special tea from Fortnum & Mason, to which he is especially addicted. Neubauer is now retired, but still retains an intense interest in motor racing, and fires off questions at me in quick succession whenever we meet.

That brilliant Targa Florio victory also brought Peter Collins into greater international prominence. He had always been an excellent driver, right from his 500s days, but I would say his arrival point as a 'big name' came with the Targa Florio of 1955. For my part, I was very pleased, because after the race he asked me if I would officially become his manager. I discussed this with Stirling, and on obtaining his consent, I agreed to take on the management of Peter Collins.

Incidentally, when Stirling's contract with Mercedes came to an end, he was very reluctant to part with the 220A saloon they had provided for him, so one of the last dealings I had with Stuttgart was to negotiate the purchase from them of Stirling's car. They let him have it at a very reasonable price, and he used it regularly right to the end of 1958.

CHAPTER EIGHT

B.R.S.C.C. AFFAIRS

DRIVING for Mercedes in Formula 1 and major sports-car events, and also having the Maserati for lesser Grands Prix, Stirling ceased to compete in 500 c.c. racing by 1955. This was not because of lack of time, which could easily have been found that season, with its big gaps between events owing to cancellations following Le Mans.

The main reason, in fact, was that people were apparently saying it was time a top-liner like Moss stopped 'taking the candy from the children' in the Formula 3 class. When Stirling got to hear of this, he decided there and then to give it up. He didn't want to, for he had a great affection for the '500s' on which he started his racing career. Furthermore, with stern opponents like Don Parker and his Kieft, and Jim Russell, Ivor Bueb, Stuart Lewis-Evans and others in Coopers, it was ridiculous to suggest that Moss alone 'took the candy'—he had often to fight jolly hard to get a bite of it against such talented specialists, as was obvious in one or two 1954 events.

Much of the criticism came from the 'Formula 3 only' factions within the B.R.S.C.C., and it accentuated the foolish 'closed shop' attitude they had adopted when the Club spread its wings and took up other types of racing as well. That same attitude has virtually wiped them out of racing today. They harbour petty jealousies, and I have, generally speaking, found them too narrowminded a crowd. It is always 'Our cars started the Club; we want this, we want that', and they never seem to realize that their position has been safe-guarded only because there were other forms of racing in the programme.

As the Formula 3 movement gathered strength and Brands Hatch circuit became available, there was no more enthusiastic supporter of the 500s than I, yet the basic design of the cars, and above all the noise, has hardly changed in the last ten years. Obviously the 1959 '500' is a better, faster car than that of 1950, but it still relies on chain drive and the ever faithful Norton or J.A.P. engine to propel it; there has been no progress, no new designs, nothing; yet the Formula 3 supporters cannot see it, and oppose any suggestions to modify the Formula to bring in new competition.

One of the biggest criticisms of the 500 c.c. racing car is the noise, and I freely admit that the sound of a '500' in the paddock at Brands Hatch is sufficient to 'send me up the wall'. That hammering note of the Norton or J.A.P. single, accentuated by the megaphone exhaust, which ought, I suppose, to be music in an organizer's ears, instead is like a series of ear-shattering blows to the head. I firmly believe that the public have grown to resent the unchanging noise of Formula 3 as much as anything else.

I have heard 500s fitted with Triumph Twin engines, with the Turner 'four', with linered-down M.G. and Simca engines, and their exhaust notes *were* music, by contrast. It is not the fault of the 500 movement, of course, that these units couldn't touch the single-cylinder J.A.P.s and 'double-knocker' Nortons on performance, yet the movement took no steps to encourage the use of 'multis', nor would they consider changing the capacity limit to bring in larger, car-type units. Today, Formula Junior is expanding rapidly, and had the 500 c.c. racing movement been more broadminded, they might well have been the pioneers of such a Formula instead of going down on a sinking ship.

The foregoing is not simply 'sour grapes' because somebody accused Stirling of 'taking candy from the children' in 1954. I merely deplore the stagnation of what was once a splendid and virile movement. In my opinion the 500 c.c. car has done its job, and is now outdated in its present form. The B.R.S.C.C. would do better, I feel, to drop it outright now, and fall in line with the Continentals by adopting Formula Junior.

It was in 1955 that the B.R.S.C.C. ran their first big international meeting at Oulton Park. We had already been associated with the owners, Cheshire Car Circuits, Ltd., in the promotion of a national meeting, but this had not produced a very big crowd, and it was my desire to see a really big sports-car meeting held there, as a parallel to the *Daily Dispatch* Gold Cup meeting for Grand Prix cars.

Oulton is a splendid circuit, worthy of greater use than it actually gets. 2·7 miles round, it has the right lap length, and the setting in parkland is unsurpassed. My first step was to see the directors of the Circuit Company, and with the valuable aid of Dennis Done, who was well acquainted with most of them, we came to a very amicable agreement about how the meeting would be run.

My next aim was to seek support from one of the newspapers, and through Tommy Wisdom I was able to gain an introduction to the promotions department of the *Daily Herald*, which belongs to Odhams Press. They agreed to take on the sponsorship of the meeting, which was to be known as the *Daily Herald* International Trophy Meeting, to be held on 27 August.

The main event would be the *Daily Herald* International Trophy for sports cars, over 221 miles, supported by the *John Bull* Trophy race for Formula 3 cars, and the *Sporting Life* Trophy for production saloons. Now the term 'International Trophy' is very overworked in motor racing today, and all too often is justified by perhaps one or two foreign drivers only. I resolved that the B.R.S.C.C.'s race would be truly international in character, and that of the thirty-two entries fifty per cent should ideally be foreign.

In the end we couldn't quite achieve that ideal, but we certainly effected a fine turn-out of foreign talent for the race. From the United States came Masten Gregory, Carroll Shelby and Mackay Fraser, all in Ferraris; from Italy came Franco Cortese (Ferrari) and Azzuro Manzini (Maserati); Louis Rosier, Jean Lucas and Harry Schell represented France, the first two with Ferraris, the latter with an H.W.M.-Jaguar; Benoit Musy of Switzerland brought a 3-litre Maserati; Nogueira Pinto from Portugal entered a Ferrari; Len Cosh (Aston Martin) represented Australia; and Joakim Bonnier (Alfa Romeo) and Gunnar Carlsson (Ferrari) came from Sweden. And opposing these was the pick of British drivers and cars.

This foreign contingent included some interesting personalities and I was proud to have brought them to England for the first time. 'Jo' Bonnier, the bearded Swede, was driving a rather evil-looking black Alfa Romeo in the big race, and a very fast '1900' Alfa Romeo in the saloon-car event. Herbert Mackay Fraser, the American, who had recently come from Brazil, owned a rather elderly 3-litre

Monza Ferrari. He was fanatically keen about racing, and had met Stirling out in Portugal, when he told him he badly wanted to come to England.

'Mac', a most likeable and friendly character, made a great impression on people over here, both with his driving and his immense enthusiasm, virtually going without food and drink in order to run his beloved Ferrari.

Altogether the 1955 *Daily Herald* International Meeting had a satisfying international flavour about it. It was, I felt, the B.R.S.C.C.'s big moment; we were 'on trial', so to speak, before the public, the other clubs and the R.A.C., to see whether we could cope with a major meeting, and we all put tremendous effort and energy into the organization.

A crowd of about 50,000 turned up; this was satisfying, although we would have liked to see many more after all our efforts. They witnessed a splendid drive by Reg Parnell, who was on top of his form, and got out ahead of Mike Hawthorn's Ferrari in a works Aston Martin, to determinedly stay there to the finish. Peter Collins (Aston Martin) was third, and Masten Gregory (Ferrari) fourth.

Stirling Moss had toyed with driving a D-type Jaguar, but eventually took over Les Leston's 1½-litre Connaught, the car he had previously driven in Paris, and finished seventh, winning his class. Les's generosity in giving Stirling his drive later brought him a return drive in the Moss Maserati at Castle Combe.

By this stage of the 1955 season, we had transferred the B.R.S.C.C.'s H.Q. to new offices at No. 35, The Strand. This was a very convenient move for me, as the office in William IV Street was now far too small to accommodate the Club staff and that of Stirling Moss Ltd. By now it had become necessary, too, for Stirling to have his own private secretary instead of sharing mine, and his first was a very pleasant and efficient girl named Judy Noot. She later became a great friend of Stirling's wife Katie, and was, in fact, a bridesmaid at his wedding. Eventually she left us to go back to her parents in Wales, but has since returned to London, joining Eagle Airways as an air hostess.

In 1955, however, with Judy and all her secretarial gear, Stirling's ever-mounting correspondence, the B.R.S.C.C.'s files and abundant paper work, plus myself, my secretary, Gwen Smith, and

Ron Smith to accommodate, the two small rooms at the back of Alfred Moss's surgery were just too small. The relief was immense when we secured new offices in the Strand, virtually next door to Charing Cross Station, and very close to William IV Street.

I could nip across from one office to the other without trouble at all, and the situation was improved still further when the Post Office arranged for us to have extension lines from the switchboard in Stirling's office to that in the new B.R.S.C.C. premises, and vice versa. No matter which office I was in thereafter, I could take calls for both businesses, an ideal arrangement.

Yet another major improvement effected that year was the installation of a concrete grandstand at Brands Hatch, opposite the starting area. This was an immense asset to the circuit, making it possible for the public to watch the racing under shelter regardless of the weather, and gave Brands the distinction of being the only motor-racing venue in Britain having a permanent grandstand in the style of the classic Continental circuits.

It is generally believed that the stand was completely new, but in fact it began life at the Northolt Pony Trotting course. When this course was taken over in order to build a housing estate, John Hall of the Brands Hatch Circuit Company and I went over to North London to look over the deserted pony track. We saw three of these magnificent stands, two being still intact and one then being dismantled.

We purchased one at a bargain figure, and arranged for it to be taken down piece by piece, with every girder member being carefully marked for reassembly. The parts were then conveyed to Brands Hatch, and re-erected by a steel gang on prepared foundations, the brickwork then being built up around the structure. It certainly looked imposing as it neared completion, and I couldn't help feeling excited at the progress Brands had made, from the original one-mile track of 1950.

While the grandstand was going up, other new amenities were incorporated, including a new timing box at the top of the stand, which gave the timekeepers a view of the entire track, less the 60 or 70 yards behind the trees at Druids Corner. We also had a commentator's box built in, between the timekeepers and the Clerk of the Course's office, so that the commentator—usually that great enthusiast John Bolster—was situated between the two sources of information which are most necessary for accurate commentary. Down below we also had included rooms for the police, for Tannoy equipment and other apparatus, even setting space by for a hospital. Tea and licensed bars were also built.

Underneath the main part of the grandstand where the public sat, there was most valuable space for storing chairs, circuit signs, advertising banners, and other miscellanea of the circuit. Here the permanent staff of Brands Hatch also have their own workshops for the maintenance of circuit equipment.

In the Clerk of the Course's control room a 15-line telephone switchboard was installed, linking him with every marshal post on the course, with the paddock and other vital points. This installation was the work of Committee-member and Chief Paddock Marshal Bert Lamkin, who is a keen and clever electrician. Later, Bert also installed a number of teleprinters which we purchased from the G.P.O., enabling us to turn out practice timesheets, race times, results and other data sheets for rapid issue to the commentator, press box, the paddock and elsewhere.

Later we were able to secure the support of several companies, Shell and Dunlop among them, in the fitting out and equipping of the hospital. As a result I would say that today Brands Hatch has some of the finest medical facilities on any racing circuit.

In all, these improvements have made Brands Hatch circuit immeasurably more professional, and marked another step forward in the ambitions of the B.R.S.C.C. and the circuit proprietors. Let me say, here and now, that amongst those ambitions is one to extend the circuit to at least three-mile lap length, and stage a Major Grand Prix—preferably the British G.P.—upon it.

As a director of the Brands Hatch Company, I can assure readers that this is by no means fantasy. We have the land—the Company owns all that on which the present circuit lies, plus a considerable amount besides; we very nearly have the money, and we certainly have the incentive and the enthusiasm.

The reason I have specified three miles as the minimum lap length to be desired is that Earl Howe, Chairman of the Competitions Committee of the R.A.C., and that Committee as a body, has always specified that the British Grand Prix, which is this country's premier racing event of the year, should be staged on a circuit of not less than three miles. This has confined it so far to the only two 3-mile circuits in the country—Silverstone and Aintree.

If we can make Brands Hatch longer than three miles, all well and good—the longer the better. But up to the present, we have only received sanction from the authorities for an extension to 2·75 miles. The major difficulty currently is that of objection by residents in the locality, and until they can be won over, and we gain official consent, our 3-mile project must rest in abeyance.

When eventually we get the 'go ahead', the plan is to retain the present 1¼-mile circuit, which is so popular with the public, and use it as before for a large proportion of the season's meetings, keeping the extended course for major international fixtures only. In 1949 the cost of laying down the circuit itself was about £14,000 for the mile, and this figure has risen appreciably today, so that it is only economic common sense to retain the original layout, and embody it in the extensions when these materialize.

At the end of the 1955 season, Stirling Moss found himself in something of a dilemma. He couldn't drive for Mercedes-Benz any more because of their total withdrawal from racing, but he knew that the Maserati people were keen for him to rejoin them for 1956. On the other hand, Stirling is extremely patriotic, and with Britain's mounting interest in Formula 1, he was torn between the known potentialities of the Italian Maserati and the unknown of the British Vanwall, B.R.M. and Connaught machines.

There is no sense in driving a car which is not fully developed, but on the other hand Moss was haunted by the feeling that he ought to do his bit at least by driving one of the British cars. For our part, Alfred Moss and I were in no doubts that he should sign with Maserati for 1956; the cars were right, the team was mature and experienced, and they were very keen to have Moss, whereas the British cars had some way to go yet before they reached racing maturity.

But Stirling tried them all—B.R.M., Connaught and Vanwall— one day at Silverstone, and while I think he knew then that the Maserati was a better proposition, he still was uncertain in his mind as to what course to take. So we took the novel step of holding a dinner-party in London, inviting leading members of the motoring press, and Stirling put his problem to them, fully and frankly. It was a step which I think many of them appreciated, since he was, of course, at complete liberty to drive for whom he wished.

By a narrow vote, they chose Maserati as his best bet, and with this confirmation of his, and our, views, steps were taken without delay to sign up with Officine Maserati for Grand Prix racing, plus a number of sports-car events, in 1956. I was unable to go to Modena to effect this, but Alfred Moss and Felix Nabarro flew out to Italy instead, and negotiated a very satisfactory contract on Stirling's behalf. This took into account an agreement we had recently reached for Stirling to drive Aston Martins in certain 1956 sports-car events, and it is a measure of Maserati's esteem for him that they were prepared to have him competing against their own sports cars in some races, in order to secure his services in others.

During the Earl's Court Motor Show in October 1955, I had been introduced to a distinguished visitor from Nassau, Sir Sydney Oakes. Sir Sydney was the son of the famous Harry Oakes, a very wealthy man who lived in Nassau, and who had the misfortune to be murdered in his bed during the war years. There had been considerable publicity in the newspapers of late on this subject, there being a possibility of reopening the case in an effort to find the murderer, who to this day has gone undiscovered.

Sir Sydney Oakes is one of the guiding lights of the Bahamas Automobile Club, together with Donald Healey who, credit where credit is due, is largely responsible for the growth in importance of the Nassau road races. These had first been held in 1954, when there was severe criticism from the R.A.C. steward on the conduct of the meeting. It was felt that an experienced race promoter should be invited to go out there and organize the meeting on a more professional basis in an effort to improve its status, and this task fell to me.

The meeting was taking place from 9 to 11 December, and the main events were the Governor's Cup and the Nassau Trophy races. Stirling Moss was to drive an Austin-Healey, and he and I flew out together, leaving London late one evening, just when Alfred Moss and Felix Nabarro got back from Modena with the Maserati contract in their pocket.

We arrived at Nassau about a week before the meeting. I had

Study in relaxation: Peter Collins seated in the Grand Prix Ferrari at Aintree

The beginning of it all. Stirling Moss in his first racing car, the 500 c.c. Cooper-J.A.P.

Hans Hermann miraculously escapes from the somersaulting British Racing Partnership prepared B.R.M. after approaching the South Curve of the Avus circuit practically brakeless

Above: Stirling Moss, 250F Maserati, passes the burning wreckage of Tony Brooks' B.R.M. at Abbey Corner, Silverstone. *Below:* One of the rare incidents in the career of Peter Collins when he overturned his 500 c.c. Cooper Norton at Woodcote Corner, Silverstone

Above: We three: Alfred Moss, myself and Stirling. *Below:* Study in perfection: Fangio in the works 250F Maserati at Rouen

Above: Ghost car or special? An unusual mount for an unusual driver. Stirling is probably remembering his first car. *Below:* Stirling Moss negotiating Melling Crossing, Aintree, in the British Racing Partnership prepared B.R.M. in the British Grand Prix 1959

Above: Moment of victory. I enjoy a smaller success when winning the Junior Championship at Brands Hatch in 1950. *Below:* Moment of victory. Stirling and Jenks belatedly share the success of the 1955 Mille Miglia

Above: One of the bitter moments known to most drivers. Stirling pushes his crippled works Maserati on the verge at Stowe Corner, Silverstone.
Below: Harry Schell in the Grand Prix Vanwall at Aintree

agreed to act as Clerk of the Course and general organizer, and once there had quickly to get down to the job. The racing was to be over a 3·5-mile layout at Windsor airfield, which had first been used the previous year.

From the Bahamas Club side, things were being run by a man named Sherman ('Red') Crise, a large, voluble, ginger-headed American, extremely popular by virtue of his personality, but having no knowledge of racing promotion whatsoever. No British motor club would tolerate so low a standard of organization as that which prevailed at Nassau when I arrived.

Circuit arrangements were really primitive; there were no time-keeping facilities, and in fact right through the practice period no lap times for competitors were officially taken, the only times being provided by the various pit crews. The course is laid out over vast runways and perimeter tracks of confusingly varied width, very meagre 'safety' fencing, consisting of 50-gallon oil drums filled with shale, into which steel spikes were thrust, these supporting lengths of rope. It was very difficult to stop people going on to the circuit whenever they felt like it, and I was horrified to see Americans actually driving their cars along the circuit in the wrong direction, while practice was in progress!

The Chief Steward of the Meeting, appointed by the R.A.C., was that world-famous 'record-man' Captain George Eyston, one of the grandest persons one could ever wish to work with. Also down to watch over things from the United States' point of view was Colonel Hetherington, one of the executive officers of the American Automobile Association, now withdrawn from race promotion and the F.I.A.

Marshals and helpers were all too few, and instead of the large body of able and willing assistants we could rely upon at any British meeting to help sweep the corners, put out the marker cones and so on, George Eyston, Colonel Hetherington and I did all this ourselves. It was beneath the dignity, it seems, of the white residents on the island to do anything which they felt the coloured inhabitants ought to do, so the only way to make sure vital tasks were done was to do them ourselves.

I had to sort out flag positioning, check on the fire and ambulance arrangements, find more marshals and observers and instruct them in their duties, and improve communications between the corners and race control. It all had its funny side; I well remember when one of the telephones broke down, we sent one of the coloured linesmen along to find out what was wrong. He found the break, 'repaired' it, and duly reported the line as O.K. We tried again, but it was useless. So I sent another man along who discovered that the wire, which had been broken by a car going off the road, had been joined together by holding the two ends and tying them into a knot, our coloured helper firmly believing that this would restore telephone communication!

There was a tremendous field for the main race, ranging in size from a 4·9-litre Ferrari which took second place in the 1954 Carrera Pan-Americana race, to a '500' Fiat-engined special, so in view of the complete lack of practice times we decided that the best way out was to employ a Le Mans-type start. In this way, the highest capacity cars were at the front end, and the smallest at the tail end, which at least would eliminate some of the early passing problems.

My duties included the drivers' briefing which, unlike most European meetings, where it is held half an hour before the race, took place in the British Colonial Hotel on the previous evening. Amongst the ninety drivers, mostly American, were Phil Hill, Sherwood Johnston, Lou Brero, Jim Kimberly, Ed Crawford, Masten Gregory, Art Bunker and Jack MacAfee, all 'names' in American motor racing. These and the rest had been having a whale of a time on the famous Bahamas 'vacation' island, with boating, fishing, water-skiing, dancing, and what one American journal described as 'some of the fiercest, most violent, dangerous cocktail parties ever to grace a "sporting" week-end' to keep them happy.

Now they were ready for some racing, and I had to stand up in front of them and announce our decision to use Le Mans-type starts for the races. The result was pandemonium. The Americans are very keen on using safety belts for racing, and immediately began protesting in most violent fashion, some almost calling what amounted to a strike, others shouting, 'Let's vote on it—let's see how many want it.'

It was here that Stirling came to the rescue. He stood up and pointed out that if anyone wanted to use a safety belt, he had plenty of time to put it on when he'd sprinted across the track into his car. They'd lose a few seconds, but if they felt so strongly about it, there was nothing to prevent them using belts. It didn't alter the fact, he said, that the Le Mans start was the safest way of starting the race, and he was sure they all agreed that safety was the most important thing.

This helped to sway them, and while we had fully intended to enforce the Le Mans start whether they liked it or not, this was a much better way of securing agreement, and the ruling was accepted much more easily than it might have been.

Some 10,000 spectators had turned up to watch the racing, and in the three days of the so-called Nassau 'Speed Week' we had eleven races making up the programme. 'Fon' de Portago won the 30-lap Governor's Cup race with his Ferrari after a tense scrap with Sherwood Johnson's D-type Jaguar and Californian Phil Hill's Ferrari. In the longest event of all, the 60-lap, 210-mile Nassau Trophy race, Phil Hill got his Monza Ferrari out ahead of de Portago's and won by 23 sec. despite Fon lapping at a fantastic 104·2 m.p.h., while Masten Gregory was third with a 3-litre Maserati. It is noteworthy that all three drivers subsequently took up Grand Prix racing.

Amongst numerous other events was the Bahamas Auto Club Trophy, for Bahamian residents only. Now it happens that in Nassau, the few car-hire concerns operating favour small open sports cars, these being more popular in that hot and balmy climate than saloons. Most of these cars were Singer '1500s', and one or two local residents hit on the idea of using these for their race by hiring them for a few days, flogging the poor things to death in the race, then returning them to the self-drive hire company!

It was when this race got going that something occurred which required an immediate Stewards' decision; we looked round for them, and found George Eyston but not 'Red' Crise or Sir Sydney Oakes. Then it dawned on me—they were also out on the circuit, racing for the Club Trophy!

Organizing that 'Speed Week' might have brought its headaches, but it was certainly a wonderful commission. I should very much like to have undertaken it subsequently, but unfortunately my temperament is such that, if I see something is radically wrong, I cannot personally take part in it or support it. I am afraid there were some very strong words and an even stronger clash of personalities between Sherman Crise and myself. As he was Chairman of the Club Competitions Committee, with a large financial interest in the meetings, it was quite obvious that we would never come to terms again.

During our stay in Nassau I was able to put in some time at deep-sea fishing with George Eyston, who is a tremendous enthusiast for this sport. We went out early one morning in a very well-equipped boat, catching six or seven big fish in all, including a couple of barracuda, a shark and one or two amberjacks.

This deep-sea fishing is much more exciting than it may sound. At least a thirty-foot boat is needed, with fairly powerful engines to give a good turn of speed, to get you out to deep water without delay. At the back of the boat, in the open stern or transom, are two strong swivel chairs. A six-foot rod with a clutch reel and about 900 feet of line is used, and to the hook at the end of the line are attached some brightly coloured feathers, and the bait. This is usually a small, silvery fish which looks very much like a miniature swordfish, having a sharp, pointed nose with a formidable collection of serrated teeth.

The lines are trailed behind the boat, Eyston and I sitting next to each other in the swivel chairs; one line has a weight on it to make it sink six or eight feet deeper than the other, so that when the boat deviates from a straight course the lines curve out behind the boat, one under the other, without fouling.

The big thrill comes when suddenly you get a bite. The rod almost bends double under the pull, and the line starts to run out as the fish exerts a greater pressure than the friction clutch on the reel. You just let it run out and out, until the fish tires and slows down. At this, you begin jerking the rod backwards, at the same time winding the line in. It is known for people to fight for two or three hours to bring a fish in sometimes, depending on how powerful he is. Then, as you wind him gradually in to the last few yards of the line, comes the great speculation as to what you will see when he breaks surface. Shark? Barracuda? Tuna? What will it be? If he's big, and they mostly are in those waters, you will have to use the gaff to bring him into the boat—and believe me, the sight of a four-foot shark or a fierce-looking barracuda writhing on the hook can be quite intimidating.

All too soon the time came to end my second visit to Nassau. Stirling's next destination was not London, as mine was, but Auckland, New Zealand, where he was to drive his faithful old 250F Maserati to its last victory in the New Zealand G.P. on 7 January, 1956.

Although he received many invitations to stay and be fêted in New Zealand, Stirling left the very next day. This annoyed some people out there, but was, in fact, unavoidable as he had to get to Buenos Aires in good time for the Argentine G.P., where he was to drive a works Maserati on 22 January. He flew via America, covering a tremendous distance within a few days.

Aircraft travel may seem very glamorous if you are taking a three-hour trip to Nice for your annual holidays, but believe me, when you travel from one side of the world to the other, it can become extremely boring and fatiguing. Personally, I find that the very slight, high-pitched vibration from the floor of an aircraft always makes my ankles swell, and my limbs become very restless. Just sitting, trying to do something, and not knowing quite what to do, is also tiring, so how a particularly active and restless person like Stirling puts up with it, I can't think.

When Stirling and I parted after Nassau I took a plane to New York, spent a few days there, then returned to London. Christmas loomed ahead, and with it the second Boxing Day meeting at Brands Hatch of the B.R.S.C.C. This time our gamble with the weather, which we so pleasingly won the previous year, did not come off. Oh dear, how it rained! From an early hour it poured depressingly down, but the crowds still turned up to watch the racing, and the drivers, the marshals and all the other officials gave of their gallant best under adverse conditions.

We didn't roast an ox that year, but we had a barbecue of two of Alfred Moss's 'White Cloud' pedigree pigs, with U.S.A.F. personnel from Manston airfield to do the roasting. Father Christmas called in again, this time from the sky via a helicopter. We chartered the machine to fly from Gatwick, carrying that cheerful character Duncan Hamilton, who was to be our Santa Claus. Unlike Stirling, Duncan was large enough to do without padding!

But the weather was so bad, and the cloud so low, that the helicopter had difficulty in reaching Brands Hatch. Then, just when we were getting very anxious, we heard the familiar 'whish-whish' of the helicopter, and it popped into view over the misty Kentish hills, hovered over the circuit, and landed. Out came Duncan Hamilton in flowing white beard, exuding real Santa Claus *bonhomie*—though he was very glad to down a quick glass of whisky to drive out the cold after his flight.

Colin Chapman and Mark Lund scored wins, Ivor Bueb won the main Formula 3 race, split into two heats; Archie Scott-Brown won the Formule Libre event with a works Grand Prix 2½-litre Connaught, while Tony Brooks, making his first visit to Brands Hatch, took second place in John Risely-Prichard's privately owned 2-litre Connaught.

The public were delighted to see Tony in action, for he had made headlines three months before, when he won the Syracuse G.P. in Sicily with a Connaught, beating the works Maseratis and Gordinis fair and square, and giving the first hint of many fine performances to come. We persuaded him to drive two demonstration laps in the actual winning Connaught, and the crowd showed their hearty approval by blowing their car horns loud and long.

It was at this particular meeting that we experimentally insured against loss of revenue through rain. We paid a premium of about £200, but even though it rained like fury for most of the day, we still didn't collect any benefits under the policy, as there was not sufficient 'fallage' of rain within a set period of time!

CHAPTER NINE

THE DIZZY ROUND

So 1955, that black year for motor racing, was past, and 1956 got under way. After his Auckland win, Stirling's next date was the Argentine G.P., and this event also marked Peter Collins's first drive for the Scuderia Ferrari. Neither of them had any luck. A wheel of Stirling's works Maserati ran over his foot while being pushed to the start, giving him considerable pain, and although he led the race for a short while, his engine went on to five cylinders and then packed up altogether.

As for Peter, he was given a Ferrari Squalo instead of one of the Lancia-based V8s, and though this ran reliably it was too slow. Then Piotti got in his way before a corner and both cars had to retire, sadly dented. Fangio, now in the Ferrari team, won the G.P.

The 1000 Kilometres of Buenos Aires for sports cars came next in the *Temporada* series, and this time Stirling won the race, sharing a 3-litre 6-cylinder Maserati with that versatile Argentine sportsman Carlos Menditeguy, who plays tennis, polo, golf and squash as well as doing motor racing. Peter co-drove a 4·9-litre Ferrari with Luigi Musso, but the car chewed its rear axle up shortly after half distance; Peter managed to raise the lap record to over 102 m.p.h., and I think Ferrari were pretty pleased with their latest recruit.

The third and final race of the *Temporada* was the Buenos Aires City G.P., which you might reasonably expect to have been held in that city. But it wasn't—it took place at Mendoza, some 650 miles away from Buenos Aires! There was some fun about this, the Argentine press suggesting that in future the Argentine G.P. might well be held at the Nurburgring or Silverstone!

Anyway, Fangio scored his usual victory, and Stirling came home second, after having one of his very rare spins early on while trying to hold the Lancia-Ferraris. Peter Collins was given the Squalo Ferrari again, and plodded home fifth after driving very consistently.

I was amongst several people who had hoped that Peter as well as Stirling would have joined the Maserati team for 1956. He had driven the disc-braked 250F Maserati of the Owen Organization very well during 1955, and drove for the works team in the Italian G.P. at Monza, when he had to retire. It was, in fact, due to a strange and unfortunate coincidence that Peter Collins did not join Maseratis. Acting on his behalf, I had sent them a telegram which said, in effect, 'Are you interested Collins driving Maserati?' Now it happened that, a little while before, Colin Davis, who began racing the previous season with Formula 3 Coopers, had called at the Modena factory, and Maseratis mistakenly assumed that my telegram referred to him, and sent a wire back to the effect that they did not require 'Colin' to drive for them. By the time we had got this lot disentangled Ferrari, who had got wind of the nego-tiations, had nipped in quickly and snapped Peter up for his team.

So Peter Collins found himself in the position Stirling had occu-pied with Mercedes, i.e. running in the same team as the great Fangio. Whereas, however, Stirling was No. 2 for Mercedes, Peter had those two excitable Italian rivals, Eugenio Castellotti and Luigi Musso, coming between him and the World Champion. As 1956 was to show, it did not prevent Peter from making a splendid showing, and establishing himself as the third of the big three British racing drivers—namely Mike Hawthorn, Stirling Moss and Peter Collins.

I had little hand in arranging Peter's contract with Ferrari that first year, as they 'rushed' him into it before he could contact me. But thereafter I took on the task of 'managing' him, looking after his correspondence, travelling arrangements, etc., and opening a bank account for him in London. For this Peter gave me a single power signature on his account, so that I could sign a cheque on his behalf for any sum necessary to meet his business requirements.

I soon found that, whilst it was one thing to be 'manager' to Peter Collins in title, it was another to be one literally. Stirling is an admirable subject for management because he wants, and needs, to be managed; but Peter was not of the same temperament.

He was a fun-loving youngster who drove racing cars primarily for enjoyment; Stirling enjoys it too, but treats it as a serious pro-fession. Peter was the swashbuckling, buccaneer type of person, very much like Mike Hawthorn; that is why the pair became such close friends when they were in the Ferrari team together, both sharing similar outlooks on driving and life in general.

Now Peter was somewhat unreliable. He was vague, delightfully vague. He would make appointments, then forget them completely; not purposely, but accidentally. Whereas lesser people could get themselves disliked in this way, Peter's charm very soon turned away the wrath of the person he had let down. He had such a cheerful, infectious grin, on top of which he refused to be serious about anything, so that people took it in the spirit it was meant, and he always got away with it.

To 'manage' a person really successfully, of course, there has to be an exceptionally deep bond of friendship and understanding, and although I was a friend of Peter our friendship was never so close as that between Stirling and me. My management of Peter's affairs was much more a formal commercial affair than with Stirling.

With Peter I had a contract, not because Peter would ever go back on his word, but because it was a proper business arrangement. With Stirling, however, I never had, nor ever wanted, a contract. Our relationship has been too close for too long to need such a formality. Not that the Collins contract was signed until a little later in the year anyway, since the first thing to do was to sort out Peter's affairs and to 'get his house in order' according to our standards. This took quite a bit of doing, and only then, when Peter was sure in his mind that he wanted me to manage him, did we draw up the contract.

There was an initial misunderstanding between Stirling and myself regarding Peter's contract. Stirling thought my intentions were solely to arrange Peter's air travel, his hotel bookings and that sort of thing. He had not fully realized that at the same time I would negotiate Peter's contracts, and he foresaw that I might find myself in a position where I would have to divide my loyalties.

He was very right in this respect, for such a position might easily have arisen, had I not had sufficient staff to assist in all my duties. But it never did happen, since by 1956 I had built up quite an organization at 35 The Strand, in addition to William IV Street, and was able to delegate much of the work on behalf of Collins to Ron Smith, my personal assistant.

For Stirling, 1956 proved to be a highly successful year so far as race victories were concerned. He drove G.P. and sports Maseratis, a G.P. Vanwall, sports Aston Martins and, on rarer occasions, Porsche and Cooper sports cars. He won two Grande Epreuves—those of Monaco and Italy—for Maserati. He also won the New Zealand and Australian G.P.s and Formula 1 events at Goodwood and Aintree for the Italian marque. He won the *Daily Express* International Trophy race at Silverstone with the new Vanwall. He won the Argentine 1000 km. and the Nurburgring 1000 km., both Sports Car Championship events, and also the Bari and Venezuelan G.P.s, the Australian T.T. and the Nassau Trophy with sports Maseratis. He won the *Daily Herald* Trophy at Oulton Park and the Easter Goodwood unlimited sports-car race with Aston Martins. And he won the British Empire Trophy at Oulton Park, and a shorter up to 1500 c.c. race at the same circuit in August, with a Cooper-Climax.

But he didn't win the World Championship, which was his greatest goal. That honour fell, for the fourth time, and the third consecutive year, to Fangio the Great, and none, I think, will dispute the Argentinian's supremacy as a driver. But close behind him in talents came Moss, Hawthorn and Collins—place them in what order of merit you wish—and it was very clear that, even though Britain had no cars worthy as yet of winning the Championship, we certainly had the only drivers worthy to be future World Champions.

And the cars were on the way. Connaught had given the first hint of mounting British potentiality at Syracuse in 1955, followed by Vanwall at Silverstone in May 1956, when Stirling won the B.R.D.C./*Daily Express* race despite the presence of Fangio and Collins with Ferraris.

Maseratis had decided not to support this 176-mile, non-Championship event as the all-important Monaco G.P. came a week later and they were concentrating on that race, rather than splitting their efforts. This left Stirling without a Formula 1 car for Silverstone, but eventually we fixed up with Tony Vandervell for him to drive one of the two new Vanwalls. These were a great improvement on the 1955 cars, had new chassis designed by Colin Chapman of Lotus, and remarkably clean aerodynamic bodies designed by streamline expert Frank Costin.

Driving that Vanwall marked a great turning point in Moss's career. From the time he first sat in it, the pair seemed to go together like eggs and bacon. Both Stirling and Schell set up the fastest practice lap at 1 min. 42 sec., with Vanwalls. Mike Hawthorn set the initial pace with the remarkably fast B.R.M., but after the usual Bourne luck prevailed on the thirteenth lap, Stirling took the lead, never to lose it.

I remember standing up on the balcony above the pits, talking to several pressmen before the race started. We were all saying what a wonderful thing it would be to have a British car, driven by a British driver, able to meet anything which Italy could offer on equal terms. And there, before our eyes, this miraculous thing happened, with Stirling in the Vanwall winning the race after roundly beating the Ferraris. It took another season before the British car regularly trounced its Italian rivals, but Silverstone, 5 May, 1956, marked the first round, and strengthened within Stirling his greatest ambition—to win the World Championship in a British car.

After the Vanwall performance, doubts assailed us as to whether Stirling had, in fact, made the right choice in signing with Maserati, but subsequent mishaps on tougher circuits than Silverstone proved that Tony Vandervell's new car was still immature as a Grand Prix challenger.

Monaco came next, where Stirling showed his mastery by seizing an early lead and holding it throughout, to win his first major Continental Grand Prix, despite the menace of Fangio roaring round in pursuit, first in his own Ferrari until that wilted under the strain and then in Peter Collins's.

At Spa, the next Championship round, Peter came into his own and won the race for Ferrari, watched by Fangio whose car broke its transmission. Stirling had a lucky escape when the rear hub on his Maserati sheared and he lost a wheel. He then took over Perdisa's car and finished third.

Cesare Perdisa never made much impact in Grand Prix racing, but he was a very pleasant, amusing character. His father publishes one of Italy's best glossy motoring magazines, called *Quattroruote*, and his son is quite a humorist in his way. Stirling and I picked up quite a bit of Italian from him, and were able to converse quite happily. One of his habits was to eat raw eggs, it being his boast that he always ate two first thing every morning. On several occasions he made Stirling feel sick by taking an egg from his car—or from his pocket—cracking it on the wing of the car, and consuming it raw in front of him.

Championship round 4 brought the biggest money prize of the lot—the French G.P. at Rheims, which was heavily sponsored by British Petroleum Ltd. The first prize was ten million francs, an unprecedented sum in European motor racing, equivalent to something like £10,000. Moss's Maserati didn't take to Rheims at all well and retired, but Peter, who was quite a strategist, just as Stirling was, decided that Fangio was certain to go all out for a win, and reckoned that the best thing he could do was to sit behind and see what happened. Plenty did. First his team mate Castellotti decided to hang on to Peter all the way, hoping to pip him near the end, while Harry Schell put the Vanwall cat amidst the Ferrari pigeons with a vengeance, sending the Italian team aflutter when he forced his green car up and split the trio up.

Fangio went all out and had fuel-pipe trouble for his pains, Schell dropped back and Peter and Castellotti went hell for leather to the finish, Peter just beating the Italian to it, and winning his second Grand Prix in a fortnight. There was no question of team orders; Ferraris just left Peter and Eugenio to fight it out; I don't think the latter was very pleased at the end, for he was desperately ambitious to win a major Grand Prix. But Collins drove that little bit better, and thwarted his ambitions.

Neither Stirling nor Peter could do anything about Fangio in the German G.P., though Peter hung on to the Champion and twice broke the lap record before his fuel tank split. Then he took over de Portago's car and overdid things near the Karussel, abandoning the car. Stirling took second place for Maserati.

For sheer excitement, drama, tension and glamour, for everything that can ever be described as the *desiderata* of a motor race, the Grand Prix d'Europe at Monza on 2 September was *the* race for me. Both Stirling and Peter were star performers in this unforgettable event, and Stirling's ultimate victory brought such jubilation to the Maserati mechanics and the Orsi family that I saw people unashamedly weeping in the pits with sheer joy.

At that stage, Peter Collins still had a chance to win the World

Championship, provided Fangio did not finish or make the fastest lap. Well, Fangio didn't make the fastest lap, and his car broke down, precipitating an action on Peter Collins's part which made him the undying hero of Italian motor racing and earned him a popularity he was never to lose.

It was steering trouble, occasioned by the rough conditions on the new banking they had incorporated into the Monza circuit, which brought Fangio to the pits. They made a jury-repair to his car and gave it to Castellotti to nurse round. Then Musso brought his Ferrari in for tyres, well up and hoping to win his country's Grand Prix before his countrymen. Fangio expected to take the car over, as the Championship was at stake, but Luigi, all strung up, refused to hand over and shot back into the fray.

Then Peter, who had seen Fangio sitting on the pit counter, came in and offered his car to the Maestro. He did this quite off his own bat; nobody in the Ferrari pit signalled him to do so. By this sudden, spontaneous act of sportsmanship, he threw aside his own chances of becoming World Champion in order that Fangio could secure the honour. Fangio was delirious, embraced Peter and hopped into the Ferrari, tearing off to take second place only 5 sec. behind Stirling in a most memorable race.

Although Peter was so delightfully casual on the surface, sub-consciously he took that Monza race as seriously as anybody. I had an alarming demonstration of this on the night before the event. The Ferraris were suffering serious tyre troubles on that very fast circuit. Great chunks of tread were being flung off their Englebert tyres owing to the tremendous stresses imposed on the banking, and this preyed on their drivers' minds.

Peter and I were sharing accommodation at the Palace Hotel in Milan, and two or three times during that night I was woken up by Peter's voice crying 'The tyres! the tyres!' as he threshed unhappily through a nightmare. Just what mental torture he was going through at the time, I don't know, neither could he remember in the morning, but, like the rest of the Ferrari drivers, he was obviously terribly worried about the tyre position.

Not surprisingly either; the prospect of a burst tyre on the Monza banking at 170 or 175 m.p.h. was enough to give anybody nightmares. That the fears were justified was demonstrated by

Castellotti and Musso, who both threw treads early in the race. Castellotti's tyre burst on the banking, the Ferrari hurtling down the banking on to the inner track in the path of oncoming cars, his escape being breathtakingly remarkable. The strain on the banking later revealed itself in a different manner on Musso's Ferrari, which broke its steering and just missed crashing into the pits. Poor Luigi was leading at the time, and burst unashamedly into an emotional flood of tears.

Stirling very nearly missed victory at the eleventh hour owing to a slight miscalculation, for he ran out of fuel on the back section of the circuit. As the Maserati's speed dropped, Stirling looked desperately back and saw Piotti's Maserati coming up. He signalled frantically that he wanted a push, and the obliging Italian came up behind Stirling's car until they made gentle contact, then shoved him all round the banking, accelerating as fast as he could to give sufficient impetus for Stirling to coast into the pits, yell for 'Benzina', and get going again under his own power without losing the lead!

Now this was both ingenious and extremely lucky, but unfortunately the Italian television coverage caught the dramatic incident from start to finish, so that everybody knew what Moss and Piotti were up to, and there was a great deal of excited speculation on the unpleasant subject of disqualification. It so happened, however, that there was nothing in the race regulations expressly to forbid such tactics, and Stirling's first place for Maserati could not be challenged. After his cruel luck in this same race in 1954, I feel that few, if any, begrudged Moss his 1956 victory in the Grand Prix d'Europe.

Turning to the sports-car races of 1956, both Stirling and Peter enjoyed highly interesting and successful seasons. I have already listed Stirling's main successes, which were so numerous that season that there is no space to deal with them in detail. Some, however, must not go unmentioned, and one race in particular, the Mille Miglia, ended in inglorious failure.

Having won this event in 1955 with a 300SLR Mercedes, you might expect that Stirling would have been keen to repeat his success. But he wasn't. Back in 1951, when he first drove in this world-famous Italian road race, Stirling said he thought the Mille Miglia was the greatest race in the calendar. This, however, I put down to his more youthful enthusiasm of that time, because by 1956 he had decided, like many other drivers, that it was a highly dangerous affair. He had won it once, and that was enough, thank you.

However, Officine Maserati felt very differently about it. As an Italian company, they were naturally keen to pit their new competition cars in Italy's famous town-to-town race against the rival Ferraris. In Moss they felt they had the ideal driver; after all, what he and Denis Jenkinson could do in 1955 for Mercedes, they surely could repeat in 1956 for Maserati?

Unfortunately, the Italian concern could not match the mighty Daimler-Benz organization when it came to resources, planning and organization, and although Stirling and Jenks were to have a brand-new 3·5-litre Maserati, it was very much a rush job. Mechanics were working on the car right up to the last hour before the start, which did not increase the confidence of its crew.

Stirling and Jenks left Brescia in very bad conditions, feeling far from happy but determined to make the best of it. They were well on the way to Rome when, approaching a right-hand corner, the incredible 'understeer' of the Maserati took charge in the wet, and the car just went straight on.

The car went off the road in the biggest fashion ever, mounted a small parapet, and charged down a steep slope, its headlong plunge being arrested only by a small but very tough tree. Stirling and Jenks leapt out, awed at their escape from what looked like certain and painful death, thanks only to a single tree, growing in the right spot. They gazed at the scene in mingled horror and relief, then Jenks said: 'Crikey! And I haven't even got my camera.'

So Maserati's aspirations in the Mille Miglia were not realized, and Ferrari scored a rousing one, two, three victory, with Peter Collins finishing second. Peter followed the fashion in having a bearded partner too, that well-known racing photographer and journalist Louis Klemantaski. Louis enjoyed the 1000 Miles tretremendously, taking some wonderful pictures which were later published throughout the world.

The Mille Miglia winner was that extremely courageous driver Eugenio Castellotti, who drove the finest race of his career, and gained if possible further endearment in the hearts of the Italian public. I would say that, of all the Italian drivers who have met their fate in a racing car apart from Alberto Ascari, Eugenio Castellotti's death while practising at Modena early the following year created the most sorrow in the hearts of the Italian public.

Stirling's luck with the sports Maserati changed for the Nurburgring 1000-kilometre race, a month after the Mille Miglia. This is a race in which Stirling always revels, first because it is a sports-car race, which he likes, and secondly because it is at Nurburg, on Europe's most difficult circuit. Over those sinuous, winding, plunging fourteen miles of the Ring, any disadvantages of a car can be balanced out, or at least materially reduced, by brilliant driving.

That year Stirling's own car broke down, and he took over the second car in the Maserati team, whisking past the Ferraris in an epic drive to win. The victory was shared by three other drivers, Jean Behra, Harry Schell and Piero Taruffi, although none will deny that it was Moss's magnificent spurt which gained the day.

When Stirling wasn't driving Maseratis in sports-car events, he drove Aston Martins, and as Peter Collins was a long-established member of the Feltham équipe, he and Stirling found themselves as team mates on occasions. They were paired together for Le Mans, 1956, and I think that but for slight mechanical bothers they would almost certainly have won the race. As it was, they finished second after leading for a time in pouring rain.

It was in the Rouen G.P. that we had a further insight into Peter's sportsmanship. Rouen is a beautiful circuit, in some ways similar to Nurburg although nothing like so long; it has a very fine road surface, and the sort of corners in which the real drivers revel. Aston Martin were running there against Ferrari, and at this stage Astons were beginning to fit disc brakes to their cars. These had not achieved the stage of perfection they have reached today, and slightly affected the steering of the cars. Now Peter, who was quite a technician in his way, had worked things out and decided that the drum-braked car would be better at Rouen, specifically asking team manager John Wyer if he could have such a car.

When the team got going at Rouen in practice, it was found that Peter's car had by far the best handling of the four entered. On the other hand Stirling proved to be the fastest driver, and, on learning of this, Peter promptly handed his drum-braked car to

Stirling, and took over the disc-braked one. Moss was certainly happier in Peter's car, but despite this, he could do nothing about the leading Ferrari. This was most ably driven by Castellotti, who took Fangio's place when the 'old man' decided to have a break from racing, and won by 3·9 sec. from Stirling. Peter had to retire from the race with engine trouble.

There was also an up to 1500 c.c. race at Rouen, and by then we had purchased and built up a Cooper-Climax. Instead of Stirling driving this, we nominated Peter Jopp, an old friend of ours. Unfortunately Peter had an accident early in the race, going off at a corner on the first lap, and overturning. His shoulder was dislocated and the Cooper quite badly damaged, but just why the accident happened we have never found out. Peter thought it might have been due to an unscrubbed new tyre which had been fitted, and if the uninitiated find this puzzling, I would tell them that until a new tyre has been taken round a few laps so that the tread has been slightly roughened and the 'gloss' removed, adhesion is very poor, and can quickly cause trouble at racing speeds.

Writing of Coopers reminds me that earlier in the season Stirling had won the British Empire Trophy race at Oulton Park, driving a borrowed 1500 c.c. Cooper-Climax. This belonged to a young driver called Mike McDowel, who was running with the Cooper works team at the time, although he owned the car.

Stirling also drove a 1½-litre Maserati on one occasion during 1956, in the sports-car race at Nurburg preceding the German G.P. The 1500 c.c. Maserati was perhaps one of the worst sports cars the Modena concern ever produced. It is strange, but the Italians, like the Americans, seem unable to produce a really satisfactory small car, and much of Britain's success in the smaller capacity classes is attributable to our use of ultra-light chassis and components, for the Lotuses, Coopers and so on certainly hadn't the power output of the Italian cars then.

At Nurburg, only Stirling's driving ability enabled him to hold off Roy Salvadori in the works 1500 c.c. Cooper-Climax, but even so, he couldn't do anything about Hans Herrmann in a works Porsche.

It was after the German G.P. meeting that Moss flew back to England to compete in a race which many would prefer to forget, so bad were the conditions. This was the second *Daily Herald* International Trophy race, organized at Oulton Park by the B.R.S.C.C. The old weather clerk was definitely not on our side this time, and I have seldom if ever seen more rain at one meeting. Only the notorious *Daily Express* Formula 1 race at Silverstone in 1951, which had to be stopped after six laps owing to the terrible rainstorm and flooded track, could compare.

At Oulton Park, the morning's weather forecast said 'rain and gales', and how right they were! It was raining when the first race started, and by the time the big race was due to start the heavens just opened and dropped the lot. Our organization was stretched to its very limit in our efforts to cope, for the entire circuit became waterlogged, and lakes began to form at some of the corners. At Old Hall a particularly large one collected, all the drainways becoming blocked with leaves, grass and other litter which was washed down. The only way to get rid of it was to take the fire tender down there and pump the water away from the corner into a ditch some twelve or fourteen yards off the road.

Other fire pumps performed similar tasks elsewhere on the course, all appropriately fitted with Coventry Climax engines! The flood of water brought other troubles, washing large areas of mud on to the course, and adding to the drivers' difficulties. Gallant marshals swept as much of this away as possible, but as fast as they swept, more mud collected.

As a result of all this, the race was nearly an hour late in starting, so we cut the distance from 56 to 40 laps, and arranged to take drivers on a tour of inspection before sending them off. David Murray of the Ecurie Ecosse decided not to run his two Le Mans-winning D-type Jaguars, an action few if any understood, for none of the other cars withdrew, while the crowd endured their prolonged soaking stoically, determined to see the racing.

They certainly witnessed some splendid driving, particularly from Stirling in one of the four works Aston Martins. He won after what can only be described as a remarkable drive, adding further to his great reputation as a wet-road driver.

Yet I must stress that, despite this reputation of his, Stirling does not like wet circuit conditions any more than any other driver; it is simply that he wholly applies himself to the task, and utilizes all his delicate 'feel' in controlling the car under slippery conditions. That wet-road driving is perhaps his greatest forte was already demonstrated six years earlier when he won his first major victory, the 1950 T.T. at Dundrod, and all who witnessed him in action at Oulton Park at the *Daily Herald* meeting will agree to his greatness.

Starting off on streaming roads, he had pulled out a lead of over 6 sec. on the very first lap, practically hidden in flying spray. By the fifth lap he was lapping the tail-enders and had 23 sec. lead over Tony Brooks in another Aston Martin. By the twelfth lap he had lapped every car apart from his three team mates, Brooks, Salvadori and Parnell, and eventually he won by over 1¾ min. from Brooks, the other two Astons being third and fourth, over a lap behind.

Not content with this remarkable performance, Moss then took out the 1500 c.c. Cooper-Climax, which had been repaired after its Rouen prang, and won the 1½-litre race for the *Sporting Life* Trophy by nearly two minutes from the second man. It was so dark by then, and the course still so slippery, that we of the B.R.S.C.C. decided to cut the distance from 25 to 10 laps.

I don't think Stirling was quite so happy in the Aston Martin team that season as Peter was. He was less familiar with the methods of the Feltham équipe, and in some ways found them irksome. Many people wondered why he chose to join Astons in 1956, rather than Jaguars, for he had always got on extremely well with 'Bill Lyons, 'Lofty' England and the rest of the Coventry team.

It was, in fact, a question of leadership, for when Stirling joined Mercedes-Benz in 1955, his place as First Driver in the Jaguar team was taken by Mike Hawthorn. Mike did extremely well for the team that season, and, understandably, Jaguars were not prepared to demote him to No. 2 in order that Stirling could rejoin them in 1956. We had some long discussions on the subject, and although I am sure that the two drivers could have reached a satisfactory compromise, and would have enjoyed driving together, it was eventually decided that Stirling would join Aston Martin, who had asked him to lead the team.

This 'No. 1' business may sound 'big-headed', but it should be remembered that Stirling was a very fast, experienced driver, of great value to any team, and it meant that he would be fully given his head to tackle the formidable opposition in sports-car racing in those days.

At any rate, it gave him the chance to drive a British car, for although he had chosen to join Maserati for World Championship events, and they had wanted him to drive for them in certain sports-car races as well, the desire to drive British was strong within Stirling, and growing stronger all the time.

Even so he did not find it easy in the Aston Martin set-up, largely, I think, owing to differences of personality. Now the head of the Aston Martin Competitions Department, and the racing manager at that time, was that notable figure John Wyer. John is a pleasant, very serious person, but I think in my own mind that he and Stirling were at completely opposite poles, and seldom saw eye to eye.

John Wyer at that time was, in my opinion, entirely overworked; he was responsible for the technical development of the Aston Martin production cars and for almost the entire development and running of the racing team. I have always found him a very fair and understanding person to negotiate with, but I can imagine him also to be very much misunderstood by his team. Modelling his methods perhaps too literally on the world-famous Mercedes-Benz organization, he tended to be too much the strict disciplinarian. He lacked the keen sense of humour possessed by Neubauer, which is so necessary to control a team. Racing drivers as a group tend to be boyish, and readily give way to their sense of humour, otherwise they don't enjoy life, and unless the manager can match their mood, and cloak his demands in good humour, he is in for a difficult time from the word 'go'.

I remember we had several minor difficulties with Aston Martins. They always made it a principle that ninety per cent of all prize money would be divided equally amongst the team. Thus, if three cars were entered, two retired, and the other won the race, its driver shared the winnings, less ten per cent for the mechanics, equally amongst the other team drivers regardless of individual merit in that particular race.

This, in some ways, is a very fair way of doing things, but it is unusual, and Stirling for one preferred to rest on his own laurels and nobody else's. If he's going to win, he likes his full share of the prize money and doesn't want to share it with others. On the other hand, he is completely adamant that, if somebody else wins, he doesn't want a share of their winnings. They drove, and they won, and therefore he considers that they alone are entitled to the benefits, less any taken by the firm or given to the mechanics. The latter is a splendid scheme which could well be extended, as it keeps up the morale of the entire staff and gives added incentive to work well.

The Feltham team also tended to do things in a heavy, too-highly organized manner. Before each race meeting, long and detailed movement schedules were drafted, hotels were arranged, often without consideration of individual preferences, and the whole procedure resembled a military operation. Discipline is highly necessary, of course, particularly with a team contesting big races which are vitally important to its prestige, but I have always clung to the belief that, if you want the best from your drivers, they must go to the line happy, and minor pinpricks caused by excessive control do not make for complete happiness or ease of mind.

Immediately after the Grand Prix of Europe at Monza, Peter Collins and I set off for Modena, where we were to meet Enzo Ferrari, head of the most famous Scuderia in the world, to discuss the terms of Peter's contract for 1957. I had never visited the Ferrari sanctuary at Maranello before, although I had often seen the Ferrari service department in Modena itself, within a stone's throw of the Maserati establishment. Maranello, however, was the headquarters and the very heart of the Ferrari empire, and I looked forward to our visit.

When we arrived, I first met the team manager, Sculati, and was then introduced to Enzo Ferrari himself, with whom I had a most interesting discussion through an interpreter. He asked me various questions about British drivers, and talked extensively of Peter, whom he kept describing as 'buono piloto, buono piloto'. Pete, being the friendly soul that he was, got on very well with Enzo Ferrari, who developed a genuine affection for the boy from Kidderminster.

For the actual negotiation of the 1957 contract, Ferrari handed me back to Sculati, from whom I was able to gain several improvements in terms for Peter, getting him a better financial return altogether. I would observe here that several drivers, though excellent at the wheel of a racing car, show less ability when it comes to matters of contracts and business on their own behalf. At one time the offer of a contract from Ferrari was like dangling a carrot before a donkey, but I would say this is less so today. Speaking from practical experience, I don't think the Ferrari contract offers very much; it is not a particularly worthwhile contract, and although to drive for Ferrari may be a tremendous boost to a driver's prestige, it can also do a driver harm.

For example, although the contract reads rosily on first examination, offering the driver a certain percentage of the moneys received from events entered, it gives no guarantee of any specific number of races for that driver, nor does it give a minimum guarantee of the amount of money he will receive per event, or per annum.

This may work well in a busy Grand Prix season, but there are other types of event which are less remunerative, such as Le Mans. This long-distance classic requires plenty of pre-race work, drivers usually having to spend a full week there. Under the Ferrari contract the driver is required to pay his own travel expenses to get there, and for his own accommodation. Being Le Mans, accommodation is in heavy demand, so hotels become extra expensive.

As to the race itself, no starting money is paid at Le Mans, and a driver and his co-driver may get a car round for twenty-three of the twenty-four hours and then break down. Result: no prize money, no bonuses, no nothing, except for some heavy bills for living at Le Mans for a week, and the privilege of driving in one of the hardest and least popular races of the year.

One subject we discussed with Sculati was the forthcoming Argentine *Temporada* which opened the 1957 season, and I remember that Peter insisted on crossing by boat, rather than fly. This was not because of any dislike of flying, but because of his great love for the sea.

If Peter had not taken up motor racing so seriously, I am sure he would have spent his entire life on the water. He was a natural sailor, and was the fortunate co-owner, with his father, of a beautiful craft which they kept moored in the River Dart at Dartmouth. Called the *Genie Maris*, this was a converted trawler, beautifully fitted out.

So Sculati arranged for him to travel by Italian liner from Genoa in company with the German member of the Scuderia Ferrari, Count Wolfgang Berghe von Trips, a fun-loving youngster despite his pompous and seldom-used title, who usually went by the highly democratic nickname of 'Taffy'! Ferrari's contract, by the way, stipulated that, while the concern paid drivers' travelling expenses to places outside Europe, the journey always started from Modena. By this arrangement Pete was obliged to pay his own fares to Italy every time he went from England for a race. This seemed a bit hard and I tried to get it changed, but without success. As Peter was to live in Modena during most of the season, he didn't bother overmuch, anyway.

Whilst I was at Modena, Peter arranged for me to be shown around Maranello. This was a most interesting visit, for the Ferrari works are considerably larger than Maserati's, and the sight of numerous delectable Ferrari sports cars on the production lines was mouth-watering. During the war, and for a period afterwards, Ferraris produced machine tools, but these were later dropped in order to concentrate on car production.

There were no locked doors or 'Keep Out' notices at Maranello when I went, and they let me go where I wished. I saw the new Formula 1 team cars being prepared for Argentina, several competition sports cars, and their new Gran Turismo models. It was interesting how the Grand Prix V8s, which had been 'inherited' from Lancia when that concern withdrew from racing in mid-1955, were acquiring Ferrari 'personality'. By now they had slightly lengthened chassis, and much improved road holding, while the famous side tanks, set between the wheels, had become empty sponsons, with the exhaust pipes jutting through. Already they were planning to discard the side tanks altogether, and after the Argentine races the Lancia-Ferrari V8s began to look like orthodox racing cars again.

I also had a look round the Modena branch of Ferrari, and there beheld a sad sight. This was a Fiat '500' which had been converted by Abarth. It had belonged to Enzo Ferrari's son Dino, who had died from natural causes. Shortly before he became ill, it seems that Dino parked his Fiat there, and after his death Enzo Ferrari would not permit it to be moved. It was just covered over with a dust sheet, and, as far as I know, remains in the same place today.

Ferrari himself is a very modest man. Although a unique figure in Italy, and an important industrialist in his own right, he lives quietly in a modest flat, without any of the inflated standards which a man in his position might adopt. His tastes are simple, and he runs around in an ordinary Fiat '1100' saloon.

He has his eccentricities, and all who have a hand in the negotiation of Ferrari entries for any particular race are well aware of his financial hardheadedness. He is a man of remarkable perception, with an uncanny ability for summing up the personality of people. I once attended a private dinner-party given by Ferrari, in the company of Peter Collins, Bernard Cahier, Sculati and others. We went to a very well-known Modena restaurant called Da Finis, Enzo Ferrari talking most volubly.

I couldn't understand all that was being said, but Peter told me afterwards that Ferrari had been summing up the drivers then making up the Grand Prix circus, giving a word portrait of their characters, mentality, temperament and individual foibles. Peter said that these portraits were pinsharp and, in some instances, brutally accurate. He spoke, it seems, of Stirling's seriousness, Peter's happy-go-lucky attitude, the changing moods of Mike Hawthorn, the gay, 'schoolboy' play of Harry Schell, the talented, gentlemanly Trintignant. And so on.

That Enzo Ferrari never attends a race meeting is now almost traditional, but he goes to Monza for practice, and though he may not be seen when his cars are out on the circuit fighting for Grand Prix honours, his influence is certainly not absent. He keeps tabs on everything, virtually controlling the team from Modena. His team manager reports back at the end of each practice session, and acts on his instructions.

It is this virtual dictatorship by Ferrari which has brought him so much success, in my opinion. His knowledge of motor racing is tremendous, and his orders are backed by equal experience. Racing demands quick decisions, and for these to take immediate effect, firm control is essential. A parallel to Ferrari in many ways is Tony Vandervell, and again, it will always be my belief that the Vanwall success was largely due to Vandervell's iron will and strong personality.

It was a contrast, after the cold singlemindedness of Enzo

Ferrari, to meet a character like the Marquis Alfonso (Fon) de Portago at Modena. Fon was not only a valuable customer to Ferrari, being extremely wealthy; he was also valuable as a driver, for this colourful Spaniard had undeniable talents. After doing well with his own sports cars, he joined the team in 1956, driving both sports and Grand Prix machines with mounting skill.

He was a fascinating character, and like many who are wealthy, could get away with things which less well-endowed people would never dare to attempt. He was extremely humorous, he frequently looked like a tramp, and often lived like one too. He went about the world as if he couldn't afford a haircut; he seldom shaved until late evening, carrying a dark, unsavoury growth of stubble, yet on other occasions I have seen Fon looking as immaculate as the Spanish grandee which in truth he was.

He was a fanatical sportsman, being an accomplished athlete, an acknowledged expert on the Cresta Run, where he led the European bobsleigh team on more than one occasion, boxer, swordsman, polo and tennis player, an experienced flier and an expert horseman, being the only man who has raced at Aintree both on four legs and four wheels. In general he was one of those incredible people of the world who love danger, live dangerously, and couldn't imagine living any other way. He had other accomplishments too, and was on very good terms with many of the most beautiful women of this world.

Fon's death, like his life, was violent, but very sudden. His Ferrari was smashed to pieces when, apparently, the transmission broke, and a wheel came off at about 150 m.p.h. during the 1957 Mille Miglia, killing him, his co-driver Eddy Nelson, and, by terrible misfortune, eleven spectators at a tiny village outside Mantua. As a result the 'shock wave', which was receding after the Le Mans catastrophe of 1955, was repeated in lesser fashion, and road racing in Italy was banned. The old town-to-town Mille Miglia race has never been held since.

Opposite the Ferrari works at Maranello is a compact little roadhouse comprising a café/restaurant and a few pleasant apartments. This is owned by Ferrari, many of his employees enjoying an aperitif or a meal, while Enzo himself often entertains visitors there to lunch when out at Maranello.

For 1957, Peter Collins was to have a small flat on these premises, an arrangement which he relished. Peter loved the Continental life, and in particular life in Italy. As I have said, he was rather a lackadaisical, placid sort of character, difficult to involve in an argument of any gravity, ever ready to grin at life, fond of a glass of chianti and Italian food; so the life out there completely suited him.

He had become fluent in the language, and was right on top of his work. He undertook a lot of testing for Ferrari, and took a very close interest in the development of the Grand Prix cars.

And what facilities they have there for testing! If we want to test a racing car in Britain, we have all the paraphernalia of booking a circuit—and often, when you have booked, say, Silverstone or Goodwood, and paid quite a reasonable fee, down comes the rain, testing is impossible, and the day has been wasted.

At Ferraris, Maseratis also, the men work on the car at the factory, and when it is ready, the test driver dons a pair of gloves and a crash helmet, climbs in the car, is pushed off into the main road, and drives straight off through the village, up on to the mountain road, turns round at the crossroads and drives straight back to the works.

All is done within an hour. He gives his report and comments, further adjustments may then be made, and off he goes again up the road with a hearty bellow from the Grand Prix exhaust, to try out the new mods. And this process will be repeated until the car is right. The population don't complain—they love it. The sound of a Ferrari winding up into fifth gear as it approaches the little mountain village above Maranello brings everybody out to the windows or into the streets, to watch the car and cheer its driver. No wonder Italian cars have dominated racing for so long, with such facilities. The lack of them in Britain makes the Vanwall, Cooper and other marques' achievements all the more praiseworthy.

If Ferraris wish to do some prolonged testing on a real circuit, they simply drive the car or cars the twelve kilometres or so to the Modena Autodrome. No problem of getting them into transporters and wasting time that way; they just go roaring down the road, and come back later in the day. More serious testing can be conducted at Monza, which is some 150 miles away, and although they have driven the cars there and back on occasions, it is not really practical for Grand Prix machines, so they take them in the big grey transporters which have been seen in every circuit paddock in Europe at some time or another.

As 1956 drew to a close, Stirling notched up a remarkable score of victories for Maserati in diverse parts of the globe. He began with the Venezuelan G.P. at Caracas, which is a fantastic town, made ultra-wealthy by the oil found in the country, and an extremely expensive place to live in. Perhaps to accentuate this, or to outdo other race promotors, the organizers decided to give a very special gold cup to the winner of the G.P.

Now it is generally accepted, and more often than not laid down in the contract, that trophies which are specifically awarded to the entrants of the winning car are retained by entrants and, vice versa, that trophies awarded to the driver are kept by him. Maserati's agreement to this was their misfortune in the case of the G.P. of Venezuela, as Stirling, the driver of the winning car, was handed this cup of pure gold, believed to be the most valuable trophy ever to be awarded for motor racing.

Needless to say, this is one trophy which we do not have on display too frequently; it spends most of its life securely locked away in a strong-room.

Stirling's car was a 3-litre sports Maserati, and he beat World Champion Fangio in a Ferrari fair and square, finishing 19·2 sec. ahead of him. The American Masten Gregory was third with another Ferrari.

After Venezuela, Stirling's travels continued, for we had planned a remarkable itinerary for him involving travels of some 40,000 miles. From Caracas he made a brief visit to Nassau, and then went on to Australia, where he was competing in two races, the Australian Tourist Trophy and the Australian Grand Prix.

This was Australia's year for the Olympic Games, and Australia was flooded with world-famous athletes, journalists and others following the Games. Naturally the Grand Prix organizers wanted to make the most of their races that year, and they were staged over the $3\frac{1}{4}$-mile circuit running around the lake in Albert Park, right in the heart of Melbourne, the 'Olympic City'. The sponsors made a splendid job of the meetings, and for the first time secured works entries from a European racing concern—Maserati—with Stirling and Jean Behra as the drivers. They sent out two 3-litre 'sixes' for the sports-car T.T., and two of the newest, very sleekly bodied G.P. cars, for the Formule Libre Grand Prix, with team manager Ugolini accompanying them.

Stirling won both events, and Behra was second on both occasions, the races being watched not only by a vast concourse of the Australian public, but by most of the Olympic Games contenders as well. Amongst these was Chris Brasher, who had scored an epic victory in the 3000-metre steeplechase, winning one of the very rare Olympic gold medals. Chris was extremely keen on motoring sport, being quite a rally fan, and it happened that, some weeks later when he was back in England, he visited that London hub of all motoring sportsmen, the Steering Wheel Club. I was there with Alfred Moss, and Chris joined us. I introduced him to Alfred, and Chris began talking about the Australian races and how he had seen Stirling score that remarkable 'double', when Alfred turned to him and said, 'Oh, were you out there?'!

I feel, at this point, that I should say something about the relationship between Stirling Moss and Jean Behra. When Moss joined Mercedes-Benz in 1955, Behra became No. 1 in the Maserati team, and when Moss returned to Maserati as No. 1 in 1956, it was thought by many that there would be bad blood between Behra, displaced to No. 2, and Stirling.

This was never the case; in fact, Stirling and Jean were the very best of friends. I don't think Behra ever considered himself to be a better driver than Moss, and in 1956 found himself in much the same position that Stirling was, in 1955, following Fangio round the circuits. He accepted the situation with equanimity, putting up some splendid performances during the year.

Jean was a great tactician and a tremendous fighter, with the courage of a lion, and he and Stirling had a thorough understanding between them. Behra greatly enjoyed testing a car, and would cheerfully pass his time at Modena, staying at the hotel and going down to the autodrome for suspension, steering, shock absorber, or some other tests, day after day. He was quite a clever engineer, being one of those rare people who can explain clearly to the designer or chief mechanic what he considers is wrong with a car, or what it needs to improve it.

Stirling would always do his share of testing when required, but so much of his life was spent travelling around and living from a suit-case that he did not relish the thought of spending time down at Modena when he might be at home. He was only too glad to leave it to the enthusiastic Behra when convenient.

After his Australian tour, Stirling flew back to Nassau for the third race meeting on the 3½-mile Windsor circuit. He had hoped to have a 3-litre works Maserati to drive, but the car with which he won the Venezuelan G.P. at Caracas was sold immediately afterwards. He therefore arranged to drive an older 3-litre Maserati, owned by Bill Lloyd, with whom Stirling had co-driven to victory at the 1954 Sebring in Briggs Cunningham's O.S.C.A.

This Maserati had covered over 33,000 miles since new, and became somewhat battered when Lloyd pranged it during one of the smaller events at Nassau. They knocked it straight in time for the 210-mile Nassau Trophy race, and rather to Stirling's surprise he won the race comfortably from Masten Gregory's and de Portago's Ferraris.

Stirling's family were there to watch him. For a long time he had been trying to get them to come out to Nassau. He thought his father had been working too hard, and he wanted his mother and sister Pat to have a holiday as well. So it was arranged that the whole family would go out there, meeting Stirling when he came back from Australia, all spending Christmas together.

It had been planned originally that I should accompany the Mosses to Nassau, and we had all booked rooms at the British Colonial Hotel. By then, however, I had for some time been enjoying the friendship of a girl called Ann Tyrrell, one of the principal dancers in the musical show *Kismet*, currently on at the Stoll. Stirling and I had first been taken to see this show by a mutual friend from Rotherham, where my people live. Afterwards we invited Ann to join us for dinner at the Colony Restaurant in Berkeley Square. This proved the most important meeting in my life, for this young lady later became my wife.

Now Ann had been in *Kismet* ever since the show opened, first as one of the leading chorus dancers, then being promoted to a leading part as one of the three princesses of Ababu. *Kismet* had a very successful run lasting for two-and-a-half years, during which time Ann never missed a performance, and consequently never had a holiday. It had been agreed between us that as soon as the opportunity occurred we would take a holiday together, giving her a chance to forget the show for a while.

That opportunity came early in December 1956, when the London run at the Stoll Theatre finished, and before the show went on tour the cast were given a week's holiday. This happened quite unexpectedly, so we therefore decided to cancel my visit to Nassau and to go holidaying together instead. We hunted through a few catalogues and travel agents' brochures, finally deciding to go down to the south coast of Spain, which was the best place we could think of to find some sun in December.

We flew to Gibraltar, then hired a car and drove across the Straits and along the coast until we reached a pleasant little village called Marbellya. There we found a wonderfully modern *hacienda* type of hotel, which was run by an Austrian who had emigrated to Spain, and had a really wonderful week's holiday. There was fine food and plenty of good wine, warm sunshine and a restful atmosphere. The sea, unfortunately, was too cold to bathe in, but we greatly enjoyed our stay, Ann had a welcome break from the show, and the week passed much too quickly. Then we flew back to England, Ann went on tour with *Kismet*, starting in Glasgow, and I went back to work at the two London offices.

A few days later the country was plunged into alarm and despondency through the Suez crisis, and the introduction of petrol rationing made things black for the motoring public. I woke up on the Saturday morning and looked out of the window. It was raining cats and dogs. I glanced at the newspapers, but they carried nothing but grave news. Then I thought about the car, and realized that the tank was empty.

There and then I phoned up the travel agent and booked a flight to Nassau, then telephoned Stirling and asked him to re-book my room at the hotel. Afterwards I found I could not get a plane until Monday evening, so I sent Stirling a wire saying I would be arriving at Nassau at about 4 p.m., Tuesday. New York in December is very cold and unpleasant, so getting bookings to the South is far from easy, since everyone who can possibly manage it wants to fly to Florida. I was therefore very pleased to secure a booking to Miami, and thence to Nassau.

But on Monday afternoon thick fog descended on London, the flight to New York was cancelled, and passengers had to travel by train to Prestwick in Scotland, and fly from there. I 'phoned the London office to ask if anything important had happened. 'Yes,' said my secretary, 'a cable has just come from Stirling Moss—it says *Gregory hasn't arrived. Where is he?*' So I said, 'You'd better send him a telegram back saying '*Gregory hasn't departed; fog*'!

But at last we boarded a plane and set off for New York at about 5 p.m., making a very fast crossing of the Atlantic. We arrived at Idlewild airport at 2.30 in the morning, much too late to do anything but sit around, so I went into the barber's shop to freshen up, before fighting for a seat on one of the southbound planes.

Before I left London I had chanced through friends to get hold of the name and address of the Vice-President of Eastern Airlines, and this was to prove extremely useful. When I went up to that Company's counter and explained that I had missed my connexion to Miami owing to delays through fog, the character just laughed at me and said, 'Well, it's no good, buddy, there's about 1500 other guys waiting to get down to Miami, so you'll certainly not get on a plane today!'

I answered: 'I've got the name of your Vice-President here; here's his private telephone number. I want you to call him right away and get him out of bed, because I was told by the Pan-American Vice-President in London to ring him up as soon as I got here, so that he could look after me, and see that I was put on a plane.' This was bluff, of course, but it rather electrified the clerk, besides having the required effect. He got me on the first plane out of Idlewild that morning.

I must say that Christmas in Nassau was fabulous. It was quite unusual to be out in the sun instead of the rain or snow. Suez had caused the cancellation of the third Boxing Day Brands Hatch meeting, so I gave up worrying and just relaxed.

CHAPTER TEN

1957—WONDERFUL YEAR

AFTER our Nassau holiday, the Moss family and I all flew up to New York in time for the New Year, finding the weather a sharp contrast to that in the Bahamas. It was bitterly cold, with blustery snow and an icy wind, but we enjoyed our stay nevertheless, even though the prices in New York were enough to frighten anybody off their feet.

Then we made our way home to England by diverse means, while Stirling flew down to Argentina for the 1957 *Temporada*, where he was to have his final drive in a Grand Prix Maserati before joining the Vanwall team. Yes, Stirling was to drive a British Formula 1 car at last, and was very happy to be doing so. He, Alfred and I had much debating on the subject before we left for Nassau, and the upshot was the signing of a contract with Tony Vandervell.

It has often been said that Mr. Vandervell is a difficult man to deal with. He certainly has a reputation as a 'tough egg', as one might expect of a big businessman, but we encountered no major difficulties in negotiating Stirling's contract with him. It took five or six hours of earnest discussion to settle all points, but it was concluded much more easily than some others we have made.

Vandervell knew what he wanted of Stirling, and what he wanted to pay, conducting the negotiations with keen professional interest. We on our part knew what we wanted; there was no dithering, and I can say, without divulging any figures, that the Vanwall contract was an extremely fair one.

It was with Vandervell's ready consent that Stirling drove in the Argentine races for Maserati, as it had been decided that the Vanwalls could not be ready in time. I was deputed to go to Modena, sort out the accounts side of things with Maseratis, and explain that Stirling would not be driving for them any more as a full-time team member. They were extremely sorry to lose his services, but I think they understood the patriotic motives behind his move, and always maintained the friendliest relationship with him.

So it was that Moss and Fangio found themselves team mates again during the *Temporada*. Fangio won the Argentine G.P.—for the fourth consecutive year!—but Stirling had trouble and could only finish eighth, despite breaking the lap record.

Ferraris had a bad day, and though Peter Collins left Castellotti behind and took the lead from Behra, he was soon out with clutch trouble. Then he took over Perdisa's Ferrari, which was also driven awhile by Von Trips, the trio sharing sixth place. Four Ferraris ran, and all four had clutch trouble, and this, plus the obvious pace of the latest Maseratis, didn't cheer the Maranello team up very much.

They felt better after the 1000-kilometre sports-car race, when no less than four drivers—Perdisa, Castellotti, Musso and Masten Gregory—shared the winning Ferrari. Stirling drove the new and very powerful $4\frac{1}{2}$-litre V8 Maserati with Fangio, but retired, having cracked the lap record three times. Then he took over the Behra/Menditeguy 3-litre Maserati and shared second place with them.

America's qualifying event for the Sports Car Championship, the Sebring 12 Hours, came next. I went over on behalf of Donald Healey to manage his team of three special-bodied Austin-Healeys, which had been carefully prepared by his son Geoffrey in England, and taken out to Florida prior to my arrival.

Before I was due to fly over, Ugolini of Maseratis asked me at very short notice if I could find a driver in England to complete their team. I pondered awhile, and then thought of Roy Salvadori, who told me he would gladly drive at Sebring provided Aston Martin, with whom he had a prior contract, raised no objection. They were not running at Sebring that year, and David Brown gave his consent, so Roy and I went off to Sebring together, travelling by Pan-American to New York, and then by National Airlines to West Palm Beach, where we stayed the night.

While there we met two friends of mine from London, Beecher Moore and his wife Bobby. Beecher is in the printing and office equipment industry, trading as Moore's Modern Methods, and he was on business in America, managing to find himself down in

Florida around Sebring time. He is a tremendous sportsman, and is especially keen on dinghy racing; his enthusiasm was infectious, and a month later I was to try dinghy racing myself, back in England. But more of that later.

After a wonderful meal together at West Palm Beach, the Moores, Roy and I went out that evening to watch a fantastic game called '*Jai Allai*'. This is rather like a complicated game of tennis and is very popular out there. There was a tremendous amount of betting on the game, and the general organization was most impressive. To start with, when we drove up, we were met by a team of youngsters of between sixteen and eighteen, one of whom gave us a disc, then jumped into our car and raced off to park it for us. Once inside and installed in balcony seats, we found two buttons in front of each seat. If you wanted a drink, you pressed button A, when up came a waiter or waitress to take your order. If you wanted to bet on the game, you pressed button B, and another waitress came up, took your bet and your money, placed it on at a sort of tote window, then brought a ticket back to you. If you won, you pressed the button again, up she came for your ticket, collected your winnings, and brought them to you.

The entertainment lasted about two-and-a-half hours, after which we left the arena, gave our disc to one of the car boys, who dashed off like mad and fetched our car. No parking problem, no rushing to the tote, no crush at the bar or other inconveniences— in fact, everything planned the way it ought to be over here.

Next day Roy and I drove out to Sebring, and went our respective ways, he to the Maserati garage, and I to the Austin-Healey team, which was based at one of the motels on the highway leading into Sebring. The three cars were driven by all-American crews, but unfortunately only one finished the 12-hour race. This was driven by a U.S. Air Force major named Gil Gietner and a young Brooklyn second-hand car dealer called Ray Cuomo.

Ray was an extremely amusing character, a typical Brooklyn boy who had been brought up in the tougher section of cosmopolitan New York, and who kept us laughing most of the time. One delightful story of his tells of how, on one of his car deals, he acquired a beautifully maintained Buick undertaker's hearse, resplendent in the traditional black with silver fittings. When he collected it, he drove this hearse in his normal sports-car style, squealing the tyres and generally enjoying himself until he pulled up with a screech of brakes and tyres at a set of traffic lights.

Next to him was a smart sedan, the driver of which looked across disapprovingly, wound his window down and said, 'You ought to be ashamed of yourself, tearing around town like that in that kind of vehicle.'

'Listen, buddy,' answered Ray, 'my passengers ain't complaining!'

In the race at Sebring, Ray Cuomo nearly put out the only Austin-Healey that survived the race, when he lost it on a bend and hit some marker cones. I have seen a photograph of the car, virtually standing on its nose at about 45 degrees, yet it landed back on the track hardly damaged, save for slightly shunted bodywork.

Stirling Moss drove a 3-litre Maserati with Harry Schell, finishing runner-up to Fangio and Behra in the big new V8 4½-litre Maserati. Roy Salvadori co-drove another 3-litre with Carroll Shelby, but they were disqualified for an early refuelling stop. It was not Scuderia Ferrari's day at all, and the best they could manage was Peter Collins's sixth place, shared by Trintignant. The Maranello team were not in the best of spirits, for their driver Eugenio Castellotti had been killed at the Modena Autodrome while testing a G.P. Ferrari just a few days before Sebring, and his loss was very keenly felt.

Immediately after the 12 Hours, I flew from West Palm Beach to Nassau, where Stirling and I were to sort out various legal problems concerned with a plot of land he had purchased on Camperdown Heights, with the intention of building a house there. I also had a long talk with Donald Healey, who was there to look into the question of opening a factory in Nassau to produce his Healey speedboats for the American market.

It was then that Donald and I arranged for further talks later on, when he returned to London, on the business of my handling his public relations work. Thus, by May 1957, I had taken on further responsibility, becoming Press Officer and Public Relations Manager of the Donald Healey Motor Co. Ltd., the Healey Marine Co., and the Healey Car Sales Co. in North Audley Street, London.

I was to retain these offices until early 1959, when pressure of other work meant that I would have to give something up. As Donald did not really need a Public Relations man or a Press Officer by then, we agreed that I would relinquish these posts.

It was not long after I had returned to England following Sebring in 1957 that I received an invitation from Beecher Moore to sail as crew in his Championship dinghy at Burnham, to get an idea of what went on in this rugged sport. Beecher is the Commodore of the Hornet squadron, a very fast class of racing dinghy, and has business interests in the building of such boats.

Moved by his enthusiasm, I had originally bought a GP14 dinghy off the stand at the *Daily Express* Boat Show, then asked Beecher if he could give me some advice on racing it. His immediate answer was that I had bought the wrong sort of boat. The next thing I found was that I had bought a Hornet as well, which I kept with the Royal Corinthian Yacht Club down at Burnham-on-Crouch.

So it was that I 'crewed' with Beecher. Now if you think motor racing is difficult, let me say that dinghy racing is just about the end. At least in a racing car you are surrounded by a cockpit and are reasonably warm—sometimes too warm, perhaps; but in a dinghy race you need to wear oilskins and all sorts of things to protect yourself. You have to get into the water to push the boat off, then you find yourself seated on a plank over the sea; the ropes bite into your hands, the weather is freezing, you are rapidly soaked by salt spray, while the wind blows through and chills you to the marrow—none of which I reckoned was too pleasant!

I also tried a bit of dinghy racing on the Thames, sailing from the Minima Yacht Club just above Kingston Bridge, but the river was far too narrow for my liking, and involved too much complicated manœuvring on crowded waterways. In the end, though I even bought a third boat, a Firefly this time, I decided that dinghy racing was not for me, that it was too slow, and that I didn't understand it sufficiently. So I disposed of the three boats and went back to four wheels.

The European Grand Prix racing season of 1957 began early in April with the Syracuse race in Sicily. Now Moss's contract with Vanwall included a clause whereby it was agreed that before the World Championship series of races which began with the

Monaco G.P. the car would appear in two prior events, and that, should it not perform to expected standards in these, then Stirling was at liberty to cancel the agreement. There was not much chance of this happening, for Tony Vandervell is a notable perfectionist, and Vanwall engineering standards of the very highest. Nevertheless, major snags do occur, as instanced by the B.R.M. in 1956, when both Mike Hawthorn and Tony Brooks terminated their contracts by mid-season—and the idea of a contract, after all, is to cover all possible contingencies.

Well, the Vanwalls were entered for two events preceding Monaco, these being Syracuse and Goodwood, and they developed serious troubles in both. At Syracuse, Stirling was in a commanding position to win when a fuel pipe broke. This was repaired, and he tore back into the race, finishing third and breaking the lap record. The race was won by Peter Collins in a Ferrari, followed by team mate Musso.

Vanwall troubles at Goodwood were even worse, broken throttle connexions losing Moss and Brooks almost certain victory. On the strength of these disappointing performances we could have invoked the 'escape clause' in Moss's Vanwall contract, but the thought never occurred to us. The car was a potential winner, that was obvious, once these minor troubles were eliminated, and Stirling retained immense faith in it.

Tony Vandervell got down to the job of putting the Vanwall right with grim determination, and by the time Monaco came round, the broken throttle connexion bogey had been laid. But Vanwall's troubles were still by no means over, such is the uncertainty of motor racing. The story of Stirling's fourth-lap crash at the Chicane, in the Monaco G.P., and the resultant pile-up which eliminated the Ferraris of Peter Collins and Mike Hawthorn, is well known. He came through the tunnel, leading the Ferraris by a yard or two, but instead of slowing to take the Chicane leading down to the harbour road, the Vanwall careered straight on and charged the barrier, sending wooden poles flying over the course. Result: three of the fastest cars and drivers out, while cunning old Fangio and Tony Brooks picked their way through the mess, finishing first and second with Maserati and Vanwall respectively.

As is so often the case where a 'big name' is concerned, Stirling was blamed by a certain element for the mêlée at the Chicane. 'He was going too fast,' said the pundits; 'he was trying to get well away from Fangio and overdid it', 'he got rattled at Collins's Ferrari on his tail' and so on. Well, I don't have to make excuses for Stirling Moss; like everybody, he has made mistakes, and readily admits them. But he didn't make a mistake at Monaco.

Stirling and I discussed his accident into the early hours after the race, and though I confess that I, too, felt he might have over-done it slightly, it was easily proven that such was not the case. The approach to the Chicane at Monaco is down a slight grade from the tunnel, the turn itself being a quick left and right on to the water front. Had Stirling been overdoing it there, and overshot the corner, he would have put his brakes on hard, in the effort to pull up short of the pole barricade; the wheels would have locked, and left black skid marks on the road just before the turn. There were none, because, for some reason which has never yet been satisfactorily explained, the disc brakes on the Vanwall just didn't operate instantly.

Now a driver of Moss's calibre judges the moment of braking for a corner, not to a second, or half a second, but virtually to one-tenth of a second, and when he presses the brake pedal, he is relying on instantaneous braking effect. With such split-second timing, it is obvious that any delay in the brakes coming on means trouble, as the car is already past the point of safety. The only possible explanation at Monaco was that some fault in the brake circuit reduced their retarding effect, and that, instead of getting 100-per-cent braking, Stirling got only 40 or 50 per cent.

That he instantly realized this is shown by the fact that he then went straight on, instead of attempting to take the Chicane at too great a speed; had there been no barrier in the way he could have pulled up safely, no long poles would have been flung on the road, and the two Ferraris would not have been involved. The folly of erecting this barrier did, in fact, have far-reaching effects, of which more later.

But let me give Stirling, who is a merciless self-critic, the last word on this incident. Quoting from his diary for Sunday, 19 May, I find: '*Up at 9 a.m. to a b—— awful day. Had a good start and led for 3½ laps then the car just didn't stop for the Chicane. I passed it at about 70 m.p.h., crashed through two barriers, hit my nose and wrecked the car; hit my elbow and that was that. Tony Brooks drove a good race and was second to J. Fangio.'*

The following day, Monday 20th, saw the formation of the Union des Pilotes Professionels Internationale; or International Union of Professional Racing Drivers—the U.P.P.I. for short. I think that the drivers at Monaco unanimously felt the organizers were at fault in erecting wooden poles across the road at that point, instead of using spaced straw bales. They were disturbed at the consequent elimination of these cars, which could have had very much more serious consequences on the drivers, and felt it was time that they themselves took a hand in safeguarding themselves.

It was that same day, back in London, that I became engaged to Ann Tyrrell, whom I was to marry later in the year, so that 20 May was of extreme importance in my life. Judge of my surprise, then, when that same day I received a telegram from Monaco, informing me that I had been appointed Assistant Secretary to the U.P.P.I. This puzzled me greatly, until I learned that, when the drivers called the inaugural meeting at Monte Carlo, they had decided to appoint Fangio's manager, Marcello Giambertone, as Secretary of the U.P.P.I. So Peter and Stirling decided that if Fangio's manager was going to be Secretary, then their manager ought to be the Assistant Secretary, in order to watch over affairs in Britain.

So I found myself with another job, and although I have held it ever since, I must confess I have had very little to do. U.P.P.I. came in for criticism right from the start, but undoubtedly it was a good step. None can have a better understanding of the safety measures on a circuit than the drivers themselves, and I think that, with the exception of John Eason Gibson and myself, there are very few race organizers who have ever been in a racing car themselves and can, therefore, fully appreciate the driver's point of view.

Take, for example, straw bales, which are so common a feature of the average improvised circuit. Well placed, they are a very useful safety measure; badly placed, they are highly dangerous. If a car comes too close to one, the hub, and particularly the knock-on-type hub with eared cap, acts like a corkscrew and tries to wind itself in. The bale, being a compressed and solid mass, stops the spinning hub and therefore the wheel tries to climb round the hub. That automatically sends the car end over end, with disastrous results.

There have been many serious accidents caused by straw bales; John Bolster was badly injured at Silverstone in 1949; St John Horsfall met his death there; an ignorant marshal at Sebring once considered that the cars were coming in too close at a corner, so moved them out, altering the line and causing Menditeguy to crash; David Brake was killed at Boreham when his Cooper 500 went through a line of bales.

No-one can have a better idea of the best siting for bales than the actual drivers; at Clermont-Ferrand last year Stirling Moss, Chris Bristow, the late Ivor Bueb and I drove round the circuit in a Peugeot 403 saloon with the sanction of the organizers, to check on the straw bale situation; we got out at every bend and replaced bales which had just been placed any-old-where by officials, simply because they could not visualize the situation as it appears to the racing driver.

An official who has never, perhaps, exceeded 90 m.p.h. in his life, cannot envisage what it is like to approach a corner at, say, 150 m.p.h. At such speeds, an apparently normal right-hand corner is entirely changed. With today's methods of drift and power sliding, the driver is beginning to steer fifty yards before he reaches the bend, and by the time he reaches the apex of the right angle the car is already aiming down the next straight and the driver fully accelerating. No organizer or official or track marshal can appreciate the best siting for straw bales or other safety measures under these circumstances as fully as the drivers, which is where the value of the U.P.P.I. should come in.

The new drivers' organization was quickly to come under the fire of the big guns of the press. In July 1957, a new and novel event was to be organized at Monza. Called the Two Worlds Trophy contest, it was to bring American and European racing together at last, the scene being the new and very bumpy high-speed banked circuit which had been built at Monza in time for the 1955 Italian Grand Prix.

The idea was more or less that of Sig. Bacciagaluppi, Circuit Director of Monza, a man very keen to further the progress of that famous circuit. It was largely his urging which had brought the high-speed banking into existence, and he naturally wanted to justify its construction by using it as much as possible. The Italian G.P. happened only once a year, so he conceived the idea of the Two Worlds race, with America's Indianapolis track racing specialists coming over to do battle with Europe's 'best'.

Unfortunately there were snags to this dream. The Americans were willing enough to come, and everything possible was done to make their appearance worth while, but the problem was to find them some worthy rivals. The Indianapolis track-racing car is a highly specialized piece of machinery; it has only two speeds in the gearbox, one for starting, the other for racing, the whole lap at Indianapolis being covered in the same gear. The engines run at almost constant speed, on a much more restricted revs. range than a European road-racing machine. Even the chassis of many Indianapolis cars is offset, while the offside tyres are chamfered to the shape of the banking, and are of different texture, shape, and, in some cases, size to the nearside tyres, all this to take full advantage of the all left-hand nature of the $2\frac{1}{2}$-mile-long rectangular Indianapolis speedway.

The Monza high-speed circuit was far closer akin to Indianapolis than to a road circuit, main differences being that it was considerably faster and certainly a lot bumpier. Europe not only had no cars to suit such conditions; she had no drivers with track-racing experience either.

The uproar began a fortnight or so before the race, when it was widely reported that the U.P.P.I.—'The racing drivers' trade union' as some papers jeeringly termed it—had issued a statement calling upon its members not to compete in the Monza race. Certain drivers had already made known their feelings in no uncertain manner on the inadvisability of holding the event, and in announcing the so-called U.P.P.I. ban a large proportion of the press, both national and technical, leapt into print, and accused these people of being frightened of a straight high-speed fight with the Americans.

Let me say, straight away, that no such 'ban' was issued by the U.P.P.I. This fiction arose, I believe, as the result of a press statement put out on his own accord by Bernard Cahier, who attended the original meeting of the U.P.P.I. at Monte Carlo, and whose statement was taken by many journalists to be officially issued by U.P.P.I. Had an official statement been issued by Secretary Giambertone, then I, as Assistant Secretary, would have received instructions to circulate it in the British press. Not only did I receive no communication whatsoever during the 1957 Monza trouble, but I have never, during my entire term of office, been instructed to put out a single statement on behalf of the U.P.P.I. organization.

But this aside, the accusations by the press that our drivers were 'frightened' was nothing but a display of ignorance. The truth was, there were no suitable cars; as already explained, a high-speed track car is a highly specialized vehicle, and to expect the European factories to produce something suitable was as ludicrous as expecting the Americans to build a Grand Prix car at equally short notice.

In fact, no European manufacturer, nor any European driver, wanted the Monza 500 Miles to be put on, nor were they consulted when its promotion was being considered. When it was a *fait accompli* and the date, prize money and so on established, then the organizers went round seeking entries. Most of the drivers, however, weren't interested in this, to them, alien form of motor racing, especially when they had no suitable cars to drive. Just because Sig. Bacciagaluppi and his confederates decided to put on a race meeting of a certain kind without consulting the drivers, there was nothing in the world, legally or morally, to compel the drivers to compete. If some of them decided they did not wish to, they had every right to say so, without being branded as 'frightened', 'cowards', 'unsporting' and similar uncomplimentary things, which to my mind simply constituted poor journalism.

In the upshot, the sole rivals to the American specialists were a team of three Jaguar D type sports cars, entered by the Ecurie Ecosse, who, according to the popular press, 'cocked a snoot at the U.P.P.I. and gallantly upheld Europe's reputation'.

Well, they certainly performed gallantly, although, of course, outpaced by the racing single-seaters from the U.S.A. Thanks to various retirements amongst the Americans, mostly due to the bumpy track, the Jaguars finally succeeded in taking fourth, fifth and sixth positions in the aggregate of the three heats making up

the 500 miles, after completely trouble-free runs. Jack Fairman's
fourth-place D type covered 177 laps; twelve less than Jimmy
Bryan's Dean Van lines Special, which won the race outright at
160·2 m.p.h.

When, a year later, the Monza 500-mile race was run for a
second time, several European drivers did, in fact, take part, including Stirling, who drove a special 4½-litre-engined Maserati entered
by the Eldorado ice cream company of Italy. It brought Stirling his
narrowest escape ever in motor racing, the car breaking its steering
arm when he was travelling on the banking at about 180 m.p.h.

The Eldorado Special literally struck the top of the banking,
bounced off, and plunged down to the bottom, completely uncon-
trollable. I wasn't at this meeting, but I do know that Stirling got
out of the car as white as a sheet, though it takes an awful lot to
frighten him. I have seen him come out of some nasty-looking
accidents without turning a hair, but the Monza crash was certainly
not to his liking.

Back to 1957, however. I will not dwell in detail on every race
making up that Championship season, unforgettable though it was.
British ambitions, which had been frustrated for so long, were at
last realized in full measure by Tony Vandervell's splendid Van-
wall cars. Stirling Moss and Tony Brooks shared victory in the
G.P. of Europe at Aintree, and after a setback in the German G.P.,
Stirling went on to win the Pescara G.P. and the Italian G.P. at
Monza, as a result becoming runner-up to Fangio for the World
Championship for the third successive year.

In social and domestic affairs, 1957 was also a big year for
Stirling Moss, Peter Collins and myself. Peter set the ball rolling
in sensational style when without warning there appeared in the
British papers a note that he had become engaged to Louise King,
and intended to marry her at Coconut Grove, Miami, in February
1957.

Now Peter, as I have said, was extremely gay and carefree. On
the rear window of his Ford Zephyr was an amusing sticker label
saying 'I like girls'—and that was the simple truth. He liked them
very much, and the number and variety of his lady friends drew
much amused comment, not to say envy, from the motor-racing
world. Doubtless he broke a few feminine hearts, for Peter was a

handsome and charming young man, but he never took his friend-
ships too seriously, which was why we were all so astonished to
learn of his sudden engagement.

Louise was an extremely talented actress, born and bred in
America, and the daughter of Mr Andrew Cordier, the Executive Assistant to the United Nations' Secretary-General, Dag
Hammarskjold. She was well known in motor-racing circles,
being extremely keen on cars, and doing quite a bit of racing with
an Austin-Healey. Her most successful stage show was when she
played the female lead opposite Eddie Bracken in the touring show,
The Seven Year Itch.

Peter's decision was so sudden that, when I first got news of it
while staying down at Tring with Alfred and Aileen Moss, I impulsively dashed to the telegraph office and sent him a lengthy
telegram, urging him to reconsider his position, at least until he
had spoken to his father and mother about it, and had introduced
Louise to them.

Well, Peter did speak to them on the telephone, received their
blessing, and the wedding duly took place on 11 February. Peter's
marriage to Louise proved an exceptionally happy one, for they
were very well suited to each other.

Stirling was next on the list. He and twenty-one-year-old
Katherine Stuart Molson had been friendly for some time now,
and their engagement was hardly the surprise that Peter's was, for
the couple had first met in Nassau a few years before. 'Katie' is a
Canadian girl, daughter of F. Stuart Molson of Montreal, owner of
one of Canada's oldest-established breweries. Like many Cana-
dians, Katie speaks French fluently, is a great water-skiier, an
expert at snow-skiing and an excellent shot.

We put out Stirling's engagement notices on 16 April, which was
just before the B.A.R.C.'s Goodwood race meeting on Easter
Monday. It was also quite by coincidence that the B.A.R.C. held
a cocktail party for drivers and the press that same evening at the
Savoy Hotel. Stirling and Katie were attending this, and when
they walked into the room they were met by a whole barrage of
photographers and pressmen, and the Goodwood race meeting,
which was the main object of the party, was rather subjugated to
that of Stirling's engagement.

I shall never forget Stirling's priceless remark in a speech he made at this party. He said, 'Of course, I realize this is a foolish time to get engaged because Peter Collins has just got married and has released such a flood of crumpet on to the market, and now I can't do anything about it.'

After their wedding, which was to take place six months later, the couple planned to live in Nassau, in the house Stirling was to build on the rather wild but beautiful plot of land he had bought at Camperdown Heights, on the north-west part of the island.

In the designing and building of this house, Stirling revealed that his capabilities are not confined to motor racing alone by any means. He took tremendous interest in building and interior decoration, and incorporated all his ideas into this house which stands on rising ground off the coast road, looking right out on to the Caribbean Sea.

The design and specification are his own, worked out under the supervision of a qualified architect, and he did much of the building too, aided by local labour. During its construction throughout 1957, Stirling had me running about like a cat on hot bricks back in London. I had to arrange for decorating and plumbing materials, bags of nails, pots of paint, special bits of timber and all sorts of things to be sent out to Nassau. I even purchased a Jeep and had that sent out, so that after a few weeks I had acquired quite an expert shipping knowledge, and could practically quote the name and sailing date of every ship sailing from the port of Liverpool or Tilbury for the Bahamas.

Meanwhile there were further Moss activities much nearer home. Alfred, Stirling and I formed an equal partnership in a new venture, a coffee-cum-hamburger bar which we called the Beef-burger, but which, I understand, is generally referred to as the 'Mossburger' in sporting circles! We had been rather taken with the idea of opening a hamburger bar in London, suitable premises already existing virtually underfoot, beneath Alfred Moss's dental surgery in William IV Street.

These premises had been empty since the war, when Alfred Moss had used them as a dental laboratory. Situated on Crown property, they have an interesting history, having once formed part of the Royal Mews, where the coaches, horses and grooms were all housed. Visitors to the restaurant will see that the room is arched, and in fact during its construction we had to build up the floor some four or five feet to raise it to street level. The considerable depth of the original building was to accommodate the largest coaches, on which the long shafts were pushed up and over, requiring ample height.

Above the coach house the horse stables were situated, and above them, on the third floor, were the grooms' quarters. This structure proved very adaptable for our purposes, and we set to work on what was to become the Beefburger. We chose this name as a variation on the word Hamburger, which we thought too stereotyped and misleading. A hamburger contains no ham; the name derives from the town of Hamburg, and a hamburger in fact constitutes pure shredded beef, pressed into a little flat cake weighing about two ounces; this is put on to a griddle and fried for one minute on either side, and then placed in the centre of a hot, toasted, sweet bun. It can be had with or without onion, is usually served with tomato relish or sweet pickle, and is extremely popular with people in search of a quickly prepared snack or light lunch.

The Beefburger was opened early in March 1957, when we gave a champagne party to the press. Stirling was in America at the time, but his sister Pat, his mother, father and I entertained the press, and successfully launched the business. Since then it has gone from strength to strength. As a business it is relatively straightforward to run, and as a contrast with motor-racing activities is surprisingly interesting.

It was in our joint launching of this enterprise that I had further insight into the kindness and shrewd business sense of Alfred Moss. Initially, he, Stirling and I agreed that each would lay down one-third of the required capital, but as my resources were much more limited than theirs, Alfred suggested that they would put up the necessary capital on my behalf, and that, should the business prove successful, I would then reimburse them, one-sixth each, and acquire my one-third interest. This I managed to do quite quickly, though the arrangement meant that my capital was never risked as theirs was.

It was Alfred Moss's drive which very largely got the Beefburger opened on time and made it the success it is. He is extremely thorough and astute, and carefully investigated all the complications of the purchase of commodities, weight, wholesale prices, tasting and so on, before we plunged. From the start we decided that everything we sold must be the best in its class, and although this has undoubtedly stood us in good stead in the long run, it proved rather wearing on our stomachs initially! We aimed at making the best coffee in town, and apart from insisting on the use of full-cream Jersey T.T. milk, we made exhaustive tests of the many kinds of coffee beans available. Before the Beefburger opened its doors Alfred and I, the staff of the B.R.S.C.C. and of Moss's surgery, and anyone else available, must have sampled hundreds of cups of coffee, made from various types of coffee beans, in order to find the grade and taste we thought the public would like best!

Similarly, we sampled dozens of varieties of *apfelstrudel* and gateau before selecting our brands, and in the few weeks before opening I felt that if I never saw another piece of gateau in the rest of my life it would be too soon. We tried every flavour, chocolate, cream, pineapple, strawberry, honey, until we were all heartily sick of it.

But it was all very necessary for the business, and I shall always be grateful to Alfred Moss for the experience I gained through this venture, which none of us has ever had cause to regret undertaking.

I have already mentioned the sad accident to Fon de Portago's Ferrari, which brought about an end to the famous Mille Miglia series. It was in this tragic 1957 race that Stirling had one of his shortest drives ever, and Peter one of his cruellest pieces of bad luck.

Maseratis had brought out their powerful 4½-litre V8 sports car that year, and although the high brake horsepower and savage exhaust snarl suggested that this was a most ferocious beast, Stirling says that it was, in fact, a beautiful car to drive. The firm had spent considerable time and money in developing this design, and once again persuaded Stirling to drive one in the Mille Miglia.

In this instance he took considerable persuading, because, not only was he no longer keen on the race, which he considered highly dangerous, but he was very dissatisfied with the preparation of the

1956 3½-litre car, which had been so rushed that there had been no time to remedy its handling and other faults before the race.

However, Maseratis had their way, and Moss (Maserati), with Denis Jenkinson once again by his side, duly appeared on the starting ramp at Brescia. Twelve kilometres out he came up fast to a corner, pressed on the brake pedal—and nothing happened. Desperately he went down through the gearbox, getting round the corner somehow without damage to car or persons, and coasting to a stop.

The brake pedal had snapped clean off.

A few days later I was over at the Maserati factory, and had a long chat with Omer Orsi, son of the proprietor, and with the young and brilliant designer, Alfieri. They told me they had X-rayed the broken brake pedal, and established without question that the material was faulty; it was just one of those awful things which crop up, and which even concerns like Maserati cannot guard against. 'This,' said Stirling, 'is my last Mille Miglia,' and as circumstances turned out, it was everybody's, since the great Italian 1000-mile classic was 'demoted' to a rally-style event the following year.

Poor Peter Collins, whose *forte* was long-distance sports-car racing, was leading the race by ten minutes from Taruffi when a drive shaft broke with only 140 miles to go. Yet as it was also a broken drive shaft which caused the de Portago accident, I suppose we must regard his bad luck as also good, since much worse might have befallen him. Pete desperately tried to motor on with one shaft only, but only covered seven kilometres before he had to give up.

While I was at Maseratis, they spoke of their admiration for the space frame designs which British marques such as Lotus were producing so successfully. These cars regularly outpaced their heavier 1½-litre sports Maseratis, and they were becoming very concerned about it. Not being too proud to learn directly from their opponents, they asked me to arrange for them to purchase a Lotus from Colin Chapman. I did so, and eventually they sent over one of their mechanics and a 1½-litre Maserati engine, which was fitted to the Lotus chassis. The resultant Anglo-Italian hybrid was then taken to Italy.

Maseratis never actually raced this car. They purchased it as a technical exercise, to study the design in detail, and not long afterwards they sold the car again. I think Colin Chapman can take it as a big compliment that a concern of Maserati's long experience and reputation should wish to purchase one of his cars, in order to learn all they could from it. One might have expected some reluctance on his part to lay his design bare to rivals, but he supplied the car without hesitation, rightly reasoning that if they so badly wanted to study the Lotus, they could always acquire one elsewhere.

Which brings me to Le Mans, where the influence of Frank Costin of Lotus became evident in a unique Maserati—Moss's $4\frac{1}{2}$-litre V8 coupé. This was one more victim of insufficient time for preparation; the idea, which was originally Stirling's, was good, for Le Mans was one place which appreciated aerodynamic closed bodywork, but the job of constructing it to Frank Costin's designs was far too rushed to be truly efficient.

Although Moss's Maserati 'hardtop' looked grotesque, I have no doubt that aerodynamically it was excellent, and a great improvement on the normal open Maseratis. But bodywork requires development as well as chassis and engines, and the high-speed passage of air over a motor car produces some curious results; holes which are designed to take in air very often push it out instead, while an apparently well-ventilated compartment may practically suffocate its driver.

The V8 coupé brought many problems with heat, oil and petrol fumes, but as the car was only completed two days before Le Mans practice began, there just was not time to deal with all the snags which arose. Poor Frank Costin was almost in tears when he saw the Italian mechanics cutting bits out of the body with great metal shears in order to improve ventilation and fit the various bits of piping properly, and when the car turned out for the race it did not look at all the handsome machine an idealist like Costin had visualized.

In the race, all the efforts of Costin and Maseratis came quickly to naught, for Moss went out after barely two hours with a broken rear axle!

It was shortly before that Le Mans race of 1957 that Peter

Collins got in touch with me, saying that Ferrari were looking for another driver to complete their team. He suggested I approach Stuart Lewis-Evans, that most talented driver of Formula 3 Coopers and, in the early part of 1957, of G.P. Connaughts as well. Now the Connaught firm had just announced their complete withdrawal from racing, to everyone's great regret, so that when I contacted Stuart at his home in Bexleyheath, Kent, he showed immediate enthusiasm to drive. He subsequently flew to Modena and came to an agreement with Ferrari to drive both sports and Grand Prix Ferraris.

His first race was at Le Mans, and although Stuart was not a keen sports-car driver, much preferring to be in a single-seater, and able to see his front wheels, he did very well, bringing home the only Ferrari to finish, taking fifth place amidst a host of Jaguars.

It was between Le Mans and the French G.P., held that year on the splendid Rouen circuit, that Stirling decided to spend a few days in the South of France on a water-skiing and sunbathing holiday. He is extremely fond of the sea, but unfortunately it was not his friend on this occasion, for he picked up some 'bug' through his nose which caused a severe infection of the antrum, the little pouch immediately behind the nose.

By the time he was thinking about packing for Rouen, he did not feel at all well, and when he got there he was really ill. His father called a doctor, who gave Stirling an injection. This made him feel better until its effect wore off, when once again he suffered acute discomfort.

On the day before the race Tony Vandervell decided that Stirling should be taken home in his private De Havilland Dove aircraft; he was flown to Croydon, then taken by ambulance to the London Clinic. As Tony Brooks had hurt himself at Le Mans, that meant that the Vanwall team were left without their two drivers. Roy Salvadori was thereupon engaged to drive one, and then Stuart Lewis-Evans, who had turned up expecting to drive a Ferrari, but found there wasn't a car for him after all, agreed to drive the other. This meant getting Ferrari's permission, but eventually Tony Vandervell came to an agreement to 'take over' Stuart completely, and he accordingly left the Scuderia he had so recently joined and went over to the Vanwall camp.

Stirling was still not well enough to drive a week later in the Rheims G.P., having undergone a small operation to his nose. Lewis-Evans showed his prowess in a Vanwall in veteran style by leading the race for much of the distance, until leaking oil got on to his screen and goggles and forced him back to third place.

Good health returned to Stirling in time for him to win that famous victory at Aintree in the European G.P., which really marked the turning of the tide for Britain in Grand Prix racing. His own car led for about twenty-five laps, then began misfiring and had to be retired. In that year you could still switch drivers from one car to another in Championship races, and as Tony Brooks, still off-colour after his Le Mans accident, was flagging, Moss took his car over. By the seventieth lap he was in the lead, and he won the race for Vanwall after lowering the lap record to 1 min. 59·2 sec.

The German G.P. was not so good, for the Vanwall suspension just could not cope with the Nurburgring; Tony Brooks felt distinctly sick, while Stuart and Stirling, too, were tossed about unmercifully in their cockpits. Moss managed to beat Jean Behra by a car's length into fifth place.

But the Vanwall engineers worked overtime to improve things, then off went Stirling to win the Pescara G.P., which had been given Championship status that year in view of the cancellation of the Belgian and Dutch G.P.s. The week previously he had driven a sports V8 Maserati in the Swedish G.P., sharing victory with Behra, and it was between the Swedish and Pescara week-ends on 13 August that I was able to fit my stag party into our very tight schedule.

Stirling had arranged it on my behalf, and it was held at the Westbury Hotel off Bond Street in a private room. Amongst those present were Stirling, Peter Jopp, Ron Smith, Phil Gross, my brother John, Yorke Noble, David Haynes and about a dozen others; first we all enjoyed a fabulous meal, even going through the ceremony of carrying out the toast and then smashing the glasses. In order not to upset the staff of the Westbury too much, we got them to place an empty bucket in one corner, and as soon as the toast was over, we all threw our glasses at the bucket, making a fine mess.

After the meal we adjourned to another room for our own private cabaret, wherein a young girl, then in cabaret at the Embassy Club, performed a fan dance to some records on a player. By that time the party was going great guns, and eventually I found myself performing a fan dance as well; Stirling also got cracking, and I think that, had the press squeezed in for a few photographs, the results would have been startling. My stag party finished at about 2 a.m., when we all went off home, tired but happy, my impending 'doom' having been sealed by my friends.

Following Pescara, Stirling and I spent a very eventful few days together, in a sphere of speed work new even to Stirling—record-breaking on the world-famous Bonneville Salt Flats in Utah.

It was back in 1955 that I had first gone down to Abingdon, to discuss this project with John Thornley, manager of the M.G. Company. Employing some components coming straight from the production model M.G.A., and others that were very special, M.G.s were planning a new record-breaking car to be known as Ex. 181. This was to have its supercharged B-series 1½-litre B.M.C. engine mounted behind the driver, and a highly aero-dynamic all-enveloping body was to be fitted.

I found Thornley a most pleasant person to conduct business with; he is ultra-efficient, understanding, and surely one of the B.M.C. geniuses; the kind of man I sincerely hope we may always do business with in the world of motor racing. Our meeting ended in agreement that Stirling Moss would drive Ex. 181 on her official record attempts, though that was to be many, many months hence. Whilst there, I was also instrumental in signing up Stirling's sister Pat to drive in rallies for the M.G. concern.

Now, in August 1957, the time had come for Ex. 181 to attack Class F records, on the famous flats which had seen so many dramatic bids for the world's absolute land speed record. Stirling and I were due to fly from London Airport on Monday, 19 August. We took off in the early evening, landing at Shannon, where we had some food, while Stirling bought himself a Rolleiflex, the latest in a long line of cameras—he just can't resist them. Then we flew from Shannon via Detroit for Customs clearance to Chicago, then on to Salt Lake City.

When we arrived we were met by George Eyston, who was in

charge of the entire operation on behalf of M.G., and Philip Mayne, who was helping with the timekeeping. Then we drove out to Wendover, the little township closest to the Salt Flats, and used as the base of operations.

I found Wendover quite fantastic. The State of Utah is what is known as a 'dry state', which means there are no bars or public houses in which to buy alcoholic refreshment; the only place you can buy it is the store, and it has to be taken away for home consumption. On the other hand, Nevada, the neighbouring state, is 'open', and you have gambling saloons, bars with all the drinks you want, and so on—it is a real rough, tough, fast-shootin' sort of state.

Wendover itself is a border town, half in Utah and half in Nevada, so that in one half you can't get a drink, while in the other you can have all you want, with roulette wheels, pin tables, slot machines and every kind of gambling thrown in. It is notable also for its military airfield, for it was from there that the crews were trained for the U.S. bombers which dropped the atom bombs on Hiroshima and Nagasaki.

The M.G. record attempt was naturally of considerable potential advertising value, and by that time I had effected a long-term agreement between Stirling and the British Petroleum Company for the linking of his name with B.P. products. Following a meeting with their top Advertising and Sales executives, it had been decided that Stirling should send a 'personal' letter from the Salt Flats direct to every B.P. dealer in England.

The only way we could do this was to assume that the record attempts would be successful, and print the letters in advance, using a facsimile block signature, have all the envelopes addressed with the letters already inside, and take them out with us.

I was loaded with three suit-cases, two being absolutely stuffed full with air-mail letters addressed to the B.P. dealers in England. Now it happened that, when we went through the U.S. Customs at Detroit, the official asked me what my suit-cases contained. I answered, 'Personal effects', so he asked me to open one. As luck would have it, the one I opened was full of B.P. letters, and the Customs man gazed with real astonishment at hundreds and hundreds of letters. I must say that Stirling didn't help matters much at this stage by drily remarking, 'My friend writes a lot of letters!', but after explanations I was able to convince him that I wasn't trying to smuggle anything through, and was let off without any import duty or tax to pay.

The Utah Salt Flats themselves are quite incredible, being virtually the bed of a former inland sea. They lie, a vast flat valley some 120 miles in length, surrounded by mountains having three distinct levels denoting earlier seas. The actual levels are clearly discernible, one high in the strata of the rock formation in the mountain side, the second about half-way down, and the third the present one, since the Lakes are only dry in the summer.

The salt stretches for miles and miles and miles, but only near Wendover is there a smooth-enough stretch to permit car record-breaking, this measuring about 13½ miles in length. To prepare and mark out the course, they take a motorized snowplough-scraper device, and drive this along, scraping a flat surface, then a lorry trails a two-foot-wide strip of oil down the centre of the track. This oil is then burned, forming a black line for the driver to aim along —highly necessary because in that vast expanse of salt there are tremendous mirage effects, largely caused by reflection of the very strong sunlight.

Stirling and I had never seen anything like the Flats before, and spent a most interesting week. Salt Lake City is, of course, the headquarters of the Mormon religion, while the region is famous in early American history. The Donna Reed expedition which made a heroic trek westward nearly came to grief in this part of the country, and Stirling and I spent many happy hours in the company of Griff Borgeson, a Californian technical motor journalist of the first quality, going over the trail of that expedition. Griff's seemingly limitless knowledge of early American history kept us enthralled, while for contrast we three also enjoyed ourselves in the gambling saloon at the State Line Hotel. It was there that I won five silver dollars, large American coins reminiscent of the early five-shilling piece. Later I had these mounted on silver chains, giving one to Ann and the others to her bridesmaids at our wedding.

The early testing of Ex. 181 was carried out by Phil Hill of California, and this was most valuable, as the car was completely *au point* by the time Stirling arrived. Phil was also the reserve driver, and his appointment was very wise, and typical of the thoroughness of Eyston and Thornley. Thousands of pounds had been invested in this particular project, and its success obviously could not hinge on the availability of one person.

There had been storms in the area before we arrived, and the salt beds were covered in water, which took three or four days to evaporate. Each morning Stirling was up at around 5 a.m. to see if conditions had improved, and on Friday, 23 August, after getting up early in vain, we went out to the Flats again in the afternoon. The salt was still a little damp but they decided to make the attempt.

Stirling said the car felt 'O.K.' save for a slight weaving as though the wheels were crossing tramlines, and on his second run third speed in the gearbox went. After that he had to change straight from second to fourth, but was successful, nonetheless, in setting up five new International Class F records. These were the flying kilometre at 245·64 m.p.h., the mile at 245·11 m.p.h., the 5 kms. at 243·08 m.p.h., the 5 miles at 235·69 m.p.h. and the 10 kms. at 224·70 m.p.h.

Record-breaking differs vastly in technique from road racing. Many people may consider that to a man like Stirling it was mere child's play; a question of climbing in, putting his right foot down and driving in a straight line; but this was far from so. Mechanical sensitivity was vital, and Ex. 181 was not an easy car to drive.

In order to achieve its excellent aerodynamic shape, the car used very small wheels; I think they were 15 in., and like all high-speed record-breakers, required the minimum of tyre tread. There was perhaps one-sixteenth of an inch thickness of tread on the canvas, which meant a tyre change after each run through the course. Furthermore, salt has a low adhesion factor, perhaps one-tenth that of tarmacadam, so that Grand Prix-style starts were right out; speed had to be built up carefully, and Stirling needed to watch the rev. counter closely as well as hold his course, stuck beneath a perspex cover and travelling like a human bullet at around 245 m.p.h. To borrow a well-worn phrase, 'sooner him than me'!

With the records broken, Stirling's letters to the British B.P. dealers had to be posted, but when I took them to the local post office and asked for something like 5000 stamps, the old lady behind the desk just about fainted. We solved the problem by borrowing the only neo-franking machine in the town from the U.S.A.F. base, paying the post office the money while they put the letters through the machine.

The following afternoon we set off for Salt Lake City, in order to catch the Chicago plane the next morning. We booked in at a Motel near the airport, and then looked around for something to do in the evening. It was here that I had my first taste of that popular American entertainment, the drive-in open-air cinema.

We joined a great queue of cars driving in, and soon found ourselves in a row, looking at the vast screen. Next to each car bay is a post, on which hangs a loudspeaker; this you remove from the post and hang on to the dashboard of your car. That gives you the sound for the picture, which you view through or above your windscreen, and as the screen is twenty to thirty feet over the ground, vision is very good.

Not being accustomed to the ways of drive-in cinemas, we had omitted to provide ourselves with any of the popcorn, soft drinks, hamburgers, hot dogs, orange juice, milk, chewing-gum and other things the American public cannot live without, but what was going on around us, and in front and behind, was just nobody's business; quite an entertainment!

But the boys and girls watch the film as well, as became obvious during the interval, when everybody dashed forward to the pop-corn counter or the 'goody' bar, coming back loaded with sticky sweets and so on. We sat there, feet up, seats set back as far as possible, watching the film and living in the lap of luxury. It was great fun, and I only wish we could have such things in England, though I suppose our climate forbids it.

On Sunday morning we rose at seven o'clock and flew to Chicago, where Stirling and I parted. I was due to get married on 2 September, so was anxious to get back as quickly as possible. Stirling's wedding was not until 7 October, so he decided to go down to Nassau to see how his house was progressing before returning to London, where he was to be best man at my wedding.

Ann and I had a particular desire to be married in a really beautiful church. We spent many hours looking around London, and eventually decided on St James's Church in Piccadilly. When working at the R.A.C. I used to pass this church daily, and was much impressed by the spirit with which the vicar tackled restoration problems after the war had left his church a burnt-out hulk. Skilful work by the builders restored it to what I consider is one of London's most beautiful churches.

Although I wasn't a resident in the parish of St James, it was agreed that we could be married there provided I qualified for residence. This entailed sleeping at least two nights in the parish, and though at first I intended to stay at the Piccadilly Hotel, I later hit on a brighter idea, and stayed in the Jermyn Street Turkish Baths with Peter Jopp. We went there fairly late in the evening, had a really good Turkish bath, then went to sleep and got off early in the morning for breakfast.

Monday, 2 September, was wedding day, and of all the things I have ever enjoyed in life, I enjoyed my wedding most of all. The day was perfect, with glorious sunshine, and everything went smoothly. My life being virtually centred on organization and administration, we naturally had to plan our wedding to perfection, and I am happy to say that it went through without the minutest hitch.

A large crowd saw us married, and some two or three hundred friends who attended the ceremony afterwards came to the wedding breakfast at the Park Lane Hotel in Piccadilly. Here the arrangements were in the capable hands of my old friend Mr Bishop, the Banqueting Manager, who has arranged the B.R.S.C.C. annual dinners with me for many years.

For our honeymoon, Ann and I went to Italy, and stayed at a villa in Levanto, between Genoa and La Spezia.

The village of Levanto lies in a beautiful part of the coast, nestling in a tiny valley at the foot of the Bracco Pass. There are very few motor cars; just the village, the blue Mediterranean, and plenty of boats in the harbour, mainly speedboats, which I adore.

I broke my honeymoon off briefly to go from Levanto to Monza in order to see the Italian Grand Prix, happy in the knowledge that Ann fully approved; she completely understands my interest in motor racing and supports me in all that I do. And I was very pleased that I did go to Monza, for it proved a wonderful race.

The sight at the start of three Vanwalls alongside Fangio's Maserati on the front row of the grid was enough to send any Briton crazy from the very beginning. Stirling Moss, Tony Brooks and Stuart Lewis-Evans were a formidable trio in the Vanwalls, and although his team mates had trouble, Stirling got out in front and won comfortably from Fangio. This in spite of a gearbox which temporarily jammed, and a precautionary pit-stop to take on more oil and change the nearside rear tyre.

I went down to Modena the following morning for a quick, pre-arranged conference with Peter Collins on the question of his 1958 contract with Scuderia Ferrari. Then, having bought some of the famous Modena salami and mortadella, and some of the equally famous Modena grain cheese, I set off by train, back to Levanto and my wife.

While at Levanto I received a letter from Yorke Noble, who was the leading character in Noble Motors Ltd., the concessionaires for the Heinkel Cabin Cruiser. Yorke Noble occupied an office suite on the fourth floor of 211 Piccadilly, which building was also occupied by our solicitors, J. N. Nabarro & Co. It was quite by chance that Noble met Stirling in the lift there one day, and he lost no time in introducing himself, then offered Stirling the loan of a Heinkel.

Stirling accepted, for he has always been enthusiastic over small cars, particularly in London, where parking and manœuvring make size merely a nuisance. Noble subsequently offered an executive position in his company to Stirling, who was intrigued by the idea and sent me along to negotiate on his behalf.

We had almost reached the point where Stirling was to join Noble Motors, when his great patriotism decided him against it. On consideration, he felt he would rather not be associated closely with a concern marketing a German-built mini-car in Britain. I think Yorke Noble was very disappointed at his decision, but he pressed on, and later persuaded Mike Hawthorn to take an interest in his firm. Alas, poor Mike was about to join Noble when he met his death on the Guildford Bypass.

I retained an association with Yorke Noble despite Stirling's decision, and in the letter I received at Levanto he invited me to join Noble Motors Ltd. as Technical Director, offering me a

Directorship, and ten per cent of the company's shares as an inducement to take up the post. I discussed this with Ann while in Italy, and, when I got back, formally accepted the position, and became Technical Director. After our magnificent fortnight at Levanto, London seemed very much over-populated, but we had the excitement of moving into the new flat we had bought in Wigmore Street, and settling down.

When I got down to things, I found that the technical service side of Noble Motors was in a shocking state. In fact, it hardly existed at all, and although there was a depot down at Lots Road, Chelsea, and a considerable stock of spare parts for Heinkels, the management was practically nil. Service as service hardly existed at all, while I suspected that spare parts were not merely being lost but being pilfered.

Stirling's wedding to Katie Molson on Monday, 7 October, was now the absolute priority of the day, and we plunged into the hurly-burly of preparations with a will. The closeness of my wedding helped to ease arrangements in many ways, and after Stirling had consented to be my best man, I felt very honoured when he asked me to be best man at his wedding. But Stirling's marriage was to be a really big affair. As a celebrity, the 'cupids' of the press had been trying to 'marry him off' for years, and now it was really happening. Something like a thousand guests were expected, and the degree of organization necessary was on a par with a major international race meeting!

The actual service was to take place at St George's in Eaton Square, and Stirling and Kate had decided on an evening wedding, fixing the time for five o'clock. The reception was to be held at the Savoy, arrangements being made for the hire of seven luxury coaches to take those guests without cars from the church at Eaton Square to the reception.

In the midst of preparations, just before Stirling's stag party, I unfortunately went down with a very severe attack of 'flu. This laid me so low that I not only had to miss the stag party, which I was very anxious should be as good as, if not better than, the one Stirling gave me, but at one stage it was in doubt whether I could assume my duties as best man on the wedding day.

I got over it, however, and we were all fit and eager for *the* day—

and so, it seemed, was most of London! It had been planned that, as Stirling and Kate came out of the church after the ceremony, there would be a pause whilst photographs were taken, not only of the happy couple, but of the wedding groups as well.

When they came out, however, they were faced by an absolute mass of photographers; I don't think I have ever seen so many cameras in action at one time in the whole of my life. They were so densely packed that some lay on the ground, some were kneeling, some standing and not a few were on others' shoulders or stands of some kind, all of them aiming at Mr and Mrs Stirling Moss as they came out through the doors of the church.

Such was the confusion, noise, and popping of flash bulbs that, instead of having the group photographs taken there and then, Stirling and Katie deemed it wiser to get into their car immediately—it was waiting at the foot of the stairs—and flee to the Savoy Hotel for the reception.

Then followed a crush of traffic which can only be likened to a Bank Holiday jam on a busy by-pass. So many people were trying to get their cars to the front of the church that we couldn't bring the official cars to the foot of the steps, and for a hectic twenty minutes the faithful ushers, who included Mike Hawthorn and Peter Collins, had to play traffic controllers. Fortunately everyone was in a gay, co-operative mood, and eventually we managed to sort the jumble out and make our way to the Savoy.

Stirling and his wife spent that night in the Harlequin suite— a fabulous 'dreamland' sort of suite—at the Dorchester Hotel, before embarking for Amsterdam and their honeymoon.

What an eventful year 1957 was! After our weddings came more racing, with the Casablanca G.P. looming up importantly at the end of October. Vanwall, B.R.M., Ferrari, Maserati and Cooper all went, and Stirling put up the fastest practice lap on the first day of training with his Vanwall. On the following day, unluckily, Stirling felt far from well, having to stay in bed with a high temperature. It was Asian 'flu, and the following day showed no improvement.

Two doctors then decided that he was unfit to race, and with all the will in the world he certainly didn't feel fit to drive at lap speeds of around 112–113 m.p.h. under a burning North African sun. On Sunday morning he got up, was driven out to the airfield, and took a plane to Paris, then another to London Airport, where he was collected and put straight to bed.

Only Tony Brooks and Stuart Lewis-Evans started with Vanwalls, Tony retiring and Stuart finishing second to Behra's winning Maserati. Peter Collins, Mike Hawthorn, Juan Fangio and Harry Schell were all also feeling the effects of the 'flu, but elected to race. Fangio came fourth despite hitting some straw bales; Peter took the lead, had a fit of coughing and spun, got going again, then crashed into the straw bales; Mike retired, both he and his Ferrari feeling terrible, while Schell finished fifth.

I have heard that Stirling's decision to go home on the day of the race created an undertone of criticism amongst those who were there. I myself did not go, so cannot vouch for this, but with two doctors confirming his unfit condition, I am sure it would have been foolhardy for him to drive in the race.

Under conditions of adversity there is nobody who will fight more doggedly or better than Stirling—so long as his ability is not impaired by some outside factor. On the other hand, he knows his own limitations to the nth degree, and is far too sensible to attempt to give of his best when suffering an illness which affects judgment and reactions; to drive under such circumstances would not only be foolish to himself, but could also endanger the other drivers on the circuit.

Did these critics, I wonder, imagine that Moss did not *want* to race at Casablanca, when Grand Prix racing is his very lifeblood? And did they know to what degree he was ill, and how it compared with the illness affecting Fangio, Collins, Hawthorn and Schell? Nobody knew these things, but Stirling knew that racing that day was beyond him and, bitterly disappointed, went home quickly rather than edure the sounds of the Grand Prix in progress from his hotel bed, obtaining treatment from his own doctors without language difficulties.

Since 1957 I have been to Casablanca, and have seen how interesting and how extremely fast and difficult the circuit is. Certainly it is not the place to go careering round when you don't feel up to it, and under these circumstances, although Peter and Mike may have been hailed by the public as 'the heroic ones to go racing when they had Asian 'flu', I contend that Peter and Mike were the foolish ones to do so, and that Stirling was the only one to show sound professional judgment.

Not long after Casablanca, Stirling had to pack his bags once again and leave for Caracas, where he was to drive a Maserati in the Venezuelan G.P. for sports cars. Maseratis were under a cloud from the start, their popular team manager Ugolini learning on the day before the race that his brother had died of a heart attack. This news brought depression to the team despite the fact that the big 4½-litre V8s had gone very well in practice, with Moss just beating Behra for fastest lap.

It proved a disastrous race. Stirling built up over two minutes' lead on everybody in just over two hours, when an A.C. 'Ace' driven by an American pulled across his front before a corner. The Maserati cut the A.C. virtually in half, then spun wildly, Stirling miraculously emerging with nothing worse than a damaged toe.

Then Behra's Maserati caught fire in the pits. The blaze was put out, then Stirling took it over to find the seat was still burning, much to his personal discomfort! He brought it back, after which Schell took over for a spell. Harry was following Bonnier in another Maserati, when the Swede had a tyre burst, both cars collided and both were written off, Schell's blazing to a cinder. In addition to this, Masten Gregory in a private V8 Maserati crashed his car, damaging it extensively.

Thus ended Maserati's chances for the World Sports Car Championship in 1957. Four highly expensive cars taken on the expensive journey to Venezuela, two cars damaged, two of the V8s written off. It takes a strong and wealthy company to be able to withstand that sort of financial loss, for the V8s were worth at least £8000 each, and I am pretty certain they were not insured.

Caracas, 1957, was the final blow which put Maseratis out of racing; already owed considerable sums of money in Argentina, Officine Maserati announced their withdrawal from motor racing in December 1957, Omer Orsi, son of the Maserati president, observing that 'motor racing has become too expensive for a small firm like ours'.

The Modena factory is still building Grand Touring and sports cars, but their absence from the circuits has been keenly felt. Stirling has a particular affection for the firm who supplied him with his first Grand Prix car, and gave him his first works drive, and we all look forward to their early return to serious competition work.

The Venezuelan race was won by Peter Collins and co-driver Phil Hill in a Ferrari, clinching the Championship for that marque. I was particularly pleased that Peter won, for his 1957 season had hardly been as brilliant as that of 1956. I rather felt this was because he had married, and wasn't trying so hard any more, though I must admit he certainly 'had a go' in the German G.P., when the old master Fangio put it across both him and Mike Hawthorn in a simply fabulous drive.

Incidentally, before leaving the subject of the race at Caracas, it was here that the U.P.P.I. organization proved of considerable value. The circuit was badly laid out, highly dangerous, and after first practice the drivers *en masse* persuaded the organizers to make various improvements. Had these not been effected, there might have been no drivers present to make a race, for they felt strongly about the conditions.

After Caracas, Stirling went to Nassau, there to meet Katie who had flown out from England. They hoped to be able to move into the new house on Camperdown Heights, but building was slower than anticipated, and this was not possible. So they knuckled down and joined in the work, Stirling digging holes, tiling roofs, making cupboards, erecting a bar, and all sorts of other things, and, I suspect, thoroughly enjoying himself.

In the middle of it came the Nassau Speed Week, and this time Moss was to drive an Aston Martin 3·7-litre DBR2 which had been shipped out to him by the works. The car went quite well in practice, and it was decided by Reg Parnell and John Wyer, both of whom came out to Nassau, that the car should also be lent to the American woman driver Ruth Levy.

Stirling first drove it in the Nassau T.T. over 102 miles, but he couldn't match the pace of Masten Gregory's 4·5 Maserati, and was lying third when electrical trouble forced him out of the running. Then Ruth Levy drove it in the Women's race, and was doing well until she was involved in an accident with another car, turning the DBR2 over.

It was too damaged for Stirling to drive the following day, so he arranged to borrow Jan de Vroom's 3·5 Ferrari, and scored his first victory in a car of this make, taking the 100-mile race from Ginther's 4·9 Ferrari. He went on to win the 250-mile 'feature' race followed by Shelby, Phil Hill and Bonnier, so that, as he was almost a Nassau resident by then, it was a case of 'local boy making good' in a big way.

The Speed Week was eventful for Stirling in other ways than racing. Half-way through the week, a gale sprang up off the coast, and at about two or three o'clock in the morning his Healey speed-boat broke away from its moorings and was driven on to the beach. Stirling couldn't retrieve it on his own, so the long-suffering Reg Parnell was dragged out of bed, and between them they got the boat safely moored again.

It was in mid-week, too, that Stirling received his wedding present from Ann and me. It was unorthodox but, I think, most welcome, particularly at that time when they were so busy on the house. When we asked Stirling and Katie what they would like, they pondered, then decided on a really comprehensive tool kit.

As I have said, Stirling is a great handyman, and loves to do things with his own hands. My wife and I therefore set about collecting all kinds of tools and equipment, arranging for them to be installed in a special wooden box with trays and clips. The kit covered just about every possible job one could find in the house or garage. There were all kinds of spanners, woodworking tools, plumbing tools, wheelbraces, drills and so on; in fact Stirling had a free choice in a wholesale toolshop we visited in London, and when it was all complete I shipped it out to Nassau.

Peter Collins came to Nassau that year, and drove a rather special car entered by Donald Healey. This had a standard Austin-Healey 100 chassis with slightly altered suspension, into which was fitted a 2½-litre 4-cylinder Grand Prix Ferrari engine. This particular engine came from the actual car with which Maurice Trintignant won the 1955 G.P. of Europe at Monaco after the collapse of the Mercedes-Benz and Lancia teams, Donald Healey having bought the car for detailed study.

I had suggested to Donald that it might prove advantageous to experiment with the production of a 'handmade' variation of the standard Austin-Healey, to which various power units could be adapted according to the customer's wishes. I have always thought that the '100' was aesthetically one of the best-looking sports-car designs ever to go into quantity production, and that connoisseurs would appreciate the availability of 'special' versions.

The Austin-Healey Ferrari was the first experiment on this principle, but unfortunately the great power from the engine was more than the chassis could reasonable cope with, and it did not perform very well at Nassau. I gather that Enzo Ferrari was rather amused on hearing of this strange alliance, and also that he was delighted with Stirling's Ferrari victories.

One strange commission which came my way toward the close of the year was to investigate one of Juan Manuel Fangio's income-tax problems, while the World Champion was in London. This arose as a result of his driving for B.R.M. in 1952 and 1953, and I took my solicitor, Felix Nabarro, along to try and help sort things out. Peter Collins, Fangio, Felix Nabarro and his accountant-brother Eric and I all gathered in the bar of the Westbury Hotel one evening. Peter acted as interpreter, while Fangio did his best to explain things.

Unfortunately, Fangio's comparatively rare visits to Britain, and the fact that when he did come he was tied up wholly with motor racing, meant that he had never given sufficient attention to tax matters on income earned over here. We were never able to reach a really satisfactory solution, though we tried hard on his behalf, and in the end he had to meet most of the tax the Inland Revenue had demanded.

CHAPTER ELEVEN

THE BRITISH RACING PARTNERSHIP

I HAVE already written enough on the Brands Hatch circuit for readers to realize that I have a particular affection for the place. I had the privilege of joining in the organization of the first meeting ever held there, for the 500 Club in 1950, and since then have organized dozens more, seeing the circuit grow and grow until it attained a unique position in British motor racing.

As Secretary of the B.R.S.C.C. for several years, I have felt proud to have contributed materially to the rise of Brands Hatch, and it was in late 1956 that an opportunity arose to further my con-nexions with the circuit. At the A.G.M. of Brands Hatch Circuit Ltd., several shareholders expressed their dissatisfaction that the Company had not declared a dividend for some considerable time, and felt that a change on the Board was necessary.

When a vacant seat had arisen on the Board, one person was nominated who was not acceptable to all the Directors. A number of them therefore nominated me in opposition, and when it was put to the vote, I was elected to join the Board, a position which I must say I felt very proud and pleased to hold.

One year later, in November 1957, I attended the next A.G.M. of the Company as a Director, driving down with Alfred Moss, who was a shareholder, in his M.G. Magnette. It was a cheerful meeting, as by now we had managed to pay off large quantities of preference-share arrears, although we still had not paid any dividend on the ordinary shares. But the balance sheet of the Company looked far healthier, and with prospects of holding bigger inter-national meetings, and the extension of the circuit to Grand Prix length drawing nearer, the future of Brands Hatch looked bright.

Whilst driving back to town after the meeting, Alfred and I talked about motor racing in general, and of what we would do if we ourselves owned a racing car. Our ideas coincided. We didn't want to leap into the cockpit and drive it; 'Pop's' racing days had finished thirty years before, whilst I had learned enough to realize that one doesn't 'just leap into a car' to glorious success. No, our ideas centred more on running a car, on running it *properly*, on seeing that it had complete preparation, and giving an accomplished driver in the cockpit every chance of success.

And so was born the germ of an idea. Why shouldn't we try running one between us? Buy a car, have it prepared properly, organize things properly, and race it? Eagerly we discussed the pros and cons. We had seen Stirling rise from one of a number in Formula 3 to Grand Prix stardom, and now, apart from behind-the-scenes assistance, we were somewhat superfluous; Vanwall and Aston Martin had their own efficient organizations which largely looked after Stirling, and there was little we could now contribute to his success.

On the other hand, we had learned a great deal about racing through the years, and could now apply our experience and expend our energy in running our own racing car. It would not show a spectacular profit, and from a business point of view would not merit the financial outlay, but we both agreed that a racing car could be run properly without showing a loss at the end of the year, and that it would provide a great deal of interest and fun.

I was not financially strong enough, however, to find fifty per cent of the capital necessary to purchase and run a racing car, but Alfred Moss suggested that, as he and I got on well and understood each other's ideas on motor racing, he would put up the capital to buy a car, provided I would give the time to seeing that the thing was run properly. And this, in fact, marked the birth of the British Racing Partnership.

To me, the British Racing Partnership was everything. Here was my chance to prove that, with adequate financial backing, and therefore proper preparation, an off-the-counter racing car could be made to produce the right kind of results. We had decided that the best car to buy was a Formula 2 Cooper, and lost no time in motoring down to Surbiton to see Charles Cooper, explain our aims, and order a car.

Then we set about creating an organization for B.R.P., as the name of our project generally was abbreviated to. There were certain standards which we intended firmly to maintain.

We believed not only that a car should be mechanically perfect, but that it should appear on the circuit immaculate; we insisted that our car should be so prepared that no work other than routine adjustments should be carried out at the circuit. We believed that for a car to be successful, it had to be first into scrutineering and first out to practice. We believed that not only should the car be spotlessly clean, but that the mechanics and driver should be the same. We believed in the psychological effects on all of perfect preparation, in the 'one-upmanship' which this would give to our drivers.

All these were ideally, no doubt, the aims of any serious racing project, but we meant to pursue them harder than most others did; in short, we were to try to bring into the private entrant field the standards of perfection more generally associated with teams such as Mercedes-Benz or Vanwall.

It was decided to base the Partnership at Tring, where Alfred Moss had a bit of space available on his farm. One of the out-buildings served as a spacious garage, and we were able to partition off sufficient space to establish an entirely separate workshop in which to prepare the Cooper when it arrived.

Accommodation settled, the next item, vitally important, was to find some expert staff. For a single car, we needed one mechanic of proven ability, and one junior assistant or apprentice to help him. After very little thought, we settled on Tony Robinson as chief mechanic. Tony had been with Stirling Moss Ltd. for some time since 1953, and we both admired his outlook on life, his calm, seemingly unhurried methods, and his perfectionist approach to his work. Tony, in my opinion, is the ideal racing mechanic, patient, unflurried and eminently practical.

Tony was working with Bruce Halford when we approached him, but fortunately was just feeling like a change at the time, and agreed to join B.R.P. We then advertised for a junior assistant, and received over seventy replies. From these we eventually selected a young chap named Derek Spencer, who fortunately lived within a mile of Tony Robinson at Neasden, in N.W. London, so that they were able to travel together to Tring and home again each day.

Finally came the choice of a driver. And here again we had no difficulty in making our choice, Alfred and I agreeing immediately that the man best suited to our particular kind of outlook was Stuart Lewis-Evans, member of the Vanwall team, and a most polished young driver. He had proved his ability and courage on innumerable occasions, and I had watched his rise to fame from the days when he and his father first began racing in 500s at Brands Hatch.

The name of Lewis-Evans was a great attraction in any entry list, and 'Pop' Lewis-Evans and his son Stuart invariably performed with skill and great sportsmanship. So I visited Stuart one day and we talked it over; he liked our 'perfectionist' approach, and after a day or two he agreed to drive for B.R.P.

As Stuart's Vanwall commitments meant he could not always drive for us, we decided to take on another driver as well. Not an accomplished expert in this case, but a 'junior' of promise with experience in sports cars or Formula 3 only; a sort of Formula 2 'trainee', who could drive the Cooper when Stuart was engaged elsewhere.

There were many talented young men who fitted this category, but one had long caught my eye for his impeccably turned-out car, and his spirited battles with the current 'kings' of Formula 3, Don Parker and Jim Russell. This was Tommy Bridger of Knebworth, Hertfordshire, who agreed to our proposals and duly joined our team.

So we found ourselves in 'business' in a relatively short time. Tony Robinson and Derek Spencer spent much of their time at first down at Coopers, helping to build the Formula 2 Cooper, and thereby familiarizing themselves with it. We purchased an Austin Omnivan to transport the car, which was to be towed on a trailer behind. This, we felt, was the best set-up for a single-car entry, since the team, when they arrived at a circuit, could quickly unhitch the trailer with the Cooper on it, and leave them in a garage, then take the Omnivan as personal transport. It could also conveniently be employed as a collection and delivery vehicle, and general 'run-around'.

We didn't arrive at the name 'British Racing Partnership' immediately; that came after several evenings' thought, and even then we had to obtain sanction to use the word 'British'. We wanted the full title to be the British Racing Partnership Ltd., but the Registrar of Companies rejected this at first, on the grounds that it suggested too great a pre-eminence in the sport. On further application a year later, however, we were allowed to have the 'Ltd.' as well.

Three days before Christmas in 1957 I made a memorable journey to Modena with the late Mike Hawthorn, to attend the famous annual Ferrari luncheon and prize-giving. Peter Collins had gone to New York after Nassau to spend Christmas with his wife's parents, and could not attend the Ferrari function. He asked me to deputize for him, and Mike and I flew out together.

We went by B.E.A. Viscount, and had just got over Milan when we noticed a vast, thick fog spreading over almost the entirety of Northern Italy. There was no landing at Milan in this, it seemed, but eventually the pilot was able to announce that we would touch down at Turin, and that we would all be conveyed to Milan by surface transport.

After waiting at Turin airport for something like two and a half hours, drinking an interminable number of Campari bitters, we were at last jammed into a coach. By the time we were moving along the fog-bound road on to the Milan Autostrada, darkness had descended, and this, plus the cold December air, made life a bit miserable. Mike and I were well wrapped up, sitting hunched in the back of the bus, not conversing, but desperately trying to sleep above the noise.

Soon we noticed the driver was getting rather erratic, and saw three vast lorries in close formation just ahead. The coach driver was an impatient character, and kept attempting the impossible; he would try to overtake the lorries, getting half-way then having to brake violently and drop back behind again as a pair of headlights loomed out of the fog in front.

Mike, who always hated being driven anyway, was going spare, his blond hair turning seven shades whiter under the strain, until in the end, by a desperate feat of acceleration and some very tense moments, our coach just scraped past the leading lorry as yet another pair of headlights came howling at us through the mist and gloom. All the occupants of the coach, apart from us, clapped heartily in approval, but Mike's comment was, 'Don't clap, you lot of so-and-sos; you'll only encourage the silly b——!'

When at last we got to Milan, we found there were no taxis to take us down to the Central Station, from which we had to catch a train to Modena. After walking part of the way with our baggage we spotted a taxi pulling up outside a large hotel. As the passenger alighted, we decided that was the taxi for us.

But I don't think Mike had noticed that the commissionaire of another hotel opposite had already signalled to the taxi-driver—not that it would have made any difference! Mike desperately needed a taxi, and here was one. Without more ado we piled into the back, flinging our luggage in, Mike giving instructions in his Italian while the driver tried his best to tell us that the taxi was already booked.

The conversation became very heated and in the end we had to get out again, with Mike muttering some very terse remarks about the taxi-driver's parentage, at which the man became distinctly offensive. Mike drew himself up to his impressive six feet plus, slowly put his baggage down, peeled his gloves off with cold deliberation, removed his sheepskin jacket and passed it to me, then advanced upon the taxi-driver, looking as if he were about to send him from Milan to Turin with one blow.

The driver quickly decided that things looked unhealthy, rushed into his car, and picked up the starting handle. Mike stopped his advance, glared coldly, and bellowed something in most impressive Italian through gritted teeth, then took his jacket, put it on again, and with a 'Come on, Ken' stalked off down the road to a quiet hotel he knew. There we had a meal, then walked the rest of the way to the station, caught the Modena train, and arrived very close to midnight.

The Ferrari luncheon party at the famous Da Finis restaurant was a memorable affair, with all the works drivers, personnel and friends of the House of Ferrari present. The prizes themselves were given away by the Mayor of Brescia, and following a splendid lunch there were the usual Italian speeches.

When it was all over, Mike and I decided to get back to London as soon as possible. But the fog was still around and flying obviously impossible, so in the end we had to take the Paris express. Back in

England, I left Mike with real regret, for he was a most pleasant and amusing companion.

The opening of the 1958 season began with problems for Stirling Moss. After much dithering and changing of minds, the Argentine G.P. was to be held on 19 January, the organization being in the hands of Marcello Giambertone, Fangio's manager. As it was a World Championship event, we had originally anticipated that Vanwalls would be running, but it was already clear some weeks beforehand that they would not.

The sudden change in fuel regulations for Formula 1 racing in 1958, when the use of aviation spirit only became compulsory, created big problems for Vanwall with their fuel injection, and until Tony Vandervell was satisfied that his cars were working properly, he was not even prepared to state categorically that Vanwall would be racing at all in 1958.

This left Stirling in an uncomfortable state of indecision; should he sign with another team, only later to regret it, if the Vanwalls did prove race-worthy in 1958, or should he hold on, for what might mean many many weeks, before making a decision? Here I must criticize Tony Vandervell for his attitude, and for leaving Moss and the other drivers 'in the air'. If they were prepared to show faith in him, then he should have had faith in them, and told them more clearly where they stood. That he would not immediately commit Vanwalls to racing in 1958 showed his realistic approach to the sport, but was unfair to the drivers, who either had to sit and wait in the hope of again driving for Vanwall, or make sure of their 1958 Championship mount by joining another team.

But one thing was certain—there were no Vanwalls for the Argentine G.P., so we had to look around quickly to find a car for Stirling. Maserati's shattering announcement of their withdrawal from racing had been made but a month ago, so they were 'out' too, and as final confirmation that the race was to be held came very late, there was no time to lose.

After discussing the problem with Stirling in Nassau over the transatlantic telephone at something like £1 per minute, it was agreed I should approach Rob Walker, and ask if he would consider entering his 2·0-litre Cooper-Climax. Rob was tickled pink at the idea, and Alf Francis and the Pippbrook Motors racing staff promptly got down to preparation.

More transatlantic phoning, and calls to Giambertone in Milan, followed before the Cooper was finally accepted for the Argentine G.P.—so late that we missed the last ship reaching Buenos Aires in time. Eventually it was agreed between Giambertone and myself that the Cooper should be flown out to Argentina, together with Alf Francis and Tim Wall, the mechanics, at the organizers' expense. This was only fair, since it was their delay which made flying the car unavoidable. Stirling was to fly direct to Buenos Aires from Nassau.

But our troubles were not over yet. The Cooper was to be flown by Pan-American Airways via New York, and I booked space for it, giving its exact dimensions and weight, also reserving space for 5 cwt. of spares. Rob Walker decided this was far from sufficient and in fact went to the trouble of borrowing George Wicken's Formula 2 Climax engine as a reserve, in case the 2·2 failed.

He also included a spare gearbox, and a multitude of tyres and tools, so that when the crate of spares was taken, with the car, to Pan-Am's freight section at London Airport, it was found that there was an excess of something like 7 cwt.!

By complete coincidence, it happened that a good friend of mine, Bert Rees, who is on the Public Relations staff of Pan-American Airways, was coming to dinner with his wife that night, at our home in Wigmore Street. His wife, who worked in the City, had arrived alone at the flat, saying, 'Bert won't be long—he phoned to say he is just checking off one or two things at the airport before he comes along.'

Bert, as it happened, was attending to the Cooper and its spares, making sure they went safely on to the New York plane that evening, and when he arrived at the hangar and found there was an extra 7 cwt. to be put on to an already fully loaded aeroplane, he nearly had kittens! Fortunately he was able to arrange for some other freight to be taken off, and Rob's car and spares were safely stowed aboard. So, although we had a late dinner, it was in a very good cause.

The Argentinians were amused, I gather, when they had the first sight of the 2-litre Cooper. That puny, frail-looking little car looked anything but a Grand Prix challenger when compared with the massive 2·5-litre Maseratis and Ferraris, and I think it was only their great respect for Stirling Moss which prevented them from treating his entry as a laughing-stock.

I doubt if there was one single Argentinian who thought the car had a chance of finishing in the first five, let alone winning the race. Seventh best practice time rather confirmed their scepticism, but what a shock Stirling gave them all! He romped home the winner, despite having to take it easy in the final stages to conserve his tyres, knowing full well that if he had to stop for a wheelchange, the Cooper's bolt-on wheels would cost him minutes instead of seconds, and inevitably lose him the race.

Tactics, skill and bluff brought this victory of 'David' over the 'Goliaths', Alf Francis and Tim Wall in Moss's pit making an elaborate show of preparing to change the Cooper's wheels while he romped on, ahead of the Ferraris. Then the Italian pit awoke too late to the fact that Moss was planning to run the whole distance without a tyre change, and sent Musso, who was lying second, all out in an effort to catch the flying blue Cooper. Musso responded splendidly, but Stirling had him mastered, and crossed the line just 2·7 sec. ahead of the pursuing Ferrari.

I vividly remember the night of the race, when I telephoned Reuters in London to ask if the results had come through yet. When the voice from the Sports desk told me Stirling had won, I could hardly believe my ears, and in absolute joy I phoned Rob Walker at his Somerset home to tell him the news. Poor old Rob sounded almost in tears. He had hardly dared to hope that the car would finish in the first three, yet now he had achieved one of his life's ambitions—winning a World Championship event as a private entry against the works team—and on only 2 litres!

Out of our mutual pleasure at Stirling's victory there grew a close friendship between Rob Walker and myself, and later in January we came to an agreement that I should look after his team's affairs, thereby adding to my already diverse duties.

I had also undertaken for Dr Vicente D'Amico Urco, President of the A.C. Siracusa, to represent the Club in Britain and obtain entries for the Syracuse G.P. in April 1958, as I had already done in 1957; I had the management of Moss and Collins, my P.R.O.

work with Healey, the Beefburger, the B.R.S.C.C. secretaryship; B.R.P., Noble Motors, the magazine *Modern Motoring and Travel*, and various other responsibilities. Something, I felt, had to go.

By now the B.R.S.C.C. was a successful organization, running more or less to routine and requiring less and less original thought. Furthermore, relationship between myself and some Committee members was not the happy one it had been in past years. When I first joined the 500 Club in 1949, it had a membership of between two and three hundred, a negligible bank balance, and immense, unselfish enthusiasm. As a result of our mutual efforts, it was built up through the years to become the B.R.S.C.C., one of the 'big three' in British motor clubs, with over 2000 members and something like £10,000 to its credit in the bank.

As it thrived, so the Committee took more interest in the Club's activities, and a proportion of them, aware of my various other connexions in racing, convinced themselves that I was unable to work for the Club without other interests in mind. Whatever Gregory did, they argued, he did it for the benefit of himself or of the people he was connected with. If I engaged Stirling Moss to race at Brands Hatch, they said it was because I was paying him three times more than anybody else, and more than he was worth. They badly wanted him as a crowd drawer, but never took into account that he did not care to race at Brands Hatch after his early years, and only did so because I persuaded him to.

It reached the stage where I had the feeling that, whatever I might suggest at Committee meetings, it was viewed with immediate suspicion. I could sense their thoughts, 'What's he going to get out of it?', and then they would digest it, and only concede with reluctance that it might have been suggested, not for my personal gain, but for that of the Club. This was too unhealthy a situation, and I felt that the time had come for me to resign, and let someone else take on the responsibility.

After reporting my decision I offered to stay in office as long as was necessary for the Club to obtain a satisfactory replacement, and in fact it was decided that my retirement should take effect from the Annual General Meeting at the end of February 1958.

My place as Secretary was taken by Nick Syrett, who had joined

me as Assistant Secretary in April 1957, when Ron Smith had left
to go north and join Dennis Done in his motor business at Chester.

After a period of anxiety while Tony Vandervell and his team of
technicians were working hard, converting the Vanwall engine to
run on Av-gas, the welcome announcement came that the team
would be in action again for the 1958 European season. Stirling
duly signed up with Vandervell, as did Tony Brooks and Stuart
Lewis-Evans, so that the 1957 team was reconstituted. In racing
events which Vanwall would not contest, Stirling had agreed to
drive for Rob Walker in his Cooper-Climaxes, and also renewed
his sports-car contract with Aston Martin.

The B.A.R.C.'s Easter Monday Goodwood opened the European
Formula 1 season with the 100-mile Glover Trophy race. There
was also the Lavant Cup event for Formula 2 cars, and as Stirling
was to drive Rob Walker's Cooper in the Formula 1 race, and the
British Racing Partnership Formula 2 Cooper was to make its
first appearance, the meeting was of double importance to me.

During practice we experimented with the B.R.P. Cooper, using
a system of radio-relay signals instead of the usual board at the pits.
My brother John, who is an electronics engineer, had been roped
in to fix this up. Radio communication in racing cars had, of
course, been tried several times before, but in most cases this was
two-way; we planned a simpler system, transmitting to the driver
only, the advantage being that he would get his information from
the pit up to a lap earlier.

My brother devised a radio receiver which, complete with
battery, weighed only $6\frac{1}{4}$ lb., and this was installed in the nose of
the B.R.P. Cooper. The Pye radio people supplied a transmitter
similar to that used in London taxis, and we secured from the
G.P.O. the frequency and broadcasting licence, together with a
wavelength shared by certain London operators and London
Airport.

A tiny aerial, about a foot long, was fitted just behind the driver's
head, to pick up the signals, and it was with much enthusiasm that
we tried the system out at Goodwood during practice. But there
were problems we had not foreseen, the main one being the
exhaust noise, which drowned the signal to the driver when he was
travelling at racing speeds. Ambling along, he could hear us quite

clearly when up to two or three miles away, but once the Climax was wound up it was hopeless, and like other experimenters with radio communication in racing, we had to give the idea up.

Stuart Lewis-Evans drove the B.R.P. Cooper in the Lavant Cup race, finishing fourth on the car's first outing without fully extending it by any means. Then we decided that, as the B.A.R.C. were including a Formula D section in the Glover Trophy race, we would give Tom Bridger a run to accustom himself to the car under racing conditions. He made a good start, leading the Formula 2 section with very little trouble. Unfortunately, going into Madgwick on one lap he misjudged slightly, the car spun off, hit the bank at the side and was badly damaged, though Tom himself was unhurt.

Not what one could call a very brilliant conclusion to B.R.P.'s first race outing, but we were not the sole unfortunates. Stirling didn't have a good day either, retiring from the Glover Trophy race when leading comfortably in the Walker Cooper.

Next came the B.A.R.C.'s Aintree '200', with Formula 1 and Formula 2 classes running concurrently. We retrieved the wreckage of the B.R.P. Cooper and, by dint of brilliant work by Tony Robinson and close co-operation by Coopers, we rebuilt the car in time to compete.

Goodwood taught us our first lesson; we had entered the car too quickly, having taken delivery of it only a few days before, therefore being unable to devote all the time we would have wished in preparation. Although a car as built and delivered by Coopers is fully race-worthy, there are certain requirements of each driver which have to be reckoned with, and only an adequate period of testing can produce a car meeting individual wants.

The question of brake balance, for example. On the Cooper, which has twin master cylinders at the front, it is possible, by adjustment of the balance bar, to alter the braking on the front or rear wheels respectively to the desired degree. Now each driver has his own methods, and the brakes are amongst the most important factors in his getting through the corners as quickly as possible.

At Goodwood we felt afterwards that there was excessive braking on the rear wheels, and that this contributed to Bridger's crash. Coming up to Madgwick—as we surmise, a little too quickly—he braked hard, but with too much braking effect at the rear the tail tended to break away. Whereas a more experienced driver might have caught it, I think Tom was taken unawares, and lost control.

At Aintree both Stirling and the B.R.P. were to do very much better. Rob Walker had entered his Formula 1 Cooper for Stirling to handle, and also two Formula 2 Cooper-Climaxes to be driven by Tony Brooks and Maurice Trintignant.

He had a field day, Moss winning the '200' by a very short head from Jack Brabham's works Cooper, despite a badly slipping clutch. Brooks won the Formula 2 class, our Partnership Cooper came second, driven by Stuart Lewis-Evans, while Trintignant in Rob Walker's second Formula 2 entry also finished.

As both Stuart and Rob will feature considerably in this chapter, I feel this is the moment to say a little about these two great characters. Stuart Lewis-Evans was a splendid little driver, totally uncomplaining, as brave as a lion, and very, very polished at the wheel. Stuart could go very fast indeed, as was proved more than once by his practice times with a Vanwall, when he would be as quick as, if not fractionally quicker than, Stirling.

Stuart was slight in build, and suffered considerably from stomach ulcers. In fact he was due for an operation for the removal of a duodenal ulcer shortly after the 1958 G.P. of Morocco, where he so sadly met his death. Yet he was of happy disposition, and readily produced that close affinity between mechanic and driver which is so necessary for a successful team.

Indeed, Tony Robinson would often complain because Stuart so seldom had any grumbles with the car; he would come in after a practice session and say 'That's fine', and Tony, who is the sort of person who, though he strives for complete perfection, always believes that something must be a little bit wrong, would worry needlessly. I am sure that when Stuart did suggest something might be improved, Tony was absolutely delighted.

Rob Walker is a great rarity in motor racing these days; the man who is so devoted to the sport that he puts his 'all' into it despite the fact that he has promised his wife he will not personally race his cars. This is unselfishness at its greatest, and Rob is one of the true gentlemen of motor racing. He is fortunate in possessing adequate means to meet his needs, but he is very ambitious concerning his racing plans; he is quiet and calm; whereas some other people produce results by noise and bluster, Rob is the extreme opposite.

His approach to racing, like his personal turn-out, is always immaculate, and his cars, prepared by Alf Francis and others down at the Dorking racing department of Pippbrook Motors, are always in first-class condition. Rob has a delightful sense of humour too, and this, with his gentle manner, has a most soothing effect, and he is the sort of person no-one could possibly fall out with—except, of course, 'Toto' Roche, who has some argument or other with Rob annually!

After his cars won the Argentine G.P., then took both the Formula 1 and Formula 2 classes at Aintree, Rob's cup of bliss was filled to overflowing at Monaco on 18 May. It was there, in the world-famous round-the-houses Grand Prix, that Maurice Trintignant drove the canniest of races in Rob Walker's newest Formula 1 Cooper, with wishbone front suspension and a 2·2-litre Climax engine. While B.R.M., Vanwall and Ferrari successively took the lead, then lost it through retirement (including Stirling's Vanwall), 'Trint' sat amidst the leaders, goading rival team managers into fury by his rapid consistency, finally taking the lead with fifty-two laps to go. He stayed there to win a rousing victory for the Walker stable, at record speed.

Luigi Musso, whipped on by the desperate Ferrari pit staff, just could not catch the dark blue Cooper, while Peter Collins was farther back in third place, his driving seeming to lack some of that fire we had come to expect. Many observers were, in fact, tending slightly to discount Peter as a major force in Grands Prix at the opening of that season.

I don't know whether Peter got to hear of these opinions, and resolved to show just how hard he *could* try, but he certainly surprised us all at Silverstone in 1958; not once, but twice, in the *Daily Express* meeting in May, and the British G.P. in July.

Peter had told me more than once that Silverstone was one of the few circuits he really disliked. He never felt happy, it seemed, and yet, strangely enough, he scored several successes there. At the *Daily Express* meeting in 1958, he went through to win after Behra in the B.R.M. had suffered smashed goggles and lost his lead to the Ferrari. In this race Rob Walker's Coopers met a reverse, Stirling retired with gearbox trouble, and Brooks and Trintignant also retired. Perhaps the team were trying to do too much?

The third World Championship event was the Dutch G.P. at Zandvoort, and Stirling in the Vanwall was utterly unassailable. The Ferraris did not perform well, Mike Hawthorn being best in fifth place, while Peter spun out of the race when his gearbox seized up. Stirling then went on to Nurburgring for the 1000-kilometres sports-car race, scoring one of his first victories, with Jack Brabham sharing the driving of the Aston Martin for a few laps. Peter and Mike shared the second-place Ferrari, but their car was well outpaced. Next, at Spa in the Belgian/European G.P., both Stirling and Peter had to retire, and Tony Brooks was the winner for Vanwall with Mike Hawthorn second, nicely stacking up points for the Championship.

Then came Le Mans, and trouble for Peter and Mike. Like most Grand Prix professionals, neither of them enjoyed driving in the famous French 24-hour sports-car race. Mike drove the car for the first spell, but he was a little over-eager at the start and did a certain amount of harm to the clutch in getaway.

Mike, as a matter of fact, was often a bit rough on clutches, as he admitted in his wonderful book *Champion's Year*, and at Le Mans the clutch got progressively worse. Eventually it packed up altogether while Peter was driving, so he pulled in at the Ferrari signalling pit, some distance from the main pits, and explained his plight to the engineer there. What was worse, when he tried to move off, the clutchslip was so bad that he could not get under way again.

So the car was abandoned, and Mike and Peter decided there was no point in hanging around Le Mans and departed, fed up, for London straight away. When the Ferrari mechanics came to retrieve the car after the race they started it up and without too much difficulty drove off, the reason being that everything was now cold, and components which were formerly hot had now contracted.

Ferraris jumped to the conclusion that Peter Collins had not really been trying; that although the car might have continued, he was only too keen to abandon the race. They went even further, implying that Peter had deliberately spoiled the clutch in order to finish the Ferrari's run as soon as possible.

These suppositions were wholly ungrounded and most unfair to a driver as honest and sincere as Peter, but the situation had not been helped by his remarks about Le Mans in and around the pits while Mike was out in the car, from which it was quite clear that he did not enjoy racing there. These got to the ears of team manager Tavoni, who instead of understanding Peter's typically casual and 'couldn't care less' attitude took his words far too literally.

The upshot of all this was that, after driving the two pre-war Grand Prix Mercedes together with Tony Brooks in demonstration runs at the Vintage S.C.C.'s Oulton Park meeting, Peter went to Rheims for the French G.P. and found himself without a Formula 1 car. Instead, he was entered to drive a Ferrari in the Formula 2 race, this being a kind of snub adminstered by Enzo Ferrari to teach his driver a lesson.

Peter rightly resented it, and said so. Tension was high during the first day's practice, and afterwards Peter, Mike and I had a meeting with Tavoni in Peter's hotel bedroom, with Louise Collins present as well. The argument at times got pretty heated, and despite Mike's fervent protestations that it was he who had spoilt the Ferrari's clutch at Le Mans, I was never sure whether Tavoni actually believed that Peter was not responsible.

After further argument, Tavoni telephoned Enzo Ferrari at Modena the following day, and Peter was allowed to drive the Formula 1 car as well as the smaller Formula 2 model.

In the Formula 2 event—the 'Coupé de Vitesse', Peter finished second to Behra's astoundingly fast Porsche, while both Stirling and Trintignant in Rob Walker-entered Coopers had to retire. As far as the British Racing Partnership were concerned, Tommy Bridger drove our pale green Cooper, but did not shine as well as we had hoped, finishing eighth after a little bit of trouble on the first lap, when he arrived with the leaders at Thillois Corner and spun round.

The French Grand Prix itself brought both triumph and tragedy to Ferrari. Mike Hawthorn won at cracking pace, and though Stirling tried his hardest with the Vanwall, he couldn't match the pace of the 'Dino' and finished second. Poor Luigi Musso was following Mike after ten laps when he came to grief on the very fast right-hand bend which immediately follows the pits. His Ferrari went out of control and crashed, Musso being severely injured, eventually to succumb.

This was a terrible blow to the Ferrari team, and both Peter and Mike were extremely upset. Luigi was an extremely nice person, with whom I formed quite a friendship, having been able to do one or two things for him when he was in England at the instigation of Peter, who was one of his closest friends. He was extremely popular in Italy, and was a tremendous patriot, very conscious of the fact that, since Castellotti had died, he was the sole Italian left in Grand Prix racing. I think he tried too hard at Rheims and paid for his efforts with his life.

As for Peter's French Grand Prix, after all the arguments to get a drive, it was not successful. He was lying third when he had to take to the escape road at the Muizon hairpin on lap 5; this was the result of a tiny magneto airscoop coming adrift and lodging behind the brake pedal so that he couldn't fully use the brakes. Then, when he was reversing up the road, the reverse gear jammed in, and he had virtually to stand up in the seat and kick it out of gear before he could proceed.

Even then he managed to make up much of the lost time, and was lying fourth when the Ferrari ran out of petrol on the very last lap. That let Juan Fangio, driving his very last Grand Prix before making an honourable retirement, into fourth position with a Maserati, while Peter pushed his car home.

After Rheims the next big race was the British Grand Prix at Silverstone, with a lesser Formula 1 event taking place at Caen, in Normandy, the following day. I decided to forgo the Silverstone race in order to be at Caen in good time, watching after the Partnership and Rob Walker entries.

Lewis-Evans was to drive our car in the Formula 2 class at Caen, while Walker had two cars entered, one the 2·2-litre Cooper for Stirling, the other a Formula 1 car for Trintignant. As all these drivers were also engaged at Silverstone, I arranged the charter of a De Havilland Rapide aircraft, which would pick them up, together with Alf Francis and Alfred Moss, at Kidlington, near

Silverstone, after the British G.P., and take them direct to Caen after clearing Customs in the south of England.

Our stay at Caen was most enjoyable. We put up at the Hotel Malherbes, which is noted for its food and its wine cellar. As the drivers would only be able to have a short practice period on the morning of the race, I had a busy time driving the three cars, Stirling's 2·2 Cooper having to be run in, while I also practised the two Formula 2 cars as much as possible.

Our garage at Caen was owned by a very pleasant Frenchman named Léon Dumis, who had played a great part in *résistance* activities during the war. He had personally helped over eighty-five Allied soldiers or airmen to escape back to England, and had been in Caen during the whole of the bombardment following the D-day landings in Normandy. Dumis had been decorated by the French Government for his heroism during the war with the Germans, and was now peacefully occupied running his garage in the town of Caen, which had been rebuilt brick by brick.

Thus it was that Léon Dumis and I sat in my newly acquired Austin-Healey 'Sprite', accompanied by some others over for the Caen race, listening on the car radio to the B.B.C. broadcast of the British Grand Prix at Silverstone. As the excitement of the start came over the air, we wondered whether Stirling would be able to pull it off with the Vanwall, and if not, whether it would be Tony Brooks or Mike Hawthorn who would win.

We none of us gave a thought to Peter Collins, and were we surprised when Peter shot through to the front like an arrow out of a bow, never to be caught! Most of us thought this was simply an attempt by Ferrari to break the opposition—Peter probably had a half-empty tank, we said.

How wrong we were—and how delighted we were to be wrong. Peter was magnificent, showing the crowd that on his day he could drive as well as anybody in the world. The 1958 British Grand Prix was certainly one of his finest races ever, and he won by a considerable margin from Mike Hawthorn, while Stirling's Vanwall blew up in the attempt to hold him.

Shortly after this race, incidentally, I saw at the Steering Wheel Club an exceptionally fine painting by Roy Nockolds, showing Peter coming up to Abbey Curve with Stirling close behind in the early stages of the race. I am pleased to say that I was able to buy this painting from Roy, and it now graces our flat.

Late on Saturday evening the Rapide arrived at Caen with its load of drivers, and we all went off for a hearty meal whilst the full Silverstone story was told. So far as the G.P. de Caen was concerned, our three cars could hardly have done better. Stirling won the Formula 1 section and the race outright, 'Trint' won the Formula 2 section, and Stuart was second with the B.R.P. car, all of which called for a celebration, which was duly effected.

Came August Bank Holiday, and with it the German G.P. on the Sunday, followed by Brands Hatch on Monday. I did not go to Nurburg for the German race, remaining in England as we were running the Partnership Cooper at Brands in the Formula 2 race. At practice on Saturday the car went particularly well, and with Stuart Lewis-Evans driving we had high hopes for the actual race.

On Sunday afternoon I had occasion to go up to Stirling's office in William IV Street to check on some documents. When I returned to the flat in the early evening, I was dismayed to find everyone there in a considerable state of gloom. Margot Beaubien, a close friend of Katie Moss, and Peter Jopp were staying to dinner that evening, and they broke the news to me that Peter Collins had crashed at Nurburg during the German G.P., and that his injuries were grave.

I tried at once to phone Stirling up at Adenau. Eventually I got through to him, but he could tell me nothing further than that Peter's condition was very serious. Tony Brooks had won the race with a Vanwall, and Stirling had retired, but I hardly took this in, so agitated was I at the news about Peter.

Next I tried to get in touch with Peter's mother and father, who I knew were down on the yacht at Dartmouth, in case the news had not reached them yet. I telephoned the Dartmouth police, the only people I could think of who would go out to the yacht, and urged them to hurry, but we were all too late, for I think Peter had died before his parents could even reach a phone and ring the hospital.

Peter's death was a very great shock to me. I know that other drivers, all too many, have been killed in motor races, and whilst one is very sorry to hear it, and regrets that talented men in the prime of life should suddenly cease to be amongst us, it is only when you are very closely connected with somebody, and have a deep friendship, that the loss really hits home.

In Peter's case I was shattered. He seemed so absolutely the last person to get killed in a racing car. A gay, carefree, lovable person, he was both difficult and easy. Difficult because he was impossible to control; he was like a young colt in a paddock who refused to take any notice of his parents, and would scarper gaily from one side of the paddock to the other, enjoying life as he though he ought to enjoy it, instead of living the disciplined life which most of us lead. Easy because of his happy-go-lucky outlook and his tremendous zest and enjoyment of life.

I shall always remember him as a sandy-haired youngster with hair blowing over his eyes, which he had a nervous habit of constantly brushing backwards with his right hand. Certainly his passing away had a greater effect upon me than anything else which has happened in motor racing to date.

I was much too upset to go to Brands Hatch on Monday, but Stuart Lewis-Evans drove an excellent race in the B.R.P. Cooper, following Jack Brabham's works car nose to tail and finishing a close second. The race was run in two equal-length heats, the times being added together to determine the result, and it was near the end of the second heat that an oil pipe to one of the camshafts broke on Stuart's car. However, he coasted across the line, using the oil in the tank to the last drop.

The next big race was the G.P. of Portugal at Oporto. To Stirling it was a race vital to his chances for the World Championship. He won it with a Vanwall after a relatively easy drive, but unfortunately failed to make the fastest lap owing to a misunderstanding. It had been a long-standing agreement between Stirling and Vanwall team manager David Yorke that whenever a rival had set up the fastest lap in a race, David would pass on the information to Stirling by means of a signal, giving an abbreviated version of the driver's name, and his time. Thus 'HAW 1–36' would mean that Mike Hawthorn had made the fastest lap so far in 1 min. 36 sec., and Stirling would know immediately that he had to better this if humanly possible, in order to gain the extra Championship point allowed for fastest lap.

At Oporto, Stirling had things more or less his own way, and in the Vanwall could leave Mike's Ferrari practically anywhere on the circuit; so it is reasonably safe to assume that he could better Mike's fastest lap whenever he wished to. But this time David Yorke signalled 'HAW REC', which Stirling took to be 'HAW REG', meaning 'Hawthorn Regular' instead of 'Record'. In the circumstances he did not attempt to extend his pace, and won the race without being aware that he had not made the fastest lap.

His Championship score that day was 8 points instead of 9—and Stirling lost the World Championship in 1958 to Mike by 1 point! Had Moss scored 9 at Oporto, Mike would have scored 6 instead of 7, and in the year's total would have been 2 points down! I am not attempting to prove that Mike was not a worthy World Champion—we all know what a splendid driver he was—but simply to show what silly things the destiny of a Championship can hang upon. It is significant that the F.I.A. have decided not to award the extra point for fastest lap in the 1960 World Championship scoring.

Sandwiched between the Portuguese G.P. and the next Championship round—the Italian G.P.—came a new international meeting at Brands Hatch, the Kentish 'Hundred'. The Brands Hatch Company, of which I am a director, had decided that the time had arrived to widen the scope of the circuit by promoting a major international Formula 2 race. This would mean spending a considerable sum on starting money in order to get a first-class entry, but we decided to take the plunge.

Amongst the entries secured were Schell, Trintignant, Shelby and Moss—making his first appearance at Brands Hatch for four years—plus all the regulars like Brabham, Russell, Lewis-Evans in the B.R.P. Cooper, Wicken, etc. His long absence from the circuit caused Stirling to put in plenty of practice to get back 'in the groove', driving Rob Walker's Cooper-Climax.

The 'Hundred' proved an excellent race, Stirling winning after a tremendous tussle with Jack Brabham and Stuart Lewis-Evans in both the 42-lap heats which made up the total distance. Despite the high quality of the entry, however, the spectator attendance was disappointingly small. At the next board meeting, we considered this point very closely, but felt that the experience and prestige Brands Hatch had gained in presenting a meeting of this class would stand the circuit in good stead for the future.

And so to Monza, as usual the most exciting event on the Calendar; I missed Zandvoort, Spa, Nurburg and Oporto, but I wouldn't miss the Italian G.P. if I could help it. Just writing about it makes me enthuse. I like Italy, I like Milan, I like shopping there, where half the fun is in the bartering. I like Italian food, though some people say it is fattening; personally I revel in the pastas, the raviolis, the spaghettis, the canneloni, the lasagne, and other dishes.

A favourite eating place of ours in Milan is the Gigi Fatzi restaurant. Gigi is a restaurateur from Rome, where he caters for a smart class of clientele in the Eternal City. Then he decided to open up in Milan as well, and founded his wonderful restaurant on the outskirts of the town.

Gigi Fatzi serves wonderful meals, and is noted for an amusing 'gimmick', confronting the customer with a huge pair of scales when he enters the restaurant. The object is to weigh yourself when you enter, and again when you leave—and if you don't come out heavier, you have done neither the restaurant nor yourself justice!

As to Monza itself, there is the excitement of uncertainty too; uncertainty as to the sort of pass you will receive. The Italians seem to be utterly incapable of providing you with the proper pass. They just can't bear the idea, it seems, of your going anywhere without the maximum of obstruction and difficulty; there are hordes of policemen who enter into the spirit of obstruction, and in 1958 they got to the point where they pushed Fangio off the circuit—a matter which did not go unnoticed in the Italian press that evening.

But once past the various barriers—human and otherwise—and one sees Monza at its best; the colour and excitement make the Italian Grand Prix a never-to-be-forgotten spectacle, especially when the cars are wheeled out on to the starting grid in front of the great grandstands. Around the cars mill the photographers, pressmen, managers, mechanics, the inevitable police, officials, and all the other people who make up the Grand Prix scene. It is intoxicating.

Then out come the Italian soldiers, each bearing the flag of one nation represented in the race, the national anthems of the countries being played one after another. Whilst this pageant is being enacted, the grandstand is one seething mass of humanity, cheering its heroes, drinking chianti, eating sandwiches, and generally creating such a babble and hubbub that it sounds almost as if one were in the middle of the jungle.

Then, at last, the flag is dropped, the cars roar away, and the chaotic mass of people on the grid is somehow shovelled back into the pits, where despite everything orderliness begins to reign.

Stirling was not to be lucky at Monza that year. It always seems to me that the Italian G.P. either brings him dramatic victory or retirement; in this case he retired. Nevertheless, as soon as his Vanwall had been pushed away, he set about helping David Yorke, enthusiastically giving signals to Tony Brooks who, despite a bad start, was now going strongly, rapidly overhauling Mike Hawthorn's leading Ferrari.

Eventually Tony won the race, and Mike was second, having suffered with his old clutch trouble, which he had used a bit too roughly at the beginning of the race. I don't know whether Tony Brooks did it purposely, but he passed Mike's Ferrari right in front of the grandstands, to a roar of cheers from the British contingent, and an absolute groan of disappointment from the Italians.

Monza left the Championship situation as complicated as before. With one more race to go, at Casablanca, Stirling could still gain the elusive Championship, provided he won and Mike was not higher than third.

Between the Grands Prix at Monza and Casablanca, life with Stirling was pretty nearly impossible. I don't mean this unkindly; it was due to the very tension under which he was living. Stirling wanted to win the Championship badly; it was his greatest ambition in life, and none can say that, with all his achievements, he was not a worthy candidate. But more than just winning it, Stirling wanted to win it with a British car.

I have said earlier that I believe Stirling could have been the first British World Champion years ago, had he chosen to drive for Ferrari when asked to. The fact that he decided instead to drive British cars soundly spoiled his chances of achieving this ambition, but it was, and is, a measure of his patriotism that he sought to win the Championship on a British-built car.

Anyway, the immediate pre-Casablanca period was an extremely trying time for those connected with Stirling, and we all had to exercise our tact and patience to the utmost degree. We tried as far as possible to be helpful to him, by steering off *the* subject, but all were agreed that we would be very relieved when Casablanca was over, and the issue settled one way or the other.

At last race week came. A whole party of us flew to Casablanca on a charter flight in a Douglas DC6 arranged by John Webb and Alan Foster. It was my first visit to North Africa, and the trip down was most enjoyable. Another charter plane was also operating, this being a B.E.A. Viscount arranged by Tony Vandervell, and naturally there was quite a bit of friendly rivalry and chaff between the respective passengers. Just to make life really complicated, Vanwall driver Moss came down on the Webb-Foster DC6, whilst Ferrari driver Hawthorn flew on the Vandervell Viscount!

The race itself was highly dramatic. Stirling did everything that was asked of him; he could not have done more. He won the race, and made fastest lap, earning nine Championship points. But owing to trouble, his Vanwall team mates were unable to give him the support he needed, so that Mike Hawthorn finished second, becoming 1958 World Champion by one point, with Stirling runner-up—for the fourth successive year!

Accidents marred the event. First the Frenchman François Picard in Rob Walker's Formula 2 Cooper-Climax left the road at a fast bend, the Cooper being written off and Picard suffering a fractured skull and other injuries. Then, one lap later, and within fifty yards of the same spot, our B.R.P. Formula 2 Cooper driven by Tommy Bridger was hit up the back by Gendebien's Ferrari. The Cooper was bowled off to the left, bouncing nose to tail until it looked something like a squashed tennis ball, while the Ferrari shot off to the right, being practically ripped in half. Most fortunately, neither Gendebien nor Bridger were badly hurt.

Then came the worst crash of all, when Stuart Lewis-Evans's Vanwall apparently slid on some oil and went off the road into the desert, catching fire. The fuel tank burst, and poor Stuart's clothes were covered in burning petrol. Unfortunately, instead of running towards the people who could have helped him, Stuart in his confusion ran away, the speed of his running helping to fan the flames and burning him even more. When eventually he was caught and the flames extinguished, the terrible fire had done its worst.

They took Stuart to the local hospital in Casablanca by helicopter, and he was flown back to England next day with Tony Vandervell, Mike Hawthorn and others in the chartered B.E.A. Viscount. During the journey he recovered sufficiently to drink tea, and to hold quite a lucid conversation. When the plane reached England, he was immediately taken to East Grinstead Hospital and put under the care of that famous surgeon Sir Archibald McIndoe.

There, during his last few days of life, Stuart, who had the courage of every lion in the world, spoke only of his future, of the cars he would drive, and the successes he hoped to achieve. Unfortunately it was not to be so, and this popular little driver died a few days later. That it should have been the last Grand Prix of the season, and the accident seemingly not his fault, made his death all the more tragic.

Yet it was, in a way, better perhaps that Stuart died as he did, for his burns were so terrible that his life, had it been spared, could not have been a happy one. He would never have been able to drive again and, in fact, it is doubtful whether he could have walked. I think a fitting tribute to this brave and talented little driver is the fact that, in his will, he had left the cornea of his eyes to the Eye Bank, and it seems that, not many days after his death, somebody else was walking round, seeing the world through the eyes of one of Britain's finest racing drivers.

Joining the Foster-Webb charter plane party at noon on Monday, Alfred Moss, Stirling and I noticed quite a few people now wearing fezes; some also had camel saddles, oriental-looking slippers, rugs and other evidence of visits to the local markets. Many a joyous haggle had obviously been fought between the 'Eengleesh' visitors and the dusky tradesmen, who celebrated the Casablanca G.P. by doubling most of their prices to allow for the expected bartering, and still made a good profit!

Soon the DC6 took off for the six-hour flight back to London, and many people had settled down to an afternoon's 'ziz' in the plane when there came an alarming banging noise, followed by a spluttering, and the starboard outer engine completely failed. The plane began to weave about and lose height, and then, to our horror, the port outer engine also stopped, and we were running on two motors only!

It was at this extremely tense moment that a deep voice boomed out from the back, 'Anybody care to join me in a hymn?' and the tension broke in a concerted roar of laughter. The voice was that of David Haynes, Stirling's good friend and Ford distributor from Maidstone. The pilot, nursing his aircraft along on two engines only, must have wondered what caused his passengers suddenly to burst out laughing at such a moment. Anyway, he reached Paris safely, where we landed, and were transferred to another plane. We eventually reached London at around three o'clock in the morning, about six hours overdue.

With Casablanca the 1958 Grand Prix season ended, and apart from the Boxing Day Brands Hatch meeting, we could now turn our minds to things other than motor racing. The Earl's Court Motor Show at the latter end of October commanded my immediate attention once I was back from North Africa.

At that time I still retained my post as Public Relations Officer for Donald Healey, and I had for some time been considering how best to tackle the eternal problem of Earl's Court—that is, to attract the crowd to *your* stand and keep them there. Faced with the publicity guns of 'the big five', who between them were bringing out various brand-new models just before the Motor Show, it was obvious that we would need something pretty eye-opening to draw the crowds away from their stands.

In other words, putting it bluntly, we needed a 'gimmick'. My contention was that if, by some means or other, I could create sufficient interest in the Austin-Healey exhibits to bring the public to the stand, it was then up to the salesmen to make use of the opportunity, and 'push' the Company's wares. We needed something so glittering and attractive that people would make a point of visiting the stand specially to see it.

So was born the 'Gold, Mink and Ivory' Austin-Healey. I put

my idea to Donald Healey, who agreed it was an extremely sound one. Then, after thinking seriously about it for a few days, he decided that the cost of the venture would be prohibitive, and the idea would have to be shelved.

I felt very bitter about this, and accordingly asked him whether, assuming I could guarantee a purchaser of the special car at a fixed price, he would then be prepared to build the car and carry out all the special treatment it would require.

'Yes,' said Donald; under those circumstances he would, so I then approached Basil Cardew, motoring correspondent of the *Daily Express*. We had a discussion in a Fleet Street pub one evening, as a result of which Basil put the idea to his editor that their newspaper should purchase the car and announce it to be the first prize in a Motor Show competition they were promoting.

Having obtained their agreement to this proposal, I went back to Donald Healey, who undertook to begin work immediately on the special Austin-Healey. The car itself was basically an ordinary 'Hundred-Six' de Luxe model, but the entire coachwork was painted in a beautiful ivory shade. Everything that was normally chromed was 24-carat gold-plated, right down to the tiniest trimming washers and screws; the wire wheels, disc brakes, bumpers and instruments were all given the same treatment.

The seats were made of a reversed champagne kid leather with pure mink insets on the seat and the back squab, while the dashboard and the complete side trim embodied reversed champagne kid. All instrument controls and other parts normally of plastic were made of solid ivory, as was the steering wheel, which was an absolute masterpiece of the craftsman's art. The ignition key was gold-plated, also the key ring on which was a tiny, but true-to-scale, 24-carat solid gold miniature of the Austin-Healey Hundred-Six.

The 'Golden' Austin-Healey was valued at around £4000, and suffice to say proved a sensation at Earl's Court, 1958; it gained some very good press reports and generous publicity, and drew masses of visitors to the Austin-Healey stand, which was the object of the exercise.

After fulfilling his various commitments at the Motor Show, Stirling Moss and his wife Katie decided they really must get to

Nassau, to finish off their house on Camperdown Heights. At the first opportunity they flew back to the Bahamas, and pressed on with the final touches. That winter saw the house completed, and an extremely comfortable home it has proved to be, although, due to Stirling's racing and business commitments, they seldom get much opportunity to stay there any length of time during the season, usually being able only to spend November and December there.

In fact, in late November 1958, Stirling had to interrupt his stay in Nassau to compete in the Melbourne G.P. Formule Libre race at Albert Park. Driving Rob Walker's Formula 1 Cooper-Climax, he was lucky to win by the margin of 39 sec. from Jack Brabham, as the car ran very short of water in the 100-mile final, and was practically incandescent when it finished.

Just after Christmas Stirling was off on his travels again, this time accompanied by Katie, bound for New Zealand and the Grand Prix at Auckland early in the New Year. Again, Stirling's mount was the much-travelled Cooper-Climax of Rob Walker's stable, watched over by Alf Francis, and again Stirling won by a handsome margin, after being helped out by Jack Brabham, who sportingly lent him a suspension wishbone to replace one that had cracked on the Walker Cooper. Jack himself was second, and Bruce McLaren third, both in Coopers.

Stirling and Katie stayed awhile in New Zealand, then flew back to Australia, where they went on a safari in Western Australia. It was then that Tony Vandervell made his startling announcement that, because of health reasons, he would not run the Vanwall team in 1959. This came as a big shock to all in England, and as big a shock to Stirling when the news reached him while hunting crocodile and other big game in the wilds of the West Australian bush.

As Stirling's representatives in England, I would like to say that Alfred Moss and I only received news of the Vandervell retirement after it had been released to the press, and that it came as a complete and utter surprise. I felt that the least Tony Vandervell could have done, in view of the staunch support Stirling had given him since 1957, was to have informed us of his decision a few hours before the press. He should have known that when the news broke, the first thing the press would do was to contact either Alfred Moss or myself to secure statements on Stirling's behalf.

As it was, we were inundated with phone calls and inquiries when we had hardly absorbed the news ourselves. In the post next morning we each received a copy of the official statement, as issued to the press.

Meantime, Stirling and Katie were continuing their world tour, and having finished safari in Western Australia, travelled homewards by way of Singapore, Hong Kong, Siam and India.

It was while he was in Siam that Stirling heard the tragic news of Mike Hawthorn's death on the Guildford Bypass, and in spite of very poor telephonic connexions, the press quickly hunted Stirling out to obtain his comments. Yet what could he, or any of us, say about such a sad accident? That Mike should win the World Championship—the first Englishman to do so—that he should then make the hard decision to give up motor racing in order to concentrate on his garage business at Farnham, and then should meet death in his own private Jaguar saloon on a public road seemed so appallingly unfair that no mere comment was suitable.

Stirling arrived back in London feeling jaded and nervy instead of fit and refreshed after his long trip. The impact of the Vanwall withdrawal from racing, followed by the Hawthorn tragedy, had their effect upon him; whilst the press gave him little relief from inquiries. Stirling, in fact, was not a happy man, and decided to escape for a while on a brief skiing holiday in Switzerland. It was arranged that four of us would go: Stirling and Katie, myself and my wife Ann. We planned to stay at Unterwassèr, where Stirling and I had very much enjoyed a previous winter holiday.

About this time I became afflicted with that fashionable but painful malady, a slipped disc, which threatened to end my skiing holiday before it even started. Not long before, I had purchased a smashed Wolseley 1500 saloon, which I proceeded to rebuild. As by then I had resigned my positions with Donald Healey, owing to pressure of other work, I no longer had the use of an Austin-Healey for personal use. I had decided that, when the Wolseley was repaired, I would keep it for my own use; it being a compact, lively little car, ideal for use in crowded London.

A few days before we were due to leave for Switzerland, I

joined in the work of assembling the Wolseley. We were putting the engine back into the chassis, a job which proved rather a juggling feat. At one stage, it was necessary to exert that little extra strength to push the engine to one side in order to get it in, and I must have been badly positioned whilst pushing hard, because I suddenly felt a wrench in my back followed by a terrible pain.

I endured what was almost torture for two days, then went down to St Thomas's Hospital to see my old friend Dr Philippe Bauwens, director of physical medicine there. Within a short time the trouble was diagnosed as a slipped disc, and I was promptly given treatment; such treatment as I had never known nor anticipated.

I was told to lay, tummy down, on a bed, when three nurses took up station, one at each end of the bed, and one in the middle. One nurse grabbed my arms and pulled one way, while the other took hold of my legs and pulled the other way. While the two nurses were trying to tear me apart, the third practically stood on my back, and, with a whacking great thump on the spine, tried to put the disc back in place.

These methods worked wonderfully, for the disc slipped back nearly in position, and I was miraculously free from pain. But when I told the nurses that I was to go skiing in two or three days' time, they were horrified, and foretold for me a black future unless I took care of myself.

At Unterwasser there are two ski-lifts, one a funicular railway which rises to some 1500–2000 feet, and the other a chair hoist which goes right to the top of the mountain. Naturally the slopes were more severe higher up, and my whole skiing experience had been confined to the limits of the funicular railway. Then one day the Swiss National Ski School instructor decided that all his 'pupils', of which I was one, had now reached a standard where they could venture to the top of the highest run.

So, with baited breath, we went up on the chair lift. When we got to the top, it became obvious that this was an 'expert's slope', and while it was all right for Stirling, who was quite accomplished by this time, and Katie, who was an old hand at skiing, I personally viewed it with some alarm. 'Off you go,' said the instructor, and off I went, zig-zagging across the slope as much as possible to reduce the gradient, and trying Christiania turns at the end of each zig-zag.

Suddenly I lost control and went careering down the mountain-side at ever-increasing speed, until it seemed to me I must be doing 70 m.p.h.! Then I became a bundle of helpless humanity with legs, arms, skis and poles flying in every direction possible, careering down fast and furiously and finding the ground extremely hard until, miraculously, I came to rest some three hundred yards farther down the slope.

When I picked myself up, the first thing I thought was, 'Well, this has certainly done the disc no good,' but as a matter of fact, quite a remarkable thing had happened because, in the bouncing and jolting I received, the disc had been pushed back the extra twenty per cent and was now firmly in its right position!

We all thoroughly enjoyed the holiday. The weather was very kind to us; almost too kind, indeed, for the sun was so brilliant that the snow started to disappear from the mountain-sides. I am afraid that my wife Ann, who was a little bit worried about the danger of breaking a leg because of her stage dancing, did not take to skiing, but this didn't in any way diminish her enjoyment.

As for Stirling, he progressed to such an extent that by the end of the week he took part in the local weekly race meeting and won a prize. Katie Moss also took part in the same race, but in a higher-skilled class, and also won a prize, and in fact by the end of their holiday Stirling had taken his bronze medal, and Katie her silver, these medals representing Swiss national skiing standards.

CHAPTER TWELVE

THE ELUSIVE CHAMPIONSHIP

BACK again in London, I looked forward eagerly to the 1959 racing season, both with the British Racing Partnership and Stirling. Alfred Moss and I had decided to extend B.R.P.'s equipment from one to two Formula 2 Coopers. That we could do this was very largely due to the help we received from the Shell-Mex and B.P. Co. through Bryan Turle, their British racing manager. The spectators probably do not realize it, but it is the fuel companies who very largely make motor racing possible, through their support.

Mindful of the preponderance of Coventry Climax engines in the Formula 2 class, we investigated the possibilities of finding an alternative power unit. Not, I hasten to add, because of any dissatisfaction with the Climax engine. Far from it; we held it as tough, willing and reliable, and in the greatest esteem, but felt that, unless there was some variety in engines, and a wider element of competition, the formula was in distinct danger of becoming too stereotyped, and suffering the same fate as Formula 3.

I am happy to say that the Coventry Climax Company agreed with our views, and when, later on, I had a meeting with Mr Leonard Lee, the Chairman of Coventry Climax, at their London office, he heartily agreed that healthy competition was beneficial to everybody, and that monopolies in any one class of racing became boring and unconvincing.

Now it happened that during 1958 some excellent performances had been put up in Continental events by the 1500 c.c. Borgward sports car, fitted with a 4-cylinder, fuel-injection engine. These Borgwards had repeatedly duelled with the rear-engined Porsches though handicapped by excess weight, and I felt that such an engine, fitted in a lighter racing chassis, might have good results in Formula 2.

We decided to approach the Borgward Company of Bremen to see if they were interested in supplying or loaning such engines. After some extremely protracted negotiations, carried out on my

behalf by Messrs Metcalfe and Mundy, the London concessionaires for the Borgward car, and in particular by Teddy de Gebert,
one of the members of the Company, it was arranged that I should
go out to Bremen to discuss the project personally with the
Borgward Company.

I found the Borgward set-up very different to that of Mercedes-
Benz. As a company, Borgward were not wholeheartedly in motor
racing; rather can it be said that they 'dabbled' in it. They had no
racing department as such, the whole of the competition programme being governed by the Chief Experimental Engineer, Herr
Buchner. Development and preparation of their fuel-injection racing engines was carried out in the experimental department, alongside other work on Borgward private cars and lorries.

On the other hand, Borgward showed marked keenness to co-
operate, and were a fair and understanding concern to negotiate
with. They are something of a colossus in German industry, producing not only large numbers of cars and trucks under their own
name, but also owning the Lloyd and Goliath works; in addition,
they are currently engaged in developing a quantity-production
helicopter.

Ranking as they do in size and importance with any of the 'big
five' of the British automobile industry, the interesting thing about
Borgward is that their policy is dictated by one man, Carl F. W.
Borgward, who holds all the shares of the Company bearing his
name. His approval has to be obtained for every major decision,
and many lesser ones, made by his executives, and the question of
loaning the Borgward 1500RS fuel-injection engines for use in
British Cooper racing cars was certainly one for Carl Borgward
himself to answer.

Eventually, therefore, I met Dr Borgward himself, and discussed
the project in his office, through an interpreter. He was a most
courteous person, listening to all I had to say, and weighing up the
problem very shrewdly. As far as I could see, he only wished to do
what any man in his position would; that is, to further and to safeguard the interests of the very large automobile empire he had
built up.

My proposals were that Borgward engines should be used in
three Coopers for Formula 2 racing; two for the British Racing

Partnership, and one for Rob Walker's car, which would be driven by Stirling Moss. The fact that Stirling would be driving was naturally of very considerable interest, and when eventually I received Borgward's consent to the proposition, no bones were made about saying that it was only the connexion with Moss's name that persuaded them to release engines for B.R.P. as well.

There were several more trips to Bremen for me before, at last, everything was settled, the contract drawn up and signed, and the first of the three engines shipped to England. The 1500RS Borgward unit was an interesting design, produced by Carl Ludwig Brandt, and embodying several component parts adapted from the standard Isabella engine. As a racing engine, it had four valves per cylinder and twin overhead camshafts, twin plugs per cylinder, coil ignition, and Bosch direct fuel injection. The hemispherical cylinder head was an extremely complicated piece of machining, having sixteen openings for the valves, eight for the plugs, and four for the petrol injection units. Bore and stroke were 75 mm. by 84·5 mm., as on the Isabella.

The whole unit was extremely light, and even with the dynamo and ancillary equipment it weighed only a few pounds more than the 1500 c.c. Coventry Climax engine, while the power output was 150 b.h.p. at 7500 r.p.m. One advantage over the Climax was a much higher revs. range, the Climax being safe for around 7200–7300 r.p.m., and the Borgward good for 8000 r.p.m.

One of the conditions that Borgward insisted upon in the contract was that we should employ, at our expense, a skilled mechanic from the Bremen factory. So when everything was settled to our mutual satisfaction, and the first Borgward engine arrived in England, there came with it a brilliant young German engineer named Fritz Juttner, who, apart from being employed in the Experimental department at Bremen, had also driven in the works sports-car team alongside Herrmann and Bonnier.

Fritz certainly had a difficult task to perform when he first arrived. He spoke very little English, conversation being carried out in smatterings of French or German, whichever was best suited. On top of that, he was away from his wife and children, was in a strange country and had the entire responsibility for the proper functioning of the almost priceless Borgward engines.

Not surprisingly, Fritz was rather unhappy when he started to work for us, and there was a certain amount of friction, as was almost bound to happen with any arrangement of this sort. But he gamely stuck it, picked up some useful English, made many friends, and I am happy to say that by the end of the season when he returned to Germany Fritz had become one of the family, so to speak, admired by all who worked with him for his technical skill.

Although Fritz Juttner's primary responsibility was the maintenance of the Borgward engines for the Partnership and for Rob Walker, he never shirked working on the cars themselves, and always worked in line with our own mechanics late into the night, without a word of complaint. He is, in fact, a member of that uncommon breed of men, the real racing mechanics, who represent one of the finest groups of people one can ever be associated with.

So the Cooper-Borgward came into existence. The two cars for B.R.P. were new ones, the 1958 car which crashed at Casablanca having been rebuilt and sold early in 1959 to Jack Brabham. Jack put a 2-litre engine in, re-selling the car in Australia, but retained the 1500 c.c. Climax engine for his own use in 1959 Formula 2 events, having considerable success with it.

Jack kicked off well by winning the Formula 2 race at Goodwood on Easter Monday, where the Cooper-Borgwards had their first outing, driven by Ivor Bueb and George Wicken, both of whom had been signed up as B.R.P. drivers for 1959. As so often happens with a new car, the performance first time out was disappointing, and Ivor and George finished way behind the leaders.

After Goodwood, however, we were able to settle down to some very stringent testing, as a result of which the performance was improved notably. In our next race, the Aintree '200', Ivor's car was leading the Formula 2 class quite comfortably when the clutch gave out, while George Wicken's car also had clutch trouble.

But we were learning all the time, and the B.R.P. Cooper-Borgwards performed better and better as the season progressed, while at the same time Rob Walker and Alf Francis, who also had a heavy Formula 1 racing programme to cope with, joined in the fray with their Borgward-engined Cooper with special Colotti five-speed gearbox in the Syracuse G.P. a week after Aintree.

This Sicilian race was for Formula 2 in 1959, a change which reduced Italian participation to a single works $1\frac{1}{2}$-litre Ferrari and a sports Osca, the rest of the fifteen starters, apart from a Porsche, being British—either Coopers or Lotuses. Once again I had been delegated the task of inscribing the British entries, and rounded up several, including the three Cooper-Borgwards of Moss, Bueb and Wicken—the Walker car in dark blue and ours in pale green—Graham Hill's works Lotus, and two Cooper-Climaxes for Jack Brabham and Masten Gregory.

These six cars were flown out to Syracuse in a Douglas DC6 chartered through John Webb and Alan Foster from Skyways Ltd., being stowed two abreast in the front of the plane, with the remaining space utilized for passenger seats to take the drivers and mechanics. Stirling had booked a seat, but had to change his outward flight plans as he had been invited to a special dinner party at No. 10 Downing Street at the request of King Hussein of Jordan.

On race day, Stirling proved complete master of the situation in the Walker Cooper-Borgward. He won comfortably from Behra's works Ferrari, with Brabham third, Gregory fourth, Ivor Bueb fifth and George Wicken seventh, a 100-per-cent finish for the Borgward-powered Coopers.

Before leaving the subject, I must relate a story concerning Syracuse. Apart from arranging British entries, starting money, charter plane, etc., I had also fixed up through John Webb and Alan Foster for the hire of various cars when we arrived at Catania airport, including, of course, one for B.R.P.

One night Ivor, George, Tony Robinson and I went into Syracuse and parked the car in what seemed a harmless position, only to find when we returned that there was a police parking ticket stuck on the windscreen. As we were to attend the Mayor's cocktail party in the Town Hall the following morning, we decided not to report to the police at once, in the hope that we might have a word with somebody influential at the party.

At the cocktail party we got hold of the Italian Shell representative who was looking after our B.R.P. entries and giving us tremendous assistance, and got him to mention to the Mayor the fact that we had received this parking ticket—'and please'—with tongues in cheeks—'what were we to do about it? Was it to him we had to report?'

As a result, the Mayor called the Chief of Police over and soundly tore a strip off him. It emerged that the whole affair had arisen solely because of the intense rivalry between the Syracuse people and the Catanians; our hired car had a Catanian registration number so a parking ticket was natural!

Our treatment was light, it seems, compared with some. Once, when the Catanians came to play the Syracusans at football, all the cars bearing Catanian numbers were pelted with cabbages, bad eggs and rotten tomatoes, while the Syracuse cars went through scot free!

With the Cooper-Borgwards nicely launched on their 1959 season, it is time to come back to Formula 1 as it concerned Stirling. When it became known that ill health would prevent Tony Vandervell from operating the Vanwall team, Stirling's choice of Formula 1 cars was narrowed down. He didn't want to drive for Ferrari; he was uncertain about the B.R.M., and liked the idea of Rob Walker's Cooper-Climax on certain circuits but was not sure about others.

We spent many hours discussing it, not a few of them on long-distance telephones whilst he was out of England. Indeed telephone communication with Stirling became something of a trial, as I had to contact him in any corner of the world; and owing to the time differences in various countries, it was sometimes necessary for me to make the calls at two, three or four o'clock in the morning to coincide conveniently with him.

It was during one of our long-distance telephone conversations that the idea of the Cooper-B.R.M. was born. It was known that Coventry Climax were to build a full 2·5-litre twin-cam engine for Grand Prix work, and that Coopers and Lotus were banking on using these new units. But it was not known when they would be ready nor how they would perform. The first Grande Epreuve of the season, following the cancellation of the Argentine *Temporada*, was the Monaco G.P. in May, and with uncertainty about the Climax engine Stirling conceived the idea of fitting a B.R.M. power unit into a Cooper chassis. The B.R.M.'s power in such a light chassis might be the right answer, he felt, for the tight conditions at Monaco.

If an engine could be obtained on loan, Rob Walker was agreeable to having it installed in one of his Coopers, so it was at short notice that I wrote to Mr Alfred Owen, proprietor of B.R.M., asking for a meeting with him. This was arranged through his personal Public Relations representative, A. F. Rivers Fletcher, 'Rivers' being an immense enthusiast, keen to see the project materialize.

I met Mr Owen in a London hotel by appointment, he having chosen this particular venue as he had another engagement that day nearby, presiding over a meeting of the Committee of Dr Barnardo's Homes, of which movement he is a very staunch supporter.

In the short hearing he was able to give me, I came straight to the point, telling Mr Owen precisely what we sought to do. He listened patiently to all I had to say, then said, 'Within a few days I will give you the answer.' True to his word, the answer came without delay, 'Yes, the engine would be available,' and he immediately arranged for me to meet Peter Spear, his engineering executive, to tie up all the details with the Owen Racing Organization.

From that initial meeting, and subsequent encounters, I came to regard Alfred Owen as one of the most sincere people I have had the opportunity to do business with. He is tremendously interested in humanitarian problems, and is always keen to listen to the other man's story, even though time is usually pressing. He is the Chairman and Managing Director of numerous companies, and I believe it is true to say that his industrial empire, the Owen Organization, which is shared by his brother and his sister, is one of the largest private organizations in the world; certainly the largest in Britain.

When the B.R.M. engine arrived at Rob Walker's racing department in Dorking, Alf Francis and his team set to with its installation in the Cooper chassis. They encountered several problems, principal amongst them being the fact that the two magnetos were mounted on the forward ends of the camshafts, and would therefore protrude through the bulkhead into the cockpit if left there. They had to be repositioned and a new drive devised.

A further problem was that of the transmission, and particularly the gearbox. Stirling and Rob Walker had a long discussion over this; Stirling felt that a five-speed gearbox was desirable to get the best out of the car, and Rob agreed that one should be designed and constructed. For this work, the rising young Italian designer Colotti was chosen, and Alf Francis made the trip out to his establishment at Modena to discuss the problem and agree on a specification. Later the Cooper with B.R.M. engine installed was taken out there for the new gearbox to be fitted, after which Stirling tried the car on the Modena autodrome and found it satisfactory.

Car and driver came back to England in time for the Aintree '200', and in that race, although Stirling broke his old lap record by ·4 sec., the gearbox failed on lap 30. At the time the Cooper-B.R.M. was leading, which may have seemed encouraging, but in fact Stirling was not satisfied with the performance. His choice of engine for the all-important Monaco G.P. was left open while the B.R.C.D.'s Silverstone meeting in May occupied his attention.

For this event, Moss had agreed to drive a B.R.M. entered and prepared by the Owen Racing Organization. For some time B.R.M.s had been pressing Stirling to drive for them as an official member of the works team. So we suggested a test of their car, pending a decision.

This was arranged at Goodwood, on the day after the Easter Monday meeting, in which, by the way, Stirling won the Formula I race with Rob Walker's Cooper, giving the new 2·5-litre Climax engine a successful first outing. The B.R.M.s of Schell and Bonnier, which had finished third and fourth, stayed down at the circuit for Stirling's tests, during which he managed to complete one lap at exactly 100 m.p.h.—the first time ever on the Sussex circuit with the Chicane included.

As I have said earlier, some drivers get into a car and just drive it; others get into a car and learn it intimately. Stirling is one of the latter calibre, and in driving both B.R.M.s he was able to discern very slight differences in handling which combined to make one chassis better than the other, despite the fact that both were built in the same jig. In this case Stirling came to the definite conclusion that Schell's car was the better handler; its chassis number was 7— purely coincidental with 7 being Stirling's favourite racing number!

Following the Goodwood tests, it was agreed with Alfred Owen that Moss would drive a B.R.M. at Silverstone, and that he should have chassis No. 7 allocated to him. When Stirling got to Silverstone, he found that chassis No. 7 had not been brought along, and this was one of the factors which led to some degree of dissension between Moss and B.R.M.

After practice, although he succeeded in making fastest time in both sessions, and unofficially broke the Silverstone lap record, Stirling decided that, although his engine was excellent, the chassis was not so good, and accordingly he asked B.R.M.s to put his engine into the chassis of the car to be driven by Ron Flockhart. In the race, Stirling took the lead from Brabham's 2·5 Cooper on lap 2 and pulled away into the lead. Then he arrived at Copse Corner on lap 5 without any brakes, which necessitated him putting the B.R.M. into a spin and ending up in the ditch at the side of the road.

That finished his drive, and a lot of people immediately said, 'Well, that's Moss's own fault—if he hadn't insisted on that late change-over of engines, his brakes might not have failed.' Many contended that he should have been satisfied with the car as it was given him, and not try to chop and change. This is countered straight away, however, for the ultimate responsibility for all the chopping and changing rested with B.R.M. themselves.

Had they provided him with chassis No. 7, as promised, he would have been satisfied. As it was, Stirling is a perfectionist, one of the reasons why he has got to where he is today, and decided that, in order to try and achieve victory, it was necessary to have the best engine and the best chassis.

The brake failure at Silverstone can, in my opinion, be attributed to vibration. By reason of the B.R.M.'s big bore, 'over-square' 4-cylinder engine, and the means of installation of engine and gearbox in the chassis, there is a very high-pitched vibration which is in the region of 200 cycles per second. This vibration transmits itself through the chassis to the disc brakes, and also to the steering wheel.

In the case of the steering wheel the vibration is of no significance, save for slight discomfort to the driver, but when it comes to the disc brakes, things are very different. There have been occasions when the small steel pipe joining the two sides of the brake caliper has fractured through vibration transmitted from the chassis, and to overcome this B.R.M.s, with the aid of Dunlops, devised a small clip which encircled the pipe with rubber, and was then clipped to the caliper itself to break down the vibration factor. I am not prepared to say whose fault it was; the fact remains that on the car Stirling drove at Silverstone the clips were not present, and, as a result, one of the pipes from the front caliper fractured.

Some pretty powerful talks ensued between Alfred Moss, myself, Alfred Owen and other members of the Owen Organization. As a result, it was eventually decided that Alfred Owen would make available to the British Racing Partnership one complete B.R.M. The Partnership staff would prepare this B.R.M., and Stirling Moss would have first choice in driving it.

It seems to be popularly believed that the reason behind this transfer of a B.R.M. from Bourne's care was because the B.R.M. mechanics could not be trusted to prepare their cars properly; this was not so. We all of us, Stirling and Alfred Moss, myself, Tony Robinson and the other B.R.P. staff, have nothing but admiration for the B.R.M. mechanics, who are an extremely efficient and friendly crowd of people.

On the other hand, I cannot but feel that B.R.M. themselves are always endeavouring to do more than they can efficiently accomplish; they will not let the design rest and concentrate on making it completely race-worthy, but seem rather to mix development and racing at the same time.

My belief is that development can only be undertaken during the winter and non-racing months. If development must continue during the Grand Prix season, then the activities should be entirely separated; design and development on one side, and the racing programme on the other. Mix the two together and I think, personally, you are bound to meet trouble.

I may be forced to eat my words some time, but that is my opinion, shared by Alfred Moss. It was on the basis of that argument that a B.R.M. was loaned to the British Racing Partnership— so that they could prepare and race the car without any diversionary development whatsoever. We planned to concentrate on racing the car exactly as handed over to us, relying simply on careful and meticulous preparation.

Meantime there was Monaco, and the problem of which car Stirling was to drive. But after the performances of the 2·5-litre Cooper-Climax, which had won successively at Goodwood, Aintree and the *Daily Express* Silverstone, in contrast with the Cooper-B.R.M.'s failure at Aintree, there was little hesitation. Stirling chose the Cooper-Climax, and the Cooper-B.R.M. project was dropped by mutual and amicable agreement.

Moving into the lead after twenty-two laps, Stirling headed the Monaco G.P. from Jack Brabham by an ever-increasing margin, until Fate dealt him a cruel blow on the eighty-second round, when the transmission suddenly made awful grinding noises, and very soon broke up altogether. The bolts holding the crown wheel and differential cage together had sheared, the pieces getting into the gears with dire results. Brabham went on to win his first eight points for the World Championship, adding an extra one when he made the fastest lap as well.

Round 2 of the Championship was the Dutch G.P. at Zandvoort in June, but we resisted the temptation to rush the preparation of the B.R.M. for this race, concentrating instead on the subsequent French G.P. at Rheims.

Undoubtedly the handing over of a B.R.M. for preparation and racing by an outside organization was quite an occasion in the Grand Prix world. Some people saw it as a split between Alfred Owen and his designer Peter Berthon, and between Owen and B.R.M., but this was not the case. The B.R.M. team, led by Raymond Mays and Peter Berthon, continued to receive the wholehearted backing of Mr Owen, and the B.R.P. project was looked upon purely as an extra endeavour to field a car in which Stirling Moss would be happy and could give of his best.

I must say that I was considerably stirred when the B.R.M. lorry arrived at Chelsea, and the car was wheeled into the B.R.P. racing workshop. Hardly twelve months earlier Alfred Moss and I began our partnership with one Formula 2 Cooper, and now here we were preparing a full-blown Formula 1 car, for Stirling to drive. This was to be the test for all our ideals of ultra-careful preparation and good workmanship.

We spared no efforts to ensure that the B.R.P. B.R.M. would be in good fettle for its first race. It was stripped to the bare chassis and completely rebuilt. Everything possible was renewed, and all components carefully checked for faults. The rather grim dark green paintwork which B.R.M. seem to favour was removed, and the car repainted in the B.R.P. colours of pale green, with white wheels.

As at Monaco, Stirling drove Walker's Formula 1 Cooper-Climax with five-speed Colotti gearbox in the Dutch G.P., and once again met heartbreaking failure. After making a very careful start to conserve the gearbox, he encountered great difficulty in passing the stubborn Behra in his Ferrari. Managing this at last, Stirling moved up behind the leaders, Bonnier (B.R.M.) and Brabham (Cooper), and after sixty laps took the lead. Three laps later a ball race in the gearbox failed, and Stirling was out. The second Championship race had now gone by without success for him, though he gained his first point by making fastest lap at Zandvoort.

Following Moss's retirement, Joakim Bonnier went on to win the Dutch G.P. in his B.R.M. after a splendid drive. It marked B.R.M.'s first victory in a Grande Epreuve after years and years of effort, and everyone—even Stirling despite his disappointment—was delighted at Bourne's change of fortune.

The irony of his success lay, of course, in the fact that shortly before, Alfred Owen had handed one B.R.M. over to the British Racing Partnership for preparation outside Bourne, and everybody said it was this 'insult' which had spurred the official B.R.M. team into winning a race at last. This was not true, and I think it was simply the law of averages taking effect at last; B.R.M. had lost more than one race when leading, and now, at last, they had lasted the distance, and won.

Before the French G.P. in July, there was a lesser event of importance to the Partnership. At the Whit Monday meeting at Crystal Palace for Formula 2 cars we ran our two B.R.P. Cooper-Borgwards, driven by Ivor Bueb and George Wicken.

Ivor took a commanding lead in the opening laps, only to be passed by Roy Salvadori in Tommy Atkins's Cooper-Climax. Ivor eventually finished second, and George Wicken was fourth. Sandwiched between our pale green cars was a surprising young man, twenty-one-year-old Chris Bristow from Streatham, who drove a hybrid motor car called a Hume-Cooper with immense zest and commendable skill.

The driving of Bristow had been brought to my attention by

several people and as by then we felt that George Wicken, who was as good a fighter on his day as any other driver, was not able to give of his best in the B.R.P. Cooper, it was agreed that the best thing was to seek a younger driver to take George's place. Shortly after that Crystal Palace meeting, we gave Bristow the opportunity of trying out a Cooper-Borgward at Brands Hatch.

The tests were surprising, almost alarming, so fast did young Bristow prove, yet so capable was he that we lost no time in signing him up to drive for B.R.P. during the remainder of the 1959 season, as well as holding an option on his services for 1960.

His first appearance in a B.R.P. car was to be the Formula 2 race supporting the French G.P. at Rheims, but before we could finalize the preparation of the Cooper-Borgwards, an important meeting took place between Herr Buchner, Borgward's experimental engineer, Fritz Juttner and our B.R.P. mechanics, Rob Walker, Alfred Moss and myself. We all gathered to discuss the installation of the Borgward engine in the Cooper chassis, and in particular the air intake arrangements.

Because of the peculiar air intake on the 1500RS Borgward engine, we had designed a rather special torpedo-shaped intake, which lay alongside the left-hand shoulder of the driver. It was felt by Stirling Moss and Alf Francis, also by the Borgward people, that this intake arrangement was not producing the desired result, and Buchner wished to conduct further experiments at the works with the car to see if they could increase power output.

It was agreed that Rob Walker's car, which Stirling was to drive in the Rheims Formula 2 event, would be taken to Bremen with Fritz Juttner so that they could make some modifications, after which the car would go to Zandvoort for further tests.

This plan was duly carried out, and the car appeared at Rheims with an entirely new air intake which extended right to the nose of the Cooper, while a longer exhaust pipe with a megaphone at the end was also fitted. Our two light green cars were altered similarly, and results showed that the changes were well worth while.

The miraculous summer of 1959 was in full blast during the French G.P. meeting, and the heat at Rheims was terrific. To Alfred Moss and me, that meeting was of tremendous importance. Apart from our Coopers, we were running the B.R.P.-prepared

B.R.M. in its first race, and were desperately keen to vindicate ourselves in the eyes of Alfred Owen, B.R.M. and the racing *cognoscenti*. The general turnout and mechanical condition of the pale green B.R.M. would, we knew only too well, come under the closest scrutiny, and we felt that we were virtually 'on test'.

More than this, however; Stirling was dependent upon our efficiency; the French G.P. was the third World Championship event of 1959, and as he had only scored one point so far, it was vitally important to him. Tony Robinson and the other mechanics had put their 'all' into preparing the B.R.M.; now came the test of all B.R.P.'s efforts.

Amongst our company at Rheims, we were very pleased to have two expert timekeepers in Cyril and Doreen Audrey. Cyril is one of the few qualified senior international timekeepers to be recognized by the R.A.C., and we took him over to take charge of timekeeping for the B.R.P. entries. He is quite phenomenal at his job, and during practice, with two watches and the aid of his wife as spotter, he timed every single car on every lap through the entire two days of practice.

Furthermore, on race day he gave us the times of the leading seven cars throughout the Grand Prix with the intervals in between as far as Stirling was concerned. All this was accomplished with two split-second stopwatches and Cyril doing mental calculations in between, plus an ingenious little set-up for communication between himself and his wife, who did the spotting. This comprised throat microphones and earphones with a little transistor amplifier, the whole device being made by Cyril himself.

We persuaded Stirling to do the minimum of practice in order to conserve the reliability of the B.R.M. for the Grand Prix itself. This he agreed to do, though he quickly put up a time which exceeded the old lap record and won him a hundred bottles of champagne. He shared these out with B.R.P., and we in turn passed some on to the Bourne staff.

The heat was absolutely fantastic when the cars went out to the grid, and with fifty laps of that immensely fast 5·1-mile course within the confines of grilling cockpits, I did not envy the drivers the task ahead of them. In the race, Stirling, driving harder than I think I have ever seen him drive before, worked the B.R.M. into third position, and looked as if he would stay there; he might even have caught Phil Hill's Ferrari for second place, but Tony Brooks's Ferrari held an unassailable lead.

Unfortunately, in the early part of the race, the tiny rod which connects the clutch pedal to the clutch withdrawal linkage of the B.R.M. had broken, and after the first hour Stirling had been driving without a clutch at all. Then, on the road down to Thillois Corner, when trying to go just that little bit faster in an effort to catch Phil Hill, he slightly miscalculated the state of the road which, owing to the boiling sun, had been reduced to a slithery mass of tarmac, stones and gravel. The B.R.M. slid and, though Stirling struggled desperately at the wheel to hold it, spun round— a very great rarity in the life of S. Moss.

The Thillois spin wouldn't have been too bad had Stirling not been without a clutch; he would have dipped the clutch and kept the engine going, then rejoined the race. As it was, he couldn't, and the engine stalled. Despite a gallant attempt to restart the B.R.M. by pushing it down the road—in that heat!—then jumping in when some impetus was gained and shoving second gear in, it couldn't be done, and eventually he ended up lying flat on his back, exhausted.

Just when Stirling spun at Thillois, one of the straw bales at the same corner decided to catch fire, and the rising column of smoke was clearly visible from the pits, causing us tremendous anxiety. Then Stirling, realizing the hopelessness of the situation, climbed into the B.R.M., enlisted outside aid for a push-start, thereby disqualifying himself, and motored quietly back to the pits.

Our disappointment at his failure was countered by our relief at seeing him safe, and I shall always remember, with bated admiration, how Stirling, immediately he came in, said to his father and myself: 'I'm sorry—the car went beautifully. It was entirely my own fault.' At such a tense moment I thought this was an extremely gallant and sporting thing to say. We derived a crumb of comfort from the fact that the B.R.P.-prepared B.R.M. had been far ahead of the works cars while it was running, and that the cause of its retirement was a structural failure, and not a fault in preparation. But there was no denying our disappointment.

As we pushed the car away, I noticed how battered the front

was; it looked as if it had run into a hail of bullets—which, in effect, it had! The pitiless heat of the sun had melted the tar on the road and loosened the surface, and the rear wheels of other cars had flung sharp stones back on the car and into his face. All the cars and drivers in the race suffered equally, so that facial injuries were common, and the noses of all the cars were sand-blasted and battered. The pale green B.R.M., of which we had been so proud, looked a very sorry mess, but though dents could be knocked out and paintwork resprayed, Championship points, once lost, could not be regained, and Stirling's chances were diminishing.

Just to prove the driver he is, Stirling recovered sufficiently from his exhaustion to get into Rob Walker's Cooper-Borgward and roundly won the Formula 2 race, despite a very fine attempt by Hans Herrmann in Behra's single-seater Porsche to displace him. The heat conditions had perhaps worsened slightly now, and car after car dropped out, either with engine or driver overheating. Both Bueb and then Bristow were, alas, amongst those who were forced to give up, but it was not surprising, considering that the heat of the air coming into the cockpit and on to the driver's chest, face and eyes was in the region of 120° to 125° F. Stirling's victory in this 25-lap event, after enduring forty-three laps in the Grand Prix, certainly stressed his stamina and fitness. Despite his retirement, young Bristow had driven splendidly in his first race for the Partnership—and, incidentally, his first race abroad, and Alfred Moss and I were well satisfied with our new recruit.

After the French G.P., our Formula 1 mechanics, headed by Tony Robinson, had to rush back to London as soon as possible, to get the B.R.M. ready for the British Grand Prix, at Aintree. However, Fritz Juttner and Stan Collier, our new mechanic in charge of the Formula 2 cars, dashed off to Rouen for the Rouen Formula 2 G.P. the following week-end.

The Rouen meeting proved a double Stirling Moss benefit. He won the Formula 2 race in the Walker Cooper-Borgward—his third successive win in this car—and also won the sports-car race for up to 2-litre cars, over the same distance—186 miles. The interesting thing about this race was Stirling's mount, which was a works-prepared 4-cylinder 2-litre Maserati, nicknamed the 'spaghetti special' by reason of the innumerable tiny tubes, welded together, forming one of the most complicated space frames ever seen.

This car had been lent to Stirling for the Rouen race, and it was pleasing to think that, despite their financial plight, Maserati had not lost their enthusiasm for racing, and were ready to come back almost at the drop of a handkerchief, when the chance came. Let us hope that this great Italian marque will be on their feet again in time to officially contest G.P. racing to the new Formula in 1961, if not earlier.

As for the B.R.P. Cooper-Borgwards at Rouen, we were more than pleased at Chris Bristow's performance. Though a newcomer to the splendid circuit at Rouen, he 'mixed it' gallantly with older hands, and fought a spirited duel with Maurice Trintignant in Rob Walker's Cooper-Climax, finally beating him into fifth place by half a length.

Ivor Bueb made a terrific start, but unfortunately spun round at the hairpin on the first lap. He drove like a rocket after that to make up time, but the Borgward engine broke an oil pipe, and Ivor had to retire.

Immediately after the Rouen race, Stirling made one of his lightning departures—but there was a very special reason for this one. He and Katie dashed to the airport with Pete Ayles, and flew back to England in the Miles Messenger I had used to come out to Rouen. In turn, I took Stirling's recently acquired Facel-Vega and, accompanied by Chris Bristow, drove to Paris and back to London, leaving the Facel at Le Bourget airport.

The reason for Moss's haste was the London to Paris Centenary Air Race, promoted by the *Daily Mail*, in which Stirling was one of the first competitors to set off from Marble Arch on Monday morning. He drove a Renault Dauphine and headed straight for Ferryfield airport, there catching the Silver City Airways ferry to Le Bourget and making the final dash into Paris in the Dauphine.

Even though Stirling didn't win any prize, or approach the fantastic times which were later put up by the forces teams and various combinations in their all-out bids to cut the time down, I still think London to Paris in 2 hrs. 42 min. and 7 sec. was quite good. His objective, in conjunction with Silver City Airways, was primarily to demonstrate just how quickly you could make the journey using ordinary everyday means of transport.

B.R.P.'s second race with the B.R.M. was the British G.P. at Aintree. It had originally been Stirling Moss's intention to drive a 2·5-litre Cooper-Climax for Rob Walker in this race, but unfortunately, due to misunderstanding, neither the car nor the new Coventy Climax engine were ready, so he decided that he would drive 'our' B.R.M. which had been completely rebuilt after Rheims. The engine had been back to Bourne for stripping and maintenance, the chassis and brakes meticulously checked, and the body, following its Rheims battering, was subjected to considerable panel beating and then resprayed.

In the race Stirling finished second despite making two pit stops, a very satisfactory performance. Naturally we would have liked him to win, but quite honestly the car wasn't capable of it, the Formula 1 Cooper-Climax being much more suited to the Aintree circuit. On top of Stirling's second, however, young Chris Bristow won the Formula 2 class of the race for us in his Cooper-Borgward, finishing tenth overall.

Afterwards, there were many who seemed only too eager to see in Stirling's two pit stops the failure of the British Racing Partnership's ideals of good organization and efficient working. 'B.R.P. slipped up,' they said, 'they miscalculated on the fuel and let Moss down.' How happy I am to be able to tell our critics how wrong they were. Stirling's first stop was definitely necessary because the nearside rear tyre had worn to a stage where it was no longer gripping the road. His race lap speeds were averaging over a second faster than his fastest practice lap and he was driving really hard, trying to catch the leading Cooper; for these reasons tyre wear was greater than had been experienced in practice.

His second pit stop was quite unanticipated, and we in the pits were very surprised to see Moss come in, signalling for fuel, and although we put five gallons in and sent him off, we were all puzzled as to why it had been necessary.

After carefully conducted tests and measurements during practice, we calculated that the fuel consumption would be 8·9 miles per gallon, and for the race put the required amount in the tanks plus a five-gallon safety margin, ensuring plenty of fuel for a non-stop run.

On the B.R.M. there are three fuel tanks; two in the side and one in the tail, so arranged that you fill up through the rear main tank, which is placed higher, and the petrol first drains into the side tanks and, when these are full, fills up the rear tank. There is a three-position switch situated on the floor between the driver's legs, enabling him to select the tanks he wishes to draw off.

At Aintree, Stirling was instructed to run on the side tanks, and after a certain number of laps, he would receive a signal from Robinson to switch over on to his main tank. All this worked smoothly, and when he duly switched on to the main tank, he should have had sufficient fuel to finish the race.

After his first stop for the tyre, however, Stirling suddenly experienced slight fluffing and spitting in the carburettor, and hurriedly decided he was running short of fuel. Wisely, in view of his position in the race, he took no chances and pulled straight into the pit, took on the five gallons and went off again, to finish second —by inches—to young Bruce McLaren!

What actually happened was that, when the lower side tanks had drained, and the supply was switched over to the main, rear tank, some of the fuel had surged into the side tanks, through the air bleed pipes. When he felt the engine fluff, Stirling tried switching back from the rear to the side tanks, which cured the trouble immediately, although the side tanks theoretically should have been empty.

When we got the car back in the workshops next day, the tanks were drained, and it was found that ten gallons and one pint of petrol remained. Deducting the extra five gallons put in, this proved our calculations of the fuel consumption during the race to be accurate to within one pint.

The next round for the Partnership was the Clermont-Ferrand Formula 2 race, where both B.R.P. Cooper-Borgwards had been entered, also two cars by Rob Walker: the Cooper-Borgward for Stirling, and the Formula 2 Cooper-Climax for Trintignant. For Rob, it was to prove a very good event. For B.R.P. it proved a very black and tragic day.

The Auvergne circuit at Clermont-Ferrand is one of the finest road-racing circuits ever constructed. Used for the first time in 1958, it is all that an airfield circuit is not, a winding, twisting, plunging five miles of road, literally carved round the peak of a mountain, so that more or less all the way round there are steep drops on one side, and rock face on the other. The whole road is beautifully engineered, with contours and gradients just right, a constant width, and a billiard-table surface. In effect, it is like a miniature Nurburgring, and offers a magnificent test of cars and drivers.

The organizers received an excellent entry for their meeting, with some Porsches and Lotuses as well as the three Cooper-Borgwards, to rival the inevitable glut of Cooper-Climaxes. Stirling found the circuit extremely to his liking, and showed it by winning the main race in Rob Walker's Cooper-Borgward—which had yet to lose a race while he was driving it. For B.R.P., Chris Bristow made a fantastic start and shot into the lead, Stirling being slightly hampered by the fact that Raymond Roche stood in his way as he swept the flag down!

Stirling picked up the loss on the opening lap, coming round on Bristow's tail. Chris led for three laps, and then began to drop back. The water cap on his radiator had worked itself loose, the securing wire having started to slip round the fixing point. The pressure from the cooling system disappeared and the engine began to overheat, forcing him to retire after five laps.

By that time our other car, driven by Ivor Bueb, was already out after an accident which was to cost poor Ivor his life. It is very difficult to say how this accident happened, as it took place on the far side of the circuit, far from our vision. It was on a right-hand bend, approached from a fairly fast downhill stretch, with the road sweeping round to the right, then climbing again, more or less in a straight line.

Unfortunately, just on the apex of the corner, where the road was cambered to the inside of the course, another road dropped down to a village, and this caused a slight peak to be formed on the left-hand extremity of the road, at the junction of the cambered circuit and the downhill road to the village.

Ivor didn't make as clean a start as Chris, and was trying to make up for lost time, running in very close company with the Belgian Gendebien in a Cooper-Climax. As the pair came up to the corner in question, Ivor was on the outside, and as his car neared the apex of the corner, the back of the Cooper-Borgward began to swing out to the left. Normally this is easily corrected, but in Ivor's case we assume that his nearside rear wheel, which was taking all the cornering force, just went over the camber peak and, in so doing, momentarily lost adhesion.

As a result, the back flicked round sideways, and went crashing into a very steep earth bank at something like 100–110 m.p.h. He was thrown out of the car, suffering very serious internal injuries.

I was keeping the lap chart at the time, and I remember very clearly that when Ivor failed to come by on lap 3, although I was concerned, I didn't have any kind of worry over his personal safety. It never occurred to me that Ivor could have an accident of any severity, because he was always such a good, safe driver. Ivor had tremendous experience, beginning with the hurly-burly days of Formula 3. He had performed wonders at Le Mans in a Jaguar under the most difficult night conditions in pouring rain, had twice co-driven the winning car there, and could handle the big Lister-Jaguars with wonderful skill in the worst of weather. I really think that this particular accident was one of those million-to-one chances, where the very worst happened.

He was taken immediately to hospital in a grave condition, and we were all cast into a terrible gloom. We practically lived down at the hospital the whole time, but unfortunately all the will in the world, and all the efforts of his friends, could not save him, and poor Ivor passed away on the Friday evening, mercifully unconscious during most of his last hours.

Ivor Bueb's crash and eventual death had a terrible effect on young Bristow, who had so far not been subjected to the tragedies of motor racing, and it very nearly put him off racing altogether. Chris was due to race at Brands Hatch on the August Bank Holiday Monday meeting, but almost decided not to appear. We had to leave him to make his own decision. We couldn't really try and persuade him to race, although we all felt that he should if he wanted to continue racing as a career.

Fortunately Chris eventually decided to race, putting up such a brilliant show at Brands Hatch that he completely stole the lime-light and won the main Formula 2 event split into two heats, against such comparative veterans as Jack Brabham and Roy Salvadori.

Incidentally, it is interesting to record Stirling Moss's opinion of Bristow's driving, after the Clermont-Ferrand race. Stirling had followed closely in his wheeltracks in the opening laps, and there-fore was in the best possible position to judge.

He said that Chris had not made a mistake at any time; the only criticism he felt inclined to make was that his second lap was a bit too fast. Moss's own practice is never to go quite as quickly as on the opening lap when leading the race, since, although on the first lap one knows the track ahead is clear, on the second round there is always the possibility of some slight oil, a tail-ender in trouble, or other hazard on the road. Apart from that small point, which experience would correct, he thought Bristow drove particularly well, and considered there was a very great future ahead of him as a driver.

It was on that same August Bank Holiday week-end that the German Grand Prix took place. Not on the fabulous Nurburg-ring in the heart of the Eifel country of West Germany, but at the Avus high-speed track, outside Berlin in the Eastern Zone. We had entered the pale green B.R.M., prepared by the British Racing Partnership, for the race, but as Stirling had now elected to drive Rob Walker's 2·5-litre Cooper-Climax for the rest of the season, we had to find another driver. Initially, the name of Ron Flockhart, who has had more B.R.M. experience than any other driver, was advanced, but the organizers, the Automobil Club von Deutsch-land, were just not interested. They wanted a German driver so we suggested Hans Herrmann, who duly drove the B.R.P. entry.

What a travesty of a 'Grand Prix' Avus was! I think, without any doubt whatever, that it was the worst race meeting I have ever had the misfortune to attend. To start off, we fell foul of the organizers for various reasons, not the least of which was the fact that the Chief of Police for the City of Berlin had decreed that only three pit passes were to be issued per car, and that of these, one was for the driver. This placed us in the position where we could have just two mechanics to look after the car and nobody else near; an impossible situation and one of considerable irony when it is remembered how Germany's Mercedes-Benz team used to descend on a circuit with a positive swarm of specialists and mechanics, yet never had any difficulty in obtaining proper passes for them all.

In addition everybody wishing to get into the paddock area was subjected to an almost Fascist-type of scrutiny, necessitating the placing of a piece of coloured string around the wrist, on to the two ends of which was placed a lead seal, embossed with the crest of the A.v.D., and we were not able to remove these for the whole time we were in Berlin. The pits were about half to three-quarters of a mile from the paddock, were extremely dirty, and were certainly not up to the standards expected for a Grande Epreuve.

As for the circuit, I am surprised that the F.I.A. ever sanctioned the use of Avus for a World Championship race. Not only is it uninteresting, but it is diabolically dangerous. The F.I.A. have made known their disapproval of racing on opposing roads; that is, where two parallel strips of road are used, with cars passing within a few yards of each other in opposite directions, yet this is the principal character of the Berlin track.

Avus simply comprises two lengthy parallel straights connected by a hairpin turn at the South Curve, and an unpleasant high-speed banked turn at the North Curve, surfaced with smooth bricks which in the wet are treacherously dangerous. In between the long parallel straights is simply a strip of grass, with no barrier whatsoever for most of the length. The Formula 1 cars could wind up to 170-plus m.p.h. along these two straights, so that the cumulative speed of two cars travelling in opposite directions would be around 340 m.p.h. It only needed one car to have a partial seizure, or to run off the road for some other reason, and the results don't bear thinking about.

F.I.A. rulings stipulate that Championship events must be of a minimum of two hours' duration, or over 300 km. minimum. The German G.P. at Avus was over a distance of 498 kms., or sixty laps, but as the organizers feared the tyres might not last the pace, they decided to split the race into two heats of thirty laps, adding up the times and basing the results on aggregate.

Every car, save for a Formula 2 Porsche, admitted to give a

'National' touch to the race, was running on tyres made by Dunlop, yet another British concern which has done so much in support of motor racing. There is an amusing story concerning their technicians at Avus.

When Vic Barlow of Dunlop's Competitions Department went to the A.v.D. offices to collect passes for himself and his technicians, he was told he couldn't have the number he requested. He queried this, but was told firmly, 'Can't have them—far too many.' Vic breathed heavily, gazed at the officials, then said, 'Unless I am given passes sufficient to cover the needs of my men, whose only wish is to service the tyres used by the competitors in your race, I shall take every wheel and tyre of Dunlop manufacture, and fly the whole damn lot back to England tomorrow.'

Asked what he thought that would mean, Barlow replied, 'It means that you will have one car running in your race and that's a Porsche—not even a Formula 1 car.'

I leave readers to draw their own conclusions as to whether he got his passes!

In fairness, I don't think that Herr Schmidt, who was Secretary of the organizing club, was at all happy about the *Grosser Pries* being run at Avus. I understand that the rental for the Nurburgring is very high, and that the Berlin Senate offered the A.v.D. a generous guarantee against loss. Be that as it may, the 1959 event was a poor affair in contrast with the splendid Nurburgring races of the past.

Things began badly with the sports-car race. It rained heavily, making the steep banking of the North Curve extremely slippery, and three Porsches went off the track, Jean Behra in one being killed. His car spun round high on the banking, hit a protection wall at the top and then wrapped itself round a flagpole, Behra being flung into the air some twenty or thirty feet and landing a lifeless heap at the foot of his car.

Despite a gallant but brief attempt by the Coopers, the G.P. was a gift to Ferrari, whose cars were able to play follow-my-leader as they wished. Even this would not have mattered; it was just that the circuit wasn't interesting. It was a case of sheer brutal speed down the straights, and no real test of driving skill or tactics. This is no compliment to Tony Brooks, who won from Dan Gurney and Phil Hill, all in Ferraris, but I don't think Tony will claim the 1959 German G.P. as his most enjoyable race!

Hans Herrmann did fairly well in the first heat with the Partnership B.R.M., finishing eighth behind Bonnier's works-prepared car. In the second heat, unfortunately, he had brake failure which resulted in his entering the 55 m.p.h. South Turn at something like 140 m.p.h.-plus.

The car charged through some straw bales, turning over six or seven times end over end. Hans was very luckily thrown out and suffered superficial injuries only, but the B.R.M. bowled along the road like a mad thing and was completely and utterly destroyed in one of the most spectacular accidents ever to happen in Grand Prix racing.

As for Stirling, who was driving Rob Walker's newest Cooper with 2·5-litre Climax engine, he had no luck at all, retiring in the opening laps with gearbox trouble.

When we got back to England, we sat down and carefully considered the future as it concerned Stirling, the British Racing Partnership, and the B.R.M. Without doubt, the latest failure of the car, when Herrmann was driving it at Avus, was disturbing. The cause was traced to the fracture of a brake pipe on one of the front chassis members, which again resulted in the total failure of the front brakes.

As I have already written, this in my view was an inherent and serious fault in the B.R.M., attributable chiefly to the almost sonic vibration transmitted from the engine to every component on the chassis. Similar disc brakes are used on a multitude of other cars with complete and impressive efficiency, only B.R.M. experiencing trouble with them.

Naturally, a mistrust of the brakes on a car has a very 'off-putting' effect on its driver, but it was not solely this which decided Stirling against driving the B.R.M. any more in 1959. It was also because it was down on power, and not fast enough to compete on even terms with a well-driven Cooper, as was demonstrated at Aintree, Rheims and Avus.

In other ways, Stirling liked the B.R.M. enormously, and he considered it the finest road-holding car that has ever yet been built, much easier to drive than the Cooper, which required far more physical and mental concentration. In Moss's own words, 'The Cooper will do exactly the same as a B.R.M. round a corner; the only difference is that the Cooper does it untidily and with great effort, whereas the B.R.M. does it smoothly, with great finesse.'

But the Cooper was lighter and, with the latest $2\frac{1}{2}$-litre Climax engine, quicker on pick-up, besides having an impressive maximum. At Rheims, for example, Brabham was approaching 180 m.p.h. down the straight, and turned in the second fastest practice lap, only ·3 sec. slower than Brooks's Ferrari.

Weighing up all these pros and cons, Stirling made up his mind to drive Rob Walker's Cooper-Climax for the remainder of the 1959 G.P. season, and we of the British Racing Partnership decided there was no further point in continuing the association with B.R.M. So it was back, temporarily, to Formula 2 only for the British Racing Partnership.

With the next Championship round, the Portuguese G.P. at Lisbon looming ahead, and Stirling now committed to drive for Rob Walker, it was clear that something drastic would have to be done to cure the incessant gearbox troubles which were ruining Stirling's chances in the World Championship. Obviously something was radically wrong with the Colotti five-speed gearbox, which behaved itself on the Formula 2 Cooper-Borgward of Rob Walker, but not on the more powerful Formula 1 Climax-engined car.

It had been felt for quite a time that the input shaft bearing was too weak and was braking up during usage, causing the teeth of the drop gears to fracture. Rob Walker and Alf Francis got together on the problem, and it was Alf who eventually discovered that the gears had not been machined according to the drawings; not only was there an error in practically every gearwheel, but the errors were not constant, varying from tooth to tooth on each gear.

Normally such components are rigorously inspected at varying stages of manufacture, and it is incomprehensible how such errors arose in the precision-built Colotti box, which was a brilliant piece of designing. In defence of Colotti himself, it should be pointed out that the gear-cutting was sub-contracted to a local engineering firm in Modena.

Anyway, once the fault was discovered, there was a scurry by Alf Francis to try and get new gears cut in time for the Portuguese G.P. It was not possible to have them all renewed in time, but he was able to replace certain gears with others machined by the Maserati concern at Modena.

I did not go to Lisbon for the G.P. of Portugal, having a vast amount to do at home, and therefore cannot say much about the race. But it brought Stirling Moss his first outright victory in a World Championship race of 1959 at last, the partly improved Colotti gearbox holding out this time, to give him a comfortable win from Masten Gregory's works Cooper and Dan Gurney's Ferrari, as well as fastest lap.

Meantime, there were developments of major importance concerning the British Racing Partnership; developments which promised to expand the horizons of Alfred Moss and myself way beyond Formula 2 racing into the exalted field of Grand Prix racing as a team.

It began when I had the opportunity of entering into discussion with one of the country's leading hire-purchase finance houses, the company called Yeoman Credit Ltd. This large concern, employing a staff of some five to six hundred, and having a network of branches throughout Britain, is controlled by three young brothers, William, Paul and Fabian Samengo-Turner. So young are these brothers that their combined ages total less than 100 years, but despite this the company they control is one of the most reputable in the country today. All three are immensely keen on motor racing.

We had come to know each other well through mutual friends in the motor trade. As the Samengo-Turner brothers derived their main income from the motor industry, they felt they might well plough a proportion back into that industry. And since motor racing interested them greatly, why not in that seemingly remote but vitally important branch of the motor industry?

One day I was invited out to lunch by Fabian and Paul, and was suddenly asked, 'How much money would you require to run a Grand Prix team?'

I nearly choked, swallowed hard, then asked, 'A full three-car team?'

'Yes.'

I didn't waste time on calculations. I had the sum in my head, for running a full G.P. team had long been a dream of mine. I told them how much I thought it would cost, and virtually they answered, 'Well, let's do it.'

We then got down to some very serious estimates and plans, with Alfred Moss joining in, and the eventual result was the formation of the Yeoman Credit Racing Team. It was agreed that they would finance the purchase of three 1960 Formula 1 racing cars, sufficient transporters and equipment to operate them in the major races of the season, and meet the costs of running these cars in the best method possible under their banner.

The British Racing Partnership, in turn, would contribute our two Formula 2 cars, backed up with our experience and 'know-how', and would be entirely responsible for the management and operation of the Yeoman Credit Racing Team.

It was decided that as the Partnership had already signed Chris Bristow up for the rest of 1959 and had an option on him for 1960, he would be one of the team drivers. Negotiations were opened with the leading Grand Prix drivers of today, leaving aside Stirling Moss, who had already contracted to drive for Rob Walker in 1960. Finally we chose the mercurial Franco-American Harry Schell to lead our team.

This, then, was our big chance to do what limited resources had previously prevented us from doing—running a full Formula 1 and Formula 2 team with every possible financial assistance and no restriction on obtaining the very best of equipment to enable us to do the job. It was all tremendously exciting, and the prospect of ordering the cars, transporters and equipment, the engaging of staff, and working out detailed plans was highly intoxicating.

Alfred Moss and I are determined that B.R.P. will justify the Yeoman Credit Company's faith in us. Believe me, the British motor industry benefits so much from British motor-racing successes, so often without acknowledgement, that it is really nice to see somebody put some money back into the sport.

One week after the Portuguese G.P. came the Kentish 'Hundred' Formula 2 race at Brands Hatch. This time the winning streak of the Walker Cooper-Borgward broke, for Stirling could do no better than fourth place overall behind Brabham's Cooper, Hill's Lotus and Bonnier's Porsche. As for Chris Bristow, it wasn't his day at all; he spun the B.R.P. Cooper-Borgward on the second lap of the first heat, forcing Moss and Hill on the grass, while on top of this he was nudged by another competitor at the bottom of Druids Hill in the sports-car race, and lost control of his Cooper-Monaco.

Chris was in the 'doghouse' again at Goodwood in the T.T. race early in September, when I had arranged for him to drive in the Porsche works team. Co-driving with Hans Herrmann, he was doing well when he became involved in an incident with Alan Stacey's Lotus, practically writing off the Porsche.

But I am glad to say that the Partnership retained their faith in Bristow—not that we ever lost it, for that matter. I have always believed that he is an exceptionally fine driver, and we planned that his first drive in a Formula 1 car would coincide with the first entry in a race of the newly created Yeoman Credit Racing Team—the Gold Cup race at Oulton Park in late September.

Chris Bristow fully justified our faith in him at Oulton, taking a splendid third place to Stirling and Brabham.

September, of course, means the Italian G.P.—my favourite race—and the 1959 event was as gripping as ever, with strategy beating sheer speed and Stirling in Rob Walker's Cooper winning in the face of a five-car Ferrari team, racing on their home ground.

But few people will know of the high drama preceding this victory, and of how, at one stage, it looked as if the Walker entry mightn't start at all. A few days before the race, while still in London, I received a telephone call from the Coventry Climax people regarding the engine of Stirling's car, which was already out there. They had, it appeared, a means of machining the cylinder head on the latest 2·5-litre unit which produced an appreciable amount of extra power. Brabham's works Cooper already had its cylinder head so treated, and Coventry Climax said they would do the same to Stirling's if the head could be rushed back from Monza.

I put an urgent call through to Alf Francis down at Modena, and got him to remove the head from the Cooper, send it to Milan by road, then have it put on a plane to London Airport. I arranged for it to be collected there, and taken down to Harry Weslake's establishment at Rye Harbour where it was duly machined, then flown back to Italy and refitted to the Cooper.

All was ready the evening before first official practice was due to start, but unfortunately, when the engine was started up, either it backfired or the throttle stuck. Whatever the cause, the result was calamitous, for all the valves were bent, and Alf was almost in tears.

By then I had arrived in Italy, and was at the hotel with Stirling when Alf Francis phoned and told us the bad news. We immediately put into action emergency measures to sort the problem out. First, we had to make every effort to run in first practice next day, and Alf undertook to straighten the valves somehow so that Moss could drive the car.

Then we had to get spares over from England, in time to fit them for the Saturday practice, if possible, but certainly in good time for the race on Sunday. Accordingly I phoned up my secretary, Rosemary Seers, at her home in Croydon, and asked her to contact Wally Hassan of Coventry Climax, explain the situation and get him to arrange for the necessary parts to be ready for collection by her at the factory, first thing in the morning.

So Rosemary phoned Hassan, who had to be dug out of his bed at past midnight, and while he was ringing round to various people to arrange for the parts to be ready when the factory opened at seven o'clock, Rosemary drove up from London in her Austin-Healey Sprite. As there was a possibility of fog on the way, she had set off very early, and consequently arrived at the Godiva works with two hours to spare.

At 7 a.m. the gates opened, and Rosemary was given breakfast while the staff speedily assembled the parts needed to put Stirling's engine to rights. Next Rosemary sped to Birmingham airport with the precious parcel, caught a plane to Zürich at eleven o'clock, then took another plane to Milan.

She arrived at about four o'clock in the afternoon, absolutely exhausted but triumphant, and with the help of the B.P.'s Italian representative I was able to rush the parts through Customs and get them to Monza, where Alf Francis and Harry Spears of Coventry Climax fitted them, working through the night.

Meanwhile Stirling, Alf Francis and Rob Walker had conspired together and, realizing after first practice that the race was going to depend on tyres, had replaced the rear bolt-on wheels on the Cooper with a pair of splined hubs and knock-off wire wheels in time for Saturday.

Already, despite the straightened valves in his engine, Stirling had made fastest lap on the Friday, and he did not improve on his time during Saturday practice. Tony Brooks with his Ferrari came within one-tenth of a second, but nobody else approached Stirling's time, so that the Walker Cooper proudly occupied pole position on the starting grid.

So to race day. Once again the intoxicating atmosphere of Monza; nothing missed, in fact, if anything more intense, with Stirling out to fight a lone battle against five V6 Ferraris, the works Coopers and the B.R.M.s. We in his pit knew that Stirling, probably the greatest strategist in racing today, had calmly and carefully weighed the situation up, and had made up his mind on what tactics to adopt.

He knew the Ferraris were faster on the straights, but less wieldy than the Coopers on the bends, so it was his hope that a Ferrari would take the lead. This duly happened, for although poor Tony Brooks packed up on the first lap with a burnt-out clutch, Phil Hill moved into the lead, with Stirling following him like a shadow, using his slipstream on the straights, and easing off on the corners to conserve his tyres.

For lap after lap he kept it up, nursing the rubber by cornering gently and losing something like fifty yards on the Ferrari through the corner, then using the lighter Cooper's acceleration to catch up again, getting into the Ferrari's slipstream and following within inches of its tail down to the braking point for the next turn.

Meanwhile Hill in the Ferrari was going as hard as he could, trying to shake off that maddening Cooper and wearing his tyres away as he raced, while behind came Hill's team mate Dan Gurney, also using rubber, trying to keep up with the pair ahead.

Moss carried this on for thirty-three laps, when the thing happened which he was banking on—the Ferrari pits called in Hill for a change of rear tyres. Next in was Gurney, followed by Cliff Allison, and in a trice the fight was over and Ferraris defeated, for they could never gain the thirty-or-so seconds they had lost.

Their sole chance now was that Stirling would also have to stop for tyres, and being well aware that quick-release rear wheels had been fitted to the Cooper, Ferraris could merely hope hard that he would have to make use of them.

But he never needed to. He just ran on like a train, taking it easy wherever possible to save his tyres, and won the race with a fair amount of tyre tread left, very much the victor by strategy as well as brilliant driving. Phil Hill was second, three-quarters of a minute behind, Jack Brabham was third, stacking up more Championship points, Dan Gurney was fourth, and two more Ferraris fifth and sixth.

Stirling's victory more than repaid all the efforts made in getting the improved head and the new valves from England, and the hours of work by Alf Francis and Harry Spears in fitting them. Rosemary Seers, who had always wanted to go to Monza anyway, was entranced by it, and felt the night drive up to Coventry, the plane dash to Milan, and the lack of sleep was more than worthwhile.

But I should like to pay tribute here to Rosemary, because she is my 'right-hand man'—or my 'right hand' anyway!—and probably knows much more about my business than I do myself. She is the sort of person I can phone up at any time, night or day, 365 days in the year, for assistance, and has now become so used to my habits, my rather eccentric ways, and occasional odd requests that I doubt very much if she would worry if I told her to catch a plane to Hong Kong and fetch back a pound of rice!

With all the difficult tasks I have given her, she has never failed me once, yet through it all she retains a sense of humour, an intense enthusiasm, and still goes racing herself when she can, so that all the technical terms and jargon of motor racing come as a second language to Rosemary.

After Monza, the destination of Stirling, Phil Hill and myself was the United States, for M.G.s had sent out their Class F record-breaking Ex. 181 to Utah for further record attempts on the Salt Flats, and Stirling, once again, was down to do the driving, with Phil Hill as reserve.

Stirling, Katie and I drove down to Malpensa airport in the Facel-Vega, accompanied by Graham Hill, who was going to drive the car back to England with Katie. After a bath and a cup of tea Stirling and I then went along to the airport, where we met Phil Hill, then all boarded the Alitalia Douglas DC7 which was to fly us to New York.

On the flight over the conversation was quite fantastic, with Stirling and Phil swapping yarns about the race so recently run. Phil complained ruefully that Stirling was using all his power in slipstreaming him, and said he could do absolutely nothing about it, though he took the corners as fast as possible and slammed down the straights, trying to get away. He knew darned well that he was giving Stirling a tow, and had a good idea of what was in Stirling's mind, but just had to grin and bear it.—'But, man, was Tavoni burned up!'

On our arrival in New York, we transferred to a T.W.A. Boeing 707, one of the impressive new jet machines which took only 5 hrs. 55 min. to cross America from New York to Los Angeles. In California the party split up, Phil going to his home in Santa Monica to be near an ailing aunt, while we went on to Las Vegas, that fabulous place in the desert of Nevada about which we had heard so much, and where B.M.C.'s P.R.O. had booked us rooms at Wilbur Clark's Desert Inn, the famous hotel where Noël Coward made his very popular Las Vegas record.

I must say I found Las Vegas a most astounding place, quite beyond the conception of anybody who has never been to America. Even to blasé Americans it is fabulous, so there just isn't a strong enough adjective to describe it in the English language!

It is a tiny town, situated in the midst of nothing save barren desert for something like a hundred miles in any direction. Outside the town is what is called 'the Strip'. This is a four- or six-lane highway, and on either side of the highway are vast, sumptuous hotels with names like Tropicana, the Stardust, the Dunes, the Last Frontier, the Sands—and when I say hotels, I mean BIG hotels.

For example, the Desert Inn at which we stayed, and the Stardust across the road, also owned by Wilbur Clark, have between them 1850 rooms per day to let. Besides these, each has a form of theatre, not merely for stage presentation, but a vast and sumptuously decorated hall with room for 1000 to 2000 people to sit down to dinner and watch the show.

In addition, of course, there is the big attraction, the gambling rooms. These never close. You can gamble in every hotel along the Strip, and in all the smaller gambling houses in the town itself, 24 hours a day, 365 days a year, year in, year out. At the Desert Inn, all routes pass through the gambling room; there is literally only one entrance and one exit to the hotel, necessitating your passing the Casino every time.

There they have something like five or six roulette tables, half a dozen Crap tables, about a dozen Black Jack tables, and perhaps 200–300 One-Arm-Bandits. All these are clattering away furiously all the time, with people betting in the famous silver American dollars or in the much bigger paper money.

Apart from the gambling, however, staying at the Desert Inn or any of the other hotels is remarkably cheap. You can see the finest cabarets in the country for as little as £2 per head plus your dinner, and can stay at the Desert Inn for as little as £2 or £3 per day. Considering this is a luxury hotel of the Claridge class, with swimming pools, golf clubs, its own shopping centre and every conceivable luxury, this is extremely reasonable. But then, of course, the entire hotel business is subsidized by the profits made in the gambling room, and the whole thing is so utterly fantastic that it seems almost ridiculous!

When we arrived at Las Vegas, our first step was to phone up George Eyston at Wendover to let him know that we had arrived, and to say that we would be over the next day. Unfortunately, while we were flying to Las Vegas, a tremendous rainstorm had lashed Wendover and the Salt Flats, leaving them covered with an inch and a half of water, so George Eyston advised us to stay where we were until the Flats dried up.

Naturally Stirling and I were delighted, and as things turned out we stayed in Las Vegas for eight days. We did the rounds of all the clubs, and saw several shows, amongst them the Sammy Davies Junior Show, which is quite remarkable, the Tony Martin Show and the Zsa Zsa Gabor Show. At this last one, we met the great Zsa Zsa personally, and went out for a drink with her afterwards.

Then George Eyston called us again, saying the course was fast improving, so we set off on the 450-odd-mile drive from Las Vegas to Wendover in a self-drive Chevrolet saloon. This was a remarkable run, for the roads are so straight and smooth that very high averages can be maintained. We covered the last 83 miles in 53 minutes, which works out at around 94 m.p.h.—and that in a rainstorm, in the dark. It was not because Stirling was driving that we achieved this; it was the sort of average that anybody could put up, because roads continuing dead straight for 20 to 30 miles are nothing extraordinary.

There are, of course, hazards, and apart from engine blow-ups if one is too throttle-happy, there is the danger of tyre blow-outs. The faster one drives under the scorching sun, the sooner a tyre blows out, and what is as yet a rare occurrence in this country is commonplace in that part of America. We ourselves blew one rear tyre out on the way, and saw plenty of evidence of others on almost every mile of road.

When we arrived at Wendover, we learned that there had been an even bigger rainstorm, and that the Salt Flats were now absolutely flooded. Eyston said there could now be no chance of making a record attempt for two or three weeks, so we had no choice but to pack up, drive to Salt Lake City, and fly back to England, where Stirling had a date at Oulton Park for the Gold Cup race.

As already mentioned, he won this race in Rob Walker's Formula I Cooper from Brabham's works car and Chris Bristow. But a few days later news came from America that the M.G. Ex. 181 had broken records at Utah. The floods departed, the salt had dried out, and Phil Hill, No. 1 reserve, took over in the absence of Stirling, and went out to break six Class E (up to 2-litre) records, exceeding 250 m.p.h. for the flying mile and kilometre. The car's engine had been slightly enlarged to 1506 c.c., to bring it from Class F to Class E category, Stirling's 1½-litre records established in 1957 remaining intact.

To those gallant readers who have got this far, it will be obvious that, in all my diverse business undertakings of recent years, I could not have conducted it without considerable delegation of the work involved. I must say, therefore, that I have been extremely fortunate in having the support of a very loyal band of people.

For instance, I know that when I am away, Stirling's secretary, Valerie Pirie, is watching over his business affairs in the most efficient way; I also know that my own secretary, Rosemary Seers, will not only look after my work on behalf of Yeoman Credit and the British Racing Partnership, but will look after anything necessary on behalf of Stirling or Rob Walker.

It is similarly comforting on the mechanical side of the Partnership. I couldn't possibly afford the time to superintend the preparation of the cars—but then, I never have to. Tony Robinson is wholly capable of doing so, and I can leave him to it with complete confidence. Alfred Moss and I do not appoint his labour; he chooses his own, and a very good choice he makes, too.

We all of us believe that enthusiasm makes happy and efficient workers, and desire that whoever works for us should work happily, not just to earn a living. Consequently, I claim that today we of B.R.P. have one of the happiest bands of mechanics in motor racing, and as long as we can keep it that way, our drivers will be happy too, and will, therefore, drive that much better.

With such keen spirit within the organization, I hold out every hope that the Yeoman Credit racing team shall meet with success in 1960. Certainly the first appearances of a Yeoman Credit entry, the Cooper at Oulton Park in September, was a great credit to Tony Robinson and the four mechanics who built it under his supervision.

CHAPTER THIRTEEN

MOSS THE MAN

You all know what he looks like, with that receding hair, oval face, firm, prominent chin, stocky build and athletic gait—but what is Stirling Moss like as a person?

As an undeniable champion, though never up till now an official World Champion in motor racing, he is an interestingly complex character; just how interesting and how complex I have learned through ten years' close association with him, both in business and as a friend.

Although Stirling always looks so maddeningly calm and relaxed at the wheel, he is not a relaxed person. His mind is too alert and active to let his body relax. In his 'leisure' hours he must always be doing something, be it talking, watching a film, wiring up a room in his house, fixing up a cupboard or putting together a plastic model car—but it must be something. Inactivity is agony to Stirling.

In his single days when we shared the same flat, first in Hampstead and then in Kensington, I very soon became aware of Stirling's restlessness and his total inability to sit quietly in a chair and read. Nor could he go to sleep easily, most of his serious thinking being done between midnight and two or three o'clock in the morning.

If there was an important race ahead, with its attendant problems concerning, say, gear ratios, brakes, tyres, strategy or what-have-you, Stirling always worked out his plan of campaign in the small hours. If he had a particular worry on his mind I always knew, because after we had turned the light out I could hear him chewing at his fingers while lying on his back staring into the darkness. He didn't bite his nails, but just nibbled, and the more he was worried, the more he nibbled.

Stirling is a gregarious type. He does not like to be alone, and surrounds himself with people. He collects friends as a small boy collects postage stamps, and will talk with them on any subject anybody cares to bring up. Now that he is married and has a permanent life companion, this tendency has decreased, but in our Challoner Mansions days, things were far from easy.

I have known Stirling phone up friends at one o'clock in the morning, then slip round and have coffee with them, simply because he wasn't tired or ready for bed. His theory was that he would tire himself out by talking; the only thing was, his friends became more tired than he did!

His necessity to be the leader doesn't only apply to motor racing; he must lead in everything he does. A psycho-analyst may have a better explanation, but I put it all down as part of his genius and the driving force within him; he tends to dominate even his closest friends, and should you get into an argument with Stirling he gets quite heated and can, in fact, become quite aggressive.

But this is a very temporary attitude, and I found that a close friend of Stirling needs to fight him in spirit every inch of the way, because the moment he feels he has mastered you, he ceases to respect you and loses interest. This eternal battle of wills was one reason why I decided to move out of Challoner Mansions and take my own flat, for I found the constant fight for supremacy rather too wearing.

I don't mean 'fight' physically, of course, although Stirling and I in our time have had our rows, and in one or two of them have very nearly come to blows. We have also had many an energetic wrestling bout which helped to work off excessive 'steam' and occasional temper; Stirling liked to try his Judo out, and while I never trained in Judo, I did a certain amount of unarmed combat in the Army, which lent itself well to this kind of struggle.

Not that he is spiteful, ever, while I have never known him to harbour a grudge. Stirling being the mercurial type, when we had one of our blazing rows his temper was up like a flash, and down just as quickly, and he quickly forgets and forgives.

He is an exceptionally fast thinker, and this makes him intolerant of those with slower-moving minds. Patience is not one of his virtues and he becomes extremely restless if he has to wait for anything or anybody. One of his better subjects at school was mathematics, and he possesses the 'slide rule' type of mind, coupled with an extremely retentive memory. He can cite lap times, circuit distances, r.p.m. and b.h.p. outputs, and he keeps this mass of figures in his mind like a neatly filed card index system. Of late, with the house in Nassau and now one in Shepherd's Market, London, to occupy him, he has become deeply immersed in building lore, and is like a walking encyclopedia on the subject of materials and prices.

In contrast, he is hopeless with telephone numbers, anniversaries, names and dates, and rather forgetful about the general things in life. One reason we have always got on well together, I believe, is because we are opposites; I can easily remember all these things, and can string off a series of telephone numbers as easily as he can lap records. Although Stirling cannot remember names, he has a wonderful memory for faces, and recognizes people many years after first meeting them, even though their names escape him.

When I first knew Stirling, he was tremendously keen on dancing; it was one way of getting rid of his surplus energy, and it was nothing for him to dance every single step from 8 p.m. until the band closed at 1 a.m. But he has few tastes in music, art or literature beyond background melodies, films and television, and periodicals, preferably well illustrated, being too impatient to sit and read large tracks of type. Films he is extremely fond of, being an inveterate cinema-goer.

Like any healthy young man, Stirling enjoys feminine company. In his bachelor days he had quite a *coterie* of charming acquaintances, as I well remember when I first got to know him. When the Mosses first moved from Maidenhead to Tring in 1950, young Stirling was very glum. We reconnoitred the quiet village of Tring in advance, I recollect, in his Morris Minor, and the place looked altogether too quiet for him. There was no river, to which he had been born and bred, no friends of his living nearby, no pleasant coffee bars or dance halls or other amenities for this carefree young man.

But he set about making the best of it, resorting to various girl friends in Maidenhead when needing female company. Late in 1950 his parents decided to give Stirling a really personal twenty-first birthday party. They acted as chief cook and bottle-washer, and gave him *carte blanche* to choose his own guests. The result was an extremely hilarious and enjoyable party.

To ensure an adequate supply of girls, Stirling returned to his old hunting ground, Maidenhead. We drove over together in the Mosses' old Rolls-Royce horse box, collecting girl friends one by one and managing to get about fifteen in without too much squeezing. Driving happily back to Tring, we were stopped by a policeman on the lookout for turkey thieves.

'What have you got in the back, sir?' asked the policeman, flashing his torch, and Stirling answered, 'A load of old hens,' whereupon there was a concerted titter from inside. The policeman opened the back door of the Rolls to have a look and was practically swamped by girls falling out on top of him!

One day Stirling and I were working in his room, when his mother knocked on the door and said, 'Oh, by the way, Stirling, one of Pat's girl friends is coming to tea; she wants to meet you.'

Stirling was not enthusiastic. 'You can tell Pat to keep her horsy friends all to herself,' he said. 'We don't want to meet her, do we, Ken?'

Round about teatime, however, while we were putting up some shelving, feeling hot and clad only in shorts, there came another knock at the door and in came Mother with Pat's girl friend, who was introduced as Sally Weston. She was a very nice-looking girl, creating an immediate impression on Stirling and me. We both felt embarrassed, and after exchanging 'how do you do's', Stirling said, 'We'll be down in three minutes for tea.'

We were, too, and once seated, we fought each other to pass the jam or the butter or the cake, to the visitor, and that evening Pat, Sally, Stirling and I all went to the local cinema. But Stirling was not tied by business hours as I was, and arranged to meet Sally on Monday when I would be working. He took her out dancing that evening, beginning an association which was to last a considerable time before they came to the parting of the ways.

Stirling is a generous and trusting person, yet like many who are, he has a peculiar attitude to small sums of money. Should I use a 3d. stamp when a 2d. will suffice, for instance, he will tick me off, yet he will sign a cheque for £1000 without hesitation should I request it.

One habit of his irritates me beyond measure—though he will probably laugh when he reads this. When a group of us go to a restaurant and agree to go 'Dutch treat', Stirling will call for the bill. Then, instead of dividing it up into, say, six portions if there are six of us, he laboriously checks what each person has had, making out six separate little accounts on the back of the bill, then tells each of us what we have spent. The only thing is, by the time everyone has paid their share, Stirling often finds he is two or three shillings better off!

Although he covers an immense number of miles every year, travelling from race to race, Stirling is a home lover; he loves England and the English, and above all his family—few families can have such a deep loyalty amongst themselves as the Mosses of Tring.

He takes great care of himself physically, and apart from enjoying sports outside motor racing such as swimming, skiing, water polo, surf-riding and spear-fishing, he trains regularly and rigorously during the racing season. Like quite a number of racing men, Stirling is superstitious—exceptionally so. Some of his preferences, like the racing number 7, are well known; he regards it as his lucky number, having gained some of his earliest successes under it and since then, by the law of averages, I suppose, it might be said to have brought him 'luck'.

His favourite colour is green; not the deeper shades but a light green, and when in a non-works car he is always happiest in a car of this colour, as worn on his Morris Minor, his Coopers, and his G.P. Maserati. Yet when his green Maserati suffered a long series of breakdowns and he was searching for a reason, he worked out that the colour must be to blame after all, and changed it to grey!

Apart from this, he almost goes mad if anybody accepts or offers a third light for a cigarette, and I soon found, when staying with him before a race, that it was unwise to be too cheerful about things like the weather; if I should look out of the window and say 'It's going to be fine', he settled in his own mind that it would rain. It was better for me to gaze at the brilliant, cloudless sky and grumble, 'Hmmm—looks like rain again.' This sounds childish, but was merely a whimsy of his, parallel to the German *hals und beinbruch* philosophy of 'opposites'. When a German wishes a driver good luck in a race he says '*hals und beinbruch*', which means, in effect, 'I hope you break a leg and your neck'!

But what of his driving methods? There are no whimsies, fancies or superstitions then! Very few drivers can equal Stirling for sheer concentration and thoroughness at the job of driving a racing car. There is no question about it, he is a supreme artist at the wheel. He wins races not only by driving skill, but by tactics. He studies 'the form', decides who are his toughest opponents, considers their strong points and their weak ones, and drives accordingly.

He misses no 'tricks' of the accepted sporting kind, is an adept at such crafts as leading a rival too quickly into a corner, and readily exploits that abstract asset known as 'moral ascendancy', assuming an appearance of leading with supreme ease, so that his closest rivals tend to think, 'Oh, what's the use—Moss has got it in the bag again—I'll play safe for second,' when actually Stirling's clutch may be slipping badly, or his oil pressure dropping, so that he is nursing the car along, hoping against hope that it will hold out.

Such are the tactics learned through long experience, but they are single facets of his overall skill. His true genius lies in his ability always to extract the very maximum from his car and himself without over-extending either, his refusal to accept defeat, and his unfailing courage and determination, balanced with the wisdom of experience. A few years ago, when he suffered a considerable number of breakdowns, it was suggested that Moss was hard on his cars, and flogged them to death. This is wholly untrue.

It is very easy for the team manager to determine which are the hard drivers. It can be done scientifically yet simply, by a few observations. Send the driver out for twenty or so fast laps of a circuit, study his times and study his car afterwards. Apart from the rev. counter 'telltale' needle, the temperatures of engine and brakes and tyre wear will all help to betray the hard driver. All will be too high, because he has been doing everything to extremes, in order to get the maximum out of his car.

Stirling in a racing car is a pure scientist, with an exceedingly sensitive mechanical 'feel'. He is always kind to the engine. There are many examples of his ability to lap a circuit faster with less stress to the mechanism. In the 1958 T.T. race at Goodwood, which Stirling won in an Aston Martin, sharing with that other great driver Tony Brooks, the rev. counter telltale needle at the finish stood at 6300 r.p.m.; on the second-place Aston Martin it stood at 6600 r.p.m., and on the third-place Aston it read 7300 r.p.m. Yet Stirling made the fastest lap.

When Stirling first drove the British Racing Partnership-prepared B.R.M. at Rheims before the 1959 French G.P., he was given a revs. limit of 7800 r.p.m. In fact, he never at any time exceeded 7600 r.p.m., yet he still managed to be two seconds faster than any of the works team. In respect of rev. limits, he is completely reliable; he will use what he is told he can use but never more.

Another of his driving virtues is that he is one of the very few able to tell you exactly what revs. he is getting, in what gear, at any point on the circuit you care to ask about. Many drivers are incapable of telling you what their engine is doing, except down the straights.

Despite his strict observation of rev. limits, Stirling extracts maximum performance all the time; lesser drivers do not; they only use optimum performance spasmodically. On any circuit, and at every part of that circuit, Moss will be exacting 100 per cent from the car and himself, in braking, accelerating, cornering —and he will do it consistently, lap after lap.

He is a perfectionist, and drives and drives until he is completely familiar with every single inch of the ground he has to travel. To you and me, the Monaco circuit or Silverstone or Monza may appear identical with last year, but Stirling's knowledge of these and other circuits is so intimate that he will detect the slightest new bump or hollow. A new bump at a crucial point can materially alter one's lap time, therefore Stirling makes it his business to find it.

As manager to Moss it may seem natural that I should beat the drum on his behalf. I do indeed regard him as a genius at motor racing, and the logical successor to Fangio today. But the Moss drum needs no beating; statistics will bear me out, and to critics I would say, remember the Nurburgring 1000-km. race or the Italian G.P. of 1959, the Argentine G.P. of 1958, the Italian G.P.s of 1954 and 1956, or the Mille Miglia of 1955, as races in which his uncanny skill and strategy gained the day.

And talking of geniuses, I would also like to say that, considering the amount of publicity Stirling has had in the past few years, the adulation of the public, and his international reputation, I think he has retained a very level-headed and balanced attitude to life. Lesser persons could have become very conceited and impossible to live with. Stirling is difficult enough, but that is because of his character and not because success has turned his head.

I think we might well give the last words on Stirling Moss in this book to that grand rival of his, the late Mike Hawthorn. In the world of motor racing, the affectionate term 'the Old Man' has long been reserved for Juan Manuel Fangio, five times winner of the World Championship. After that epic Moroccan G.P. at Casablanca in 1958, however, when Stirling thrust his Vanwall ahead, made fastest lap and won the race, while Mike finished second, thus clinching the World Championship, Mike observed, 'Mind you, "the Old Man" didn't half go; I could never have got near him.'

To pass on to Stirling the illustrious Fangio's nickname was, I feel, the ultimate compliment.